Wars and Peace

The Future Americans Envisioned
1861–1991

David Mayers

St. Martin's Press
New York

ISBN 0-312-21352-2 (cloth) ISBN 0-312-22770-1 (paper)

Library of Congress Cataloging-in-Publication Data

Mayers, David Allan, 1951–
    Wars and peace : the future Americans envisioned, 1861–1991 /
David Mayers
        p. cm.
    Includes bibliographical references and index.
    ISBN 0-312-21352-2 (cloth) ISBN 0-312-22770-1 (paper)
    1. United States—Foreign relations—1865– —Philosophy.
2. United Sates—Foreign relations——1861–1865—Philosophy.
3. United States—History, Military—Social aspects.   4. Peace—Philosophy—
History—19th century.   5. Peace—Philosophy—
History—20th century.   I. Title.
E661.7.M32   1998
327.73—dc21   98-15550
                                                                              CIP

Internal design and typesetting by Letra Libre

First edition: July, 1998
First paperback edition: November, 1999
10   9   8   7   6   5   4   3   2   1

To my parents,
believers in the American promise

Contents

Preface

The dogmas of the quiet past are inadequate to the stormy present. The occasion is piled high with difficulty, and we must rise with the occasion. As our case is new so we must think anew and act anew. We must disenthrall ourselves, and then we shall save our country.

—Abraham Lincoln, December 1862

Broadly conceived, this work examines the intellectual foundations of U.S. foreign policy since 1861. Specifically, this study analyzes the way that Americans, across the political spectrum, in times of conflict have conceptualized the era that would follow hostilities. The fate of these ideas—which belong to the category, in contemporary parlance, of new world orders—is considered with reference to five national security crises: the Civil War, the 1898 operation against Spain, World War I, World War II, and the Cold War.

This history bears directly on a current problem. How should the United States fashion its policy after the Cold War? What is striking about previous attempts to create postwar orders is that they failed in the test to fulfill the hopes of their authors. Yet the cumulative impact of these ideas has been to shape collective imagination in America.

Unlike my previous books, this one does not rely upon archival holdings of formerly confidential documents or other primary materials. It is an interpretative essay based on a reading of recent scholarship. Thus my first debt of gratitude is to the many historians and political scientists whose works are listed in the Bibliography. Friends have also helped me in this writing. The following people and I have disagreed only on important questions: Peter Kenez, Igor Lukes, Stephen Lyne, Michael Joseph Smith. Additional people, who have been of equal help, if less persistently skeptical, are: Susan Abel, John Archer, Walter Connor, Robert Dallek, Hermann Eilts, Stephanie Fawcett, David Fromkin, Elizabeth Kirkland Jones, William Keylor, Murray Levin, Peter Michael Mayers, Richard Melanson, Charles Neu, Cathal Nolan, Dietrich Orlow, L. Marvin Overby, Joel Rosenthal. My heartfelt thanks to them all for their constructive criticism and encouragement. They have saved me from more than one factual error. They have obliged me to reconsider several outlandish ideas. I alone am responsible for the book's deficiencies.

Professional organizations have allowed me to make presentations of my work in progress or in other ways fostered a stimulating environment: Canada's Congress of the Learned Societies, the Carnegie Council on Ethics and International Affairs, the History and Political Science departments of Boston University, the International Studies Association.

Boston University generously provided me with sabbatical leave to write this book. Michael Flamini of St. Martin's Press has been a patient and cooperative editor.

David Mayers
Newton, Massachusetts
January 12, 1998

Introduction

My reason for writing this book is twofold. First, I want to advance the case for the power and autonomy of ideas that exist in opposition to the coercive sphere. They exert gravitational pull toward mitigation of suffering and amelioration of strife. Second, I want to analyze the course of evolving American identity and ambitions abroad. Wartime emergency provides the window through which to view these issues.

War exemplifies the realm of necessity in its purest form. Yet even here ideas matter. It is not enough that thinkers have sought to explain the recurrence of war as an intractable problem in history, tying its origins to varied phenomena: defects in human personality or the existence of odious regimes or the anarchical nature of international politics.[1] Nor is it enough to condemn war as inevitable, as when one of its foremost practitioners, General Robert E. Lee, lamented: "I fear we are destined to kill and slaughter each other for ages to come."[2]

Warring peoples have also sought high justification—rationalization, if you prefer—for their strenuous and gory actions. Homer's heroes destroyed Troy not simply for the sake of pleasure or plunder. Their goal, as they insisted, was to enforce codes of civilized conduct, violated when Paris stole his host's wife. Napoleon's legions subdued Europe for more than the glory of conquest; they persuaded themselves that they were expanding the zone of liberty. Britain's land-grabbing in the nineteenth century was not aimed solely at preempting predatory rivals from laying claim to yet another part of Africa or Asia. By fighting native peoples, Britain was also bringing enlightenment to backward races—the "white man's burden." Hitler's soldiers in Eastern Europe justified their savagery with these needs: to redress the indignities perpetrated by Versailles, to enlarge the living space *(Lebensraum)* available to an excellent but crowded nation, to save Europe from Bolshevik barbarism.

The list of examples is endless. The point is that irrespective of motive, be it immediate (the felt need to correct an imbalance in the balance of power) or underlying (relentless affirmation of the collective self), people have required justification for the hazards and cruelty inherent in war. When General William Tecumseh Sherman said that war is hell, he was both making an empirical observation and invoking moral authority for his army's action: burning and sacking in Georgia. When Stalin asked how many divisions the Pope commanded, he was not showing just the Machiavellian's contempt for weakness. He was also paying cynical tribute to the intellectual-moral power that a few decades after his death weakened (fatally in Poland) the Soviet grip on Eastern Europe.[3] Though no more than a vulgar Marxist, Stalin understood himself as occupying a place in the apostolic succession that began with the socialist master and carried through Engels and Lenin. Against capitalist cant stood the radical ideas of proletarian rights and distributive justice, which would have been mobilized had open war erupted between the USSR and its Western antagonists.

This book is motivated by other concerns: the muddled quality of post–Cold War U.S. policy and the belief that earlier experience can be useful, both as a cautionary tale and an example of what is effective in avoiding mishap in a still threatening world. In the following pages, I try to recapture how Americans have envisioned their country's course in the periods that would follow the emergencies of 1861–1991: the Civil War, Spanish-American War, the two world wars, the Cold War. For a diplomatic historian, I have taken an unorthodox approach by including the voices of a broader range than is standard of people acting on the political scene: the powerful certainly but also the marginalized, the vanquished, and the dissenting. Political imagination is not the sole property of a policy-making elite in a representative democracy; Americans of all stripes and persuasions have always flavored national discourse. Thus I have included nonconformists from the ranks of radicals, pacifists, civil rights activists, feminists, and those scholars who have lived in the faith of John Maynard Keynes's conviction—the views of practical men of affairs are derived from academic scribblers of previous generations.[4] I hope in effect to reacquaint readers with some of those thinkers whose eloquence, passion, and even wrongheadedness gave texture to the debates of their times.

Though none of the visions of these individuals has completely taken hold, many have taken root. The power of these concepts, however frustrated their application, is evidenced today as Americans contemplate their nation's diplomacy. At the same time, the inability of previous generations to give decisive shape to the politics of their day is useful reminder that exuberance alone cannot overcome complexity. As they mixed with other determinants of foreign policy (economic, bureaucratic, partisan, external) new-world-order ideas were sculpted in ways unintended by their progenitors.[5]

In all the chapters, a specific crisis and U.S. response to it are introduced. An exegesis of the government's notion of future political life (domestic and international) follows. Then I examine the postwar career of that concept, with particular reference to its domestic supporters and opponents. In this connection the attitude of foreign allies and rivals is also reviewed, but my contention is that most U.S. foreign policy is domestically anchored.[6] The crucial points of reference are U.S. institutions and habits of mind.

Appropriately, therefore, I begin with the severest test in U.S. history: the war of 1861–1865. The United States is a deliberate country. Its founding, or invention, was designed to satisfy a particular need: an alternative to monarchical rule and assertion of the republican idea. In a sense, the Civil War constituted a second founding of the United States. Issues left unresolved by the framers—the relationship of central authority to states' prerogatives and the free zone versus the slave—were settled, more or less, by the war. In this chapter, I examine Abraham Lincoln's vision for the nation and link it to problems faced by his successor, President Andrew Johnson. I also assess compatible visions, notably those of the freed (in the voice of Frederick Douglass) and those of the cooperating defeated (General James Longstreet). Those people skeptical of the Lincoln idea are also scrutinized, including Northerners who urged a punitive peace upon the South (such as Congressman Thaddeus Stevens) and those from the losing side who still resisted (such as Nathan Bedford Forrest, wizard of the Ku Klux Klan). The moral and political ambiguity of Reconstruction resulted from this massive attempt to recast America.

The next chapter concerns the 1898 war against Spain. During that conflict, to cite a wag of the time, the United States aimed at Cuba but hit the Philippines. Americans had first to decide whether to wage an intervention on behalf of the oppressed (Cuban rebels fighting Spain), then whether to break from tradition and create an overseas empire (acquisition of the Philippines). The focus of my attention is on the indecisive president, William McKinley, and the preeminent figures in national debate: Theodore Roosevelt and Captain Alfred Thayer Mahan versus Mark Twain and William James. The latter two argued against policies likely to lead to an arrogant empire that would degrade democratic practice at home. The war against Emilio Aguinaldo in the Philippines became a divisive issue among Americans.[7] They nevertheless established dominion there—with the stated intent of preparing the indigenous people for self-rule. The United States thus become an imperial republic but uneasy with this status.

The third chapter deals with Woodrow Wilson and his attempt to broker a moderate peace for the Great War. He hoped to dispense with punitive measures and create international machinery (the League of Nations) to preempt vast violence in the future. He faced the likes of Senator Henry Cabot Lodge at home, who warned against foreign snares that would trap the country in European imbroglios. At Versailles, Wilson confronted Clemenceau, whose determination was that Germany should not again harm France. The Wilsonian idea was also challenged by revolutionary socialism, embodied by Lenin and his Third International. The Kellogg-Briand pact and peace movements—in which former suffragettes like Jane Addams played a conspicuous role—were expressions of Wilsonianism that survived into the interwar period. They proved untenable by 1939. But their core ideals resurfaced in the emergency of 1941–1945.

The Second World War chapter focuses on FDR's attempt to redefine international politics, and the U.S. position therein, via the Atlantic Charter, United Nations, and the controversial Nuremberg trials. Roosevelt was buoyed in this task by his wife Eleanor, encouraged by the dreamer Henry Wallace, supported by the NAACP leadership. The advent of atomic weaponry and dissolution of the Grand Alliance demolished Roosevelt's version of liberal internationalism.

The fifth chapter looks at Harry Truman's conception of the Cold War (buttressed by Dean Acheson) and contrasts it with the anxieties of Walter Lippmann and George Kennan, and the outright dissent of Henry Wallace and Paul Robeson. Into this discussion, I weave the outlook of two prominent intellectuals of the era: Reinhold Niebuhr, Sidney Hook. Both of them sought in distinctive ways to refine further the definition of East-West contest and the interplay between power and conscience. At no time was this dilemma more starkly drawn than during the Vietnam era, when the Cold War consensus started to crack, or during the nuclear arms race, when objectors and security planners collided in debate.

The final chapter, essentially an epilogue, looks at the post–Cold War moment from several perspectives: the administrations of George Bush and Bill Clinton; governments in Europe, Russia, and developing nations; pundits and professors. To all of them, the same questions are posed. If the United States is bound to lead, what is the quality of its leadership? Where is this U.S.-led world headed? If, by contrast, U.S. power contracts, what are the implications for national security and global stability? Regardless of the answers to these questions, what is certain—I shall contend—is the resilience of America's moral promise.[8]

Earnest attempts at innovation notwithstanding, U.S. purpose remains unchanged and like that of every nation: to survive, to prosper if possible. Yet the effort by generations of Americans (variously naive, self-serving, contradictory) to transcend this narrow understanding has produced high drama—plus glimmerings of a better political life. As applicable to this day and to this study as to his own, W. E. B. Du Bois published these lines in 1935: "Nations reel and stagger on their way; they make hideous mistakes; they commit frightful wrongs; they do great and beautiful things."[9]

ONE

Malice toward None

The United States had been a visibly divided country long before the shelling of Fort Sumter. The Mason-Dixon line reflected and fostered the development of two separate societies. These coexisted within a framework of linguistic unity and historical memory, the latter bolstered by a romantic lore of patriots subduing British tyranny. Distinctive economies had emerged on either side of this national divide. The industrial North faced the agrarian South. An elaborate system of thought and values in each section buttressed its version of economic-social-political life. In the North the idea of free labor was compatible with abolitionist sentiment. In the South the theory of racial inequality helped sustain slavery.

The possibility of national dissolution concerned Thomas Jefferson, who late in life confessed that sectional animosity filled him with dread. Young Abraham Lincoln held that unchecked regional rivalry and philosophical dispute would split the country apart. No foreign power could inflict on the United States anything as fearful as what Americans could do themselves, he warned in 1838: "At what point shall we expect the approach of danger? By what means shall we fortify against it? Shall we expect some transatlantic military giant to step the Ocean, and crush us at a blow? Never! All the armies of Europe, Asia and Africa combined, with all the treasure of the earth . . . could not by force, take a drink from the Ohio, or make a track on the Blue Ridge, in a trial of a thousand years . . . If destruction be our lot, we must ourselves be its author and finisher. As a nation of freemen, we must live through all time, or die by suicide."[1] Yet the war came, precipitated by the 1860 election of Lincoln to the presidency. He could not prevent hostilities. He could not stop them once begun. He presided instead over the first modern war, its base being industrial dynamism.

View from Abroad

The Civil War was inexplicable to most foreign observers, especially as its unfolding gave rise to reckless destruction. Bafflement transcended personal preference for either the Northern or Southern cause, uniting such diverse men as William Makepeace Thackeray, Anthony Trollope, John Ruskin, Benjamin Disraeli, Thomas Carlyle, and Thomas Huxley in wondering whether the Americans had taken leave of their sense. Yet to others the reason and conduct of struggle were perfectly plain. Victor Hugo saw the war as necessary to expunge the "great evil" of slavery, as did Charles Darwin, who declared that a right outcome could vindicate even a million battlefield deaths. John Stuart Mill believed that Union victory was needed to stay the hand (in both Europe and the New World) of antiliberalism and bigotry. George Sand saw in the sanguinary effusion divine judgment on a people who had too long tolerated the sin of slavery. In her words, "God had forsaken them to punish them." As for European conservatives, such as the Russian minister to Washington, Baron Edouard de Stoeckl, the spectacle of civil war testified to the failings of popular government. Press editorials in Spain likened the carnage to cannibalism; they pronounced as unfit a nation that allowed itself to be ruled by nonsensical myths of democracy.[2]

However varied private opinion was in Europe, the attitude of governments was more predictable, corresponding to understandings of national interest. These were mostly hostile to American unity and so apprehended by Northerners, not least of whom was General Ulysses S. Grant: "Seeing a nation that extended from ocean to ocean, embracing the better part of a continent, growing as we were in population, wealth and intelligence, the European nations thought it would be well to give us a check."[3] The Anglo-French preference was for the Union to sue for peace and allow Southern secession. This end was desirable because in the place of a single republic, two smaller states would thenceforth compete for dominant influence in North America. Additionally, Mexico and British Canada would have been able to play larger parts in New World affairs. Something like a balance-of-power system would have replaced U.S. supremacy. That London and/or Paris would therefore recognize the Confederacy and intervene diplomatically—even militarily—on its behalf was a distinct possibility through the end of 1863.

For Napoleon III, a broken United States would advance his ambition of returning the French empire to North America. His scheme at its most grandiose envisioned the seizure of the Gulf Coast from Florida to Louisiana, and a French sphere in Mexico. Napoleon persuaded the reluctant Archduke Maximilian of Austria in 1863 to accept the Mexican throne and French protection. But despite his pro-Southern sympathies and Mexican adventure, Napoleon was unwilling to take unilateral action on behalf of the Confederacy. He needed Britain's cooperation for risky New World enterprise.

Prime Minister Palmerston and Foreign Secretary Russell felt that a permanently divided Union would help safeguard Canada and render North American relations more susceptible to British influence. London's support of the Confederacy would promote this worthy goal whilst guaranteeing the steady and economical supply of Southern cotton to British textile manufacturers. By summer 1862, the government was tempted to recognize the South; after a string of Union defeats, it seemed that a new nation had been created, one on the verge of breaking an unwanted political association.[4] Preliminary steps were taken by the Anglo-French in September to offer mediation on terms favoring the South. The failure, though, of Lee's army to break Federal lines in Maryland (Antietam) or to carry the war north made Palmerston adopt a more cautious policy toward the war and a conciliatory tone toward the Union's envoy in London, Charles Francis Adams.

An Anglo-U.S. clash of arms seemed imminent on at least one occasion after Antietam. A U.S. warship intercepted the British vessel *Peterhoff* (spring of 1863) and confiscated Confederate mailbags from its cargo. Just as in the earlier *Trent* episode, there was an uproar in England, which made threats to redeem the "insult" to Queen Victoria's honor. The Confederate commissioner in London, James Mason, meanwhile continued to campaign for recognition and materiel aid. Direct assistance was never forthcoming. But the British did build a number of cruisers for Southern purchase, including the *Alabama,* which took a toll on Union maritime commerce valued at more than $15 million.

Russian interests in the Civil War were exactly opposite to those of the west European powers and had as point of reference British hopes for a divided United States. Whereas from the existence of two jealous North American republics London would have feared nothing—indeed, through their conflicting ambitions might have dominated them—St. Petersburg would have lost a counterpoise to British naval power. Consequently, within the limited means at his disposal, Alexander II sought the Union's preservation. In the phrase of Foreign Minister Alexander Gorchakov, it was "an element essential to the universal equilibrium."[5]

Czarist officials declared that any Confederate envoy to St. Petersburg would be barred from court. (The would-be Southern minister, L. Q. C. Lamar, was never admitted to Imperial territory.) Only if the United States established diplomatic relations with the Confederacy would the empire follow suit, Stoeckl assured Secretary of State William Seward. The Russians also rejected Anglo-French proposals to join a mediation effort. Neither did czarist officialdom object to Union efforts to have Confederate privateers declared illegal. At the same time, Russia's press-censorship apparatus was coordinated to emphasize Union battlefield victories and play down defeats.

Northern publicists embellished the significance of Russia's benign neutrality in the absence of other great-power support. They cheerfully drew comparisons between Alexander, who in 1861 liberated approximately 20 million serfs, and Lincoln, who proclaimed emancipation two years later. Northern abolitionists argued that their cause and Russia's had been converging ever since 1852, when Harriet Beecher Stowe published *Uncle Tom's Cabin* and Ivan Turgenev produced *Sportsman's Sketches,* which depicted serfs as whole human beings. Lincoln and Seward used every opportunity throughout the war to impress upon Anglo-French diplomats that the Union enjoyed a steadfast ally. This idea was also communicated to the Northern civilian population. In the emotional atmosphere of wartime, gratitude in the North for military services provided by Russian volunteer officers such as Colonel John Turchin (the "mad Cossack") extended to the czar himself. The poet Oliver Wendell Holmes rhapsodized on Alexander after hostilities ended as "our friend when the world was our foe."[6]

Never was the Union attitude toward Russia more apparent than in September 1863, when six ships of the Imperial navy unexpectedly entered New York harbor. A month later another squadron of six entered San Francisco Bay. Press and public regarded the presence of these warships as betokening Russian sympathy—as a warning to the Anglo-French that their intervention would have ramifications reaching far beyond North America. In fact, these Russian ships, none equal to the superior vessels in the British or French navies, had anchored in U.S. ports for reasons unrelated to the Northern cause. A possibility existed in 1863 that Palmerston and Napoleon would push the issue of Polish insurrection and Russia's squelching of it to the point of war. To prevent the fleet's being trapped in the Baltic (as during the Crimean War), the chief of Imperial naval operations ordered a number of ships to find haven in North America. They might prove valuable from there in the event of war as commerce raiders against Anglo-French shipping. In New York and San Francisco, as well as in Boston and Washington, the ships' officers and men were fêted. Parades, banquets, and balls were held to honor the Union's "true friends." War-weary, its morale sapped by antidraft and race riots, the Union attitude was captured by Secretary of the Navy Gideon Welles: "God bless the Russians!" Though Welles, Lincoln, Seward, and Charles Sumner (chairman of the Senate Foreign Relations Committee) knew the real motive behind the Russian visits, they did not broadcast it.

The administration, retaining St. Petersburg's friendly neutrality, did not protest the Russian crushing of Polish rebellion. Even as a spirited debate between Seward and Sumner (the latter eager to assist Poland) ran its course, Lincoln also refused Anglo-French entreaties to help negotiate a settlement. He maintained that the United States did not presume to meddle in the internal affairs of sovereign states.[7]

Lincoln's Hope

Discomfited though he was by Russia's autocratic regime, Lincoln nonetheless viewed cordial relations with St. Petersburg as a reasonable expedient, no different from others forced upon him by necessity.[8] Indeed, to perpetuate the republic, he and his lieutenants (particularly Seward) spared no means, even those distasteful to liberal opinion. These included suspending the writ of habeus corpus and discarding sundry civil liberties. The emergency allowed military arrests and evacuations of civilians, martial law, seizure of property, tampering with the mails, curtailment of press freedom. Spies, secret societies, and other abettors of the Confederacy—real or imagined—were rooted out by detectives such as Allan Pinkerton. They exaggerated the extent of disloyal conspiracies, thereby contributing to an atmosphere of vitriol in which political discourse became circumscribed. Northern opponents of the war were denounced as treasonous ("Copperheads"); Lincoln feared that all government departments were infiltrated by Rebel sympathizers. He chose to scrap the Constitution temporarily to save U.S. democracy. He exercised quasi-dictatorial power tempered only by his innate sense of balance and decency. Confederate essayists were not merely pandering to their constituency when they damned Lincoln's reign as fatal to traditional freedom; they had a bulky record of civil liberty violations to cite.[9]

The president who doggedly prosecuted the war was in ways an unexceptional specimen of his era. As a politician, he practiced conventional patronage—a variant of which was his appointment of political generals whose conduct was seldom meritorious. As a lawyer, he accepted any client. As a personality, he was subject to violent swings of mood, lapsing at times into deep melancholia or passivity. He was hugely ambitious, occasionally crude, and never overcame the hidden injuries of the rural-poor class. Too immersed in events to have a clear perspective, he understood the momentousness of the Civil War slightly better than others of his generation. Yet Lincoln occasionally rose above himself by giving vivid interpretation to the events of 1861–1865. "He knew the American people," wrote Frederick Douglass, "better than they knew themselves and his truth was based upon this knowledge."[10]

Perhaps it was vanity to think that affirmative meaning could be found in events that killed 620,000 soldiers (of whom 360,000 served the Union), to say nothing of hardships suffered by the wounded, orphaned, widowed, and destitute. If the same percentage of the U.S. population had died violently in the 1990s, the total would equal roughly 5 million.[11] Fully a quarter of the South's white men of military age were killed, a proportion exceeding that of major European belligerents in World War I. While the war stimulated economic growth in the North, the South's economy was savaged and took decades to recover.[12] A late twentieth-century sensibility finds implausible Lincoln's conception (and Sand's) of this theodicy: that those who died or suffered were part of a collective expiation for the offense of slavery.[13] Still, Lincoln sought to discern national purpose in the carnage.

To audiences from Capitol Hill to Gettysburg, he proclaimed that the war raised this question: would the American experiment in self-government, and democracy itself, survive? Passionate for the continuation of the United States—amounting to a "mystical attachment," some historians say—he was sensitive to conservative charges of that day against republicanism. Should the United States perish, he warned, European critics would be renewed in their skepticism of the common man's ability to discharge public affairs wisely. By contrast, Union success should confirm the faith of believers in the resilience of democracy and the wisdom of defying monarchical practice: "We shall nobly save, or meanly lose, the last best hope of earth."[14]

Lincoln originally hoped to reduce the Confederacy by methods calculated not to weaken further the fabric of national loyalty. His aim was simply to suppress the insurrection—led by a minority of hotheads, he opined, who lacked broad support—and to restore Federal authority on all disputed territory. These preferences dictated a quick military campaign that would produce minimal casualties and limit the disruption to civilian life in Dixie (sparing the "peculiar institution"). Conceived originally as a police action, this strategy required no more than a blockade of Southern ports and a 90-day enlistment of 75,000 militiamen to return the Rebels to the Union (General Winfield Scott's Anaconda Plan). Stubborn Confederate resistance quickly made a hash of this approach. Consequently, the North devised a policy that entailed more than reoccupation of Federal sites in the South but included measures of total war. These were exemplified by the decision to decimate Southern armies, by Sherman's leveling march, and by a determination to extinguish the Slave Power allegedly bearing the main responsibility for starting the conflagration.[15]

Lincoln's thinking evolved dramatically on this last point of slavery. As mentioned, he at first expected to leave undisturbed the South's human chattel. But as the burden of casualties and other costs mounted, dignifying an enlargement of war aims, he adopted policies favored by abolitionists like Sumner, who had immediately perceived the war as an occasion to realize their objective. Lincoln never altered in his conviction that blacks were intellectually inferior or that a mingling of them with whites on terms of equality was impossible—witness the revulsion, he argued, felt by whites in the North for black men in Union uniforms. He also clung to the idea of compensating owners who voluntarily emancipated their slaves; he was willing even in 1865 to grant $400 million to Southerners as remuneration for the loss of slave labor. He supported emigration of U.S.-born blacks to Africa (Liberia), Central America, or the Caribbean. Nor was he fully persuaded of the merit of black suffrage, though by the end of his life he appears to have accepted it as a logical conclusion to the war.[16]

Despite his temporizing and a grudging attitude toward the African race, Lincoln eventually embraced the idea of ending bondage, if for no other than pragmatic reasons. Emancipation weakened—as he foresaw—the labor force available in the South, swelled the ranks of the Union army by paving the way for black enlistment (approximately 180,000 soldiers), and made possible the Thirteenth Amendment. His edict of January 1863 also played to that body of Anglo-French opinion that abhorred slavery, thereby weakening the Confederacy's moral standing, hitherto based on the underdog's appeal.

Having supervised a war whose achievement was the South's unconditional surrender, Lincoln's dilemma in spring 1865 centered on how to reintegrate the vanquished zone into the national body. He held (perhaps he was asserting faith born of desperation) that a hard war and a soft peace were not mutually exclusive. Even as the last battles were being fought, Lincoln urged Northerners to forswear the temptation of vengeance. Rather, in the words of his Second Inaugural address, the victors should proceed with "malice toward none, with charity for all . . . to bind up the nation's wounds." Unfortunately, apart from high hopes and a touching insistence that North and South could reconcile, Lincoln had nothing like a coherent plan for posthostilities America.[17]

Wartime Reconstruction in Louisiana, Maryland, Tennessee, and Missouri had been ad hoc. It had amounted to a series of improvisations whose haphazardness gave no reliable guidance. A shifting mix of lenient and proscriptive policies had reflected the exigencies of war, themselves influenced by the alternating needs to punish or conciliate Confederates. Each improvisation proved unsustainable by turn. Lincoln's proclamation of amnesty and Reconstruction (December 1863) had not drawn secessionists back to the Union fold. The patronage of Southern state governments-in-exile, the career of military governors in Southern districts occupied by Union forces, efforts to organize Southern Unionists, and offers of amnesty to a repentant 10 percent of the Confederates had all collapsed in 1861–1865.[18]

Though less stirring than the Second Inaugural, Lincoln's speech on Reconstruction—two days after Lee's surrender at Appomattox on April 9, 1865—does shed light on what the president had in mind for the future: namely, restoring to "proper practical relations" the would-be secessionist states to the Union. Yet the speech's admission of divided opinion in the North on how to proceed and defensiveness about wartime Reconstruction in Louisiana underscored the administration's lack of a blueprint.[19] The peace parley that Lincoln held with Southern commissioners—Alexander Stephens, vice president of the Confederacy; Robert Hunter, Virginia Confederate senator; John Campbell, Confederate assistant secretary of war—at Hampton Roads two months before his assassination also was indicative of his preference. But his words lacked the weight of policy, as endorsed either by the cabinet or Congress. Lincoln had stressed to his Southern interlocutors the need to resist harshness and to get Rebel soldiers back to their homes. Apparently he also told the commissioners that the end of slavery was not a precondition to peace. Restoration of the Union, moreover, would entail the return or compensation of Southern properties taken under the Confiscation Acts.[20] These statements, had they been widely disseminated, would have provoked howls of protest from Radical Republicans like Congressman Thaddeus Stevens. To them, the war was a crusade to smite injustice, which meant punishing the wicked and placing former slaves on a plane of equality with white masters.

Soothing words by Lincoln in early 1865—while the fighting continued—could not have eased Confederate resentment at rejoining the Union on terms that obliterated the prewar social order. Yet after Appomattox there were prominent persons in the South who urged a modus vivendi with the Reconstruction authority. Among the early adherents to this line were General Pierre Gustave Beauregard, Alabama's Governor Robert Patton, Wade Hampton of South Carolina, Henry Wise of Virginia, and Joseph Brown of Georgia.[21] The most eminent in this party was Robert E. Lee.

He set an example of dignified adjustment to Southern vanquishment by his deportment in 1865–1870 as president of Washington College (Lexington, Virginia) and in his public comments. He discouraged white violence against freedmen. He applied for pardon and a restoration of citizenship (the latter was denied). He told former Confederates that their well-being was inextricably linked to the reunited republic's destiny. Lee's actions did not obviate his unhappiness with instances of what he considered Federal misconduct in the occupied zone, such as the trial and execution of Major Henry Wirz, commandant at Andersonville prison: Wirz's hanging amounted to a "most unjust calumny." Nor did Lee think that the freedmen and women were capable of attaining a level of civilization comparable to their former owners'. But he generally approved of President Andrew Johnson's mild policy, viewing it as consistent with Lincoln's call for national healing and carrying a promise of Southern recovery.[22]

More dramatic than Lee's accommodation with defeat was that of General James Longstreet. He did not simply submit to Reconstruction. He actively cooperated with it. His reasoning was purely practical. It had nothing to do with self-aggrandizement or opportunism, as charged by his defamers, who remained willfully ignorant of his thinking. Longstreet taught, in common with Lee, that the duration of postwar Southern suffering would correspond to the intensity of the region's defiance of Northern dictate. Saving what remained of Southern civilization required working within the occupation regime and with the Republican party. The alternative, said Longstreet, would be confiscation and governance by uncouth black men: "The thing [Reconstruction] shall be done by the blacks, and we shall be set aside, if not expatriated."[23] To prevent this disaster—to control the black vote—white men had to forsake their sentimental allegiance to the Democratic party and collaborate with Washington in consolidating Federal order. Longstreet consequently joined the Republican party, asked for (and was granted) pardon, and renewed his prewar friendship with Ulysses Grant. From President Grant, Longstreet later acquired the handsome position of customs collector of New Orleans, in which city he had earlier established himself as a businessman. As head of the Louisiana militia in 1874, Longstreet tried to suppress (with mostly black troops) an insurrection instigated by the Crescent City White League against Governor William Kellog's Radical administration. Longstreet was wounded in the fighting and taken prisoner by the League, itself mostly staffed by inveterate Confederates. Only the intervention of Federal forces was sufficient to restore peace and win Longstreet's release.

Longstreet enjoyed the continuing confidence of the Republican party for both his statements to the Northern press on the desirability of reconciliation and his cooperation with constituted authority. He won further plum appointments from G.O.P. largesse, including diplomatic assignment (minister to the Ottoman Empire in 1880–1881) and sinecures, such as the United States Commissioner for Railroads. He lived long enough to see North and South compose their differences to make common cause against Spain in 1898.

Northern support caused Longstreet and his family to be ostracized by Southern society; they were periodically forced to change their domicile. Esteemed by Lee during the war as a faithful comrade ("my old warhorse"), Longstreet was villainized in the South. His detractors, of whom Jefferson Davis was one, eventually managed to saddle him with practically every calamity, from Gettysburg, to abolition, to scalawag-carpetbagger misrule. He was the Judas. He betrayed the South on the battlefield, subsequently ingratiating himself with Northern oppressors and African primitives—the latter motivated by lustful revenge.[24]

Actually, the goals of black activists had little to do with retribution against the white South. Questions of distributive justice were considerably more important to them. But even here, tentativeness was apparent. The idea of forty acres and a mule, incidentally, seems to have originated in the problems General Sherman faced as throngs of former slaves attached themselves to his army in Georgia; he meant to unburden his forces from the responsibility of caring for so many people by directing their attention to producing their own food.[25]

Black leaders during the war had concentrated their effort on political questions, which seemed more urgent than economic ones. Would the conflict really bring about the destruction of slavery or be waged merely to preserve the United States? Might reunion be purchased at the price of retaining the institution? What military role would blacks be permitted in the war—which as of 1863 was avowedly fought for liberation? After the war, would provisions for education and gainful employment be available to freedmen, who by tradition and law had been denied both? Would black Americans be entrusted with full citizenship, including suffrage, thereby repealing the Dred Scott decision? In effect, how would blacks be situated in postwar America? One could find comfort in the drumbeat of abolitionist preaching on the hypocrisy of slavery in democracy, à la William Lloyd Garrison. But the severity of antiblack riots in New York augured ill. Declarations by Northern troops—such as the officer who confessed to diarist Mary Chestnut—that they were fighting not for black freedom but to keep the nation intact were also depressing. Lincoln avoided meetings with leaders from the black community and in public messages kept discreet distance from their cause. He made only one exception: Frederick Douglass.[26]

No one better articulated the anxieties and goals of African Americans during the war. Douglass urged white authorities to admit black men into the Union army. Once allowed, he encouraged blacks to enlist, thus ensuring a sturdy basis for claiming future rights of citizenship. His own sons, Charles and Lewis, served with the Fifty-fourth Massachusetts Volunteers, for which outfit Douglass worked as a recruiting agent. He campaigned for equal pay for black servicemen. He argued too for a policy of retaliation in response to Jefferson Davis's declaration that black men captured in Yankee uniform would be summarily shot. As to slavery, Douglass shared the fear of many African Americans that the war would end without liberation—a likelihood signaled in 1864 by the predicted election of General George McClellan to the presidency. Almost certainly, McClellan's victory would have allowed slavery to survive into the postwar era—albeit compromised by Confederate defeats, the good performance of black troops, and Lincoln's emancipation edict.[27]

Douglass's concerns for the African future in America were crystallized in his ambivalence toward Lincoln. Douglass certainly felt the abolitionist dismay for Lincoln's limited aims in the first phase of warfare. He openly criticized the president for coddling secessionists, as when in September 1861 Lincoln revoked General John Fremont's decree freeing the slaves of Rebels in Missouri. Douglass charged that the president's support of black colonization to tropical countries amounted to "Negro hatred." He was equally uneasy with Lincoln's notion that blacks might have to pass through an unspecified period of apprenticeship before becoming eligible for first-class citizenship. Douglass often despaired that the president's commitment to equality after liberation would be lukewarm. A decade after the war's finale, he pronounced: "[Lincoln] was preeminently the white man's President, entirely devoted to the welfare of white men."[28]

Yet there was another side to him that Douglass appreciated. Despite Lincoln's lack of public zeal, he nevertheless *did* place the moral authority and armed weight of the federal government against Slave Power. The president's genius, in this formulation, was pragmatic rather than visionary; it had to embrace the well-being of the whole country, not just one sect of partisans, however humane their aim: "Tardy, cold, dull, and indifferent" from the genuine abolitionist's standpoint, Lincoln was "swift" and "determined" when measured against national sentiment, which as a statesman he had perforce to consult. On the basis of their two interviews (1863, 1864), Douglass was satisfied that the president loathed slavery and looked hopefully to its extinction. Responding to Douglass's petitioning, Lincoln ordered (July 1863) that Confederate violation of the laws of war—shooting black soldiers or enslaving them—would provoke reprisals, the threat of which halted Southern practice. Doubts notwithstanding and a preference for the less equivocal Fremont aside, Douglass supported Lincoln in the 1864 election. Douglass subsequently praised the president's Second Inaugural speech as a "sacred effort" for its promises of justice (for the freedmen) and mercy (to the South). Fulfillment of this first pledge, Douglass thereafter repeated, guaranteed the nation's future safety. He was stunned by the president's murder in April 1865, on which occasion he delivered an eloquent oration. He looked with trepidation on the future as Johnson assumed executive responsibility. Whereas the emancipator had personally received Douglass with unfeigned solicitude, his successor objected to him as being "just like any nigger . . . he would sooner cut a white man's throat than not."[29]

After the War

Karl Marx was not alone among foreign observers in predicting that Lincoln's assassination would amount to "the greatest piece of folly" from a Southern viewpoint. The belief was nearly universal that Johnson, who had earlier issued blood-curdling statements on the need to exterminate Rebel leaders, would wreak vengeance. Consumed by class envy, reported Marx, this petty Southern tailor hated the planter oligarchy and would use Lincoln's martyrdom to justify draconian policy.[30] Not for the last time did subsequent events confute the socialist prophet.

The awful questions that vexed Lincoln now faced his successor. By what means and at what pace should the South be reintegrated into national life? What niche should the freed people occupy? What provision, if any, ought to be made for their security against potential white depredations? Invoking his reading of Lincoln as authoritative while relying on his own experience as military governor of Tennessee, Johnson wanted to reattach the wayward region swiftly. A former slave owner himself, he was indifferent to the fate of the newly freed; he hoped fervently that it would not become an obstacle to reunion. Antiblack feeling in the North, nearly as rife as in the South, could be counted an ally by him. These attitudes, combined with his expectation of winning the presidency in 1868 as a Democrat, placed Johnson on the side of a reenfranchised South.

Johnson promoted a clement peace during the months of presidential-led Reconstruction in 1865–1866—to the dismay of Radicals, who mistakenly had thought of him as their own. Johnson's attitude entailed opposition to both black suffrage and the Freedmen's Bureau. The president also issued proclamations of amnesty for participants in the rebellion and a return of their nonslave property. He favored mild requirements for taking the loyalty oath and for receiving pardon and the right to vote or run for elected office. He urged the discontinuance of military rule; he argued that occupation violated constitutional guarantees. Johnson tried to reduce the number of black troops assigned to garrison duty in the South, calling them a provocative presence. Presidential mercy did not, however, extend to the conspirators who killed Lincoln and wounded Seward. Contrary to the recommendation of the military court that judged the assassins, Johnson did not commute the death sentence of Mary Surratt, who by virtue of her sex and status (as mother) presumably deserved better. All the same, Johnson overcame his earlier impulses and resisted demands in the North to hang Lee, Davis, Stephens, and other Rebel notables. Johnson was seen in the former Confederacy as a reasonable man for his efforts against confiscations and executions and for his support of Southern home rule; his sensibility held back the tidal wave of Northern revenge and African anarchy. Gratitude and relief, however, did not translate into clamoring political support in Dixie, where feeling never forgave Johnson's desertion to the Union in 1861.[31]

From the perspective of Republican congressmen, specifically the Radical element, Johnson's version of Reconstruction mocked the Northern sacrifices of blood and treasure. Applied to electoral politics, his approach also threatened to restore to a prewar level Southern ascendancy in Washington through a majority Democratic party. Representation in the lower house, based on distribution of population, suddenly gave advantage to Southern-Democratic standing. In antebellum days, slaves had been worth only three-fifths of a person for purposes of determining representation. Now counted as full-fledged humans beings, freed blacks justified an increase in the size of the South's legislative delegation. Might it pass laws that nullified such gains as the Emancipation Proclamation? While Radicals brooded, the South sent to Congress (December 1865) a number of individuals who had acted prominently in the Confederate cause. They included its vice president, four generals, six cabinet officers, and fifty-eight legislators, none of whom was obviously repentant.[32] Confederate officials, civilian and military, were also elected to office in overwhelming numbers at the state and municipal levels. All-white state legislatures in the South then adopted the black codes, the aim of which was to squeeze African-American liberties; the resultant subordination approached peonage.[33] Freedmen also labored under other disabilities—that denied them voting and civil rights—and they were victimized by sporadic but deadly white violence. The rise of terrorist organizations (Regulators, Jayhawkers, Black Horse Cavalry) was a manifestation of unfocused anger, fueled by a wider sense of despair and grievance. Southern law enforcement was also culpable. Policemen in Memphis in May 1866 led a mob that indiscriminately attacked black men, women, and children, leaving 46 dead, more than 80 wounded. A few months later, policemen in New Orleans joined a rampage that left 38 blacks dead, 119 injured.

Shootings, lynchings, and a resurgence of Southern electoral strength might in fact have reversed the decision won by Northern arms. To forestall this event, Radical congressmen prevented Southern representatives from taking their Senate and House seats in late 1865. The Radicals thereupon assumed responsibility via the Joint Committee on Reconstruction for presiding over Southern rehabilitation. In the process they sought to arrogate power previously exercised by the executive branch. The ensuing duel between president and Radical Congress culminated in the 1868 impeachment trial of Johnson; he escaped conviction by one vote. Against his campaigning and futile vetoes, congressional Reconstruction imposed military order on the South. Its principal goal was to control the explosion of violence against Southern loyalists, Republicans, freedmen, and that stream of Northerners—disparaged as carpetbaggers—who established schools, aid programs, and businesses. Congressional Reconstruction also resulted in the civil rights bill (Fourteenth Amendment, 1866) and additional guarantees that provided for black suffrage (Fifteenth Amendment, 1870). The white South groaned under this reversal of fortunes. Said Robert Toombs, one-time Confederate secretary of state, the Reconstruction regime was "a mass of floating putrescence," containing equal parts tyranny, corruption, and "treachery to the Caucasian race."[34]

The villains, according to Southern publicists, were concentrated among abolitionists, suffragettes, political opportunists, and—that most pathetic of figures—the black man who presumed an extensive equality. This cabal against decency counted as its mainstays Sumner, Douglass, Salmon Chase, Edwin Stanton, Susan Anthony, Wendell Phillips, and Pennsylvania's Thaddeus Stevens. From a modern standpoint, Stevens is properly seen as symbol and substance of Radical resolve, without which the history of American racial progress would be even more bleak. Yet to Southerners then, he was a freak of nature, a clubfooted "Caliban" who not only betrayed white culture in the South but offended God by living sinfully with a black woman. These and other defamations were heaped upon Stevens in his last years (he died in 1868) and by writers inclined sympathetically to the South.[35] To President Andrew Johnson, Stevens was every bit as execrable as the secessionists of 1861.

Stung by thwarted political ambition, vindictive to enemies, irascible in private life, and imprudent in his conduct of Johnson's impeachment, Stevens's passions were as defeating to himself as to his intended victims. His glee at Southern hardship, which he saw as amply earned, and his desire for retribution explain the calumny to which he was subjected. Yet he also harnessed his ferocity on behalf of human dignity, championing such outcasts as the Indians, Jews, and Chinese. He gave liberally to charities, fought for free education in Pennsylvania, and opposed capital punishment.[36] During the war, he prodded Lincoln in the direction of emancipation. Stevens also supported the enlistment of black troops. After Appomattox he and other Radicals helped give substance to Lincoln's solemn wish that the war would bring forth "a new birth of freedom." Their efforts led not only to the Fourteenth and Fifteenth Amendments—the latter quite remarkable, given that most Northerners outside of New England opposed such legislation—but also advanced these goals: founding of public schools in the South, provision of equipment and farming land for freedmen, protection of life and property against the Invisible Empire (Ku Klux Klan). To the American correspondent of Paris's *Le Temps,* Georges Clemenceau, Stevens and his colleagues had waged revolution made stern by the *ancien regime's* intransigence.[37]

Nathan Bedford Forrest personified postwar Southern resistance, which like France's earlier *Thermidor* swept reaction to triumph. Before the war, he had prospered as a slave trader in Mississippi, where he won a degree of social acceptance normally withheld from dealers in such commerce. During the war, as a cavalry general, he enjoyed Lee's admiration and was acknowledged by friend and foe as one of the most brilliant soldiers to emerge from the conflict. Forrest's daring was matched only by his cruelty, which climaxed in the massacre of surrendering black soldiers at Fort Pillow in 1864, a deed that even his defenders are hard put to justify.[38]

A psychologically complex character who eventually repented of his more virulent racial attitudes and called for dissolution of the Ku Klux Klan, Forrest is primarily remembered for leadership of that organization. It melded and superseded assorted white supremacist groups in the late 1860s. Dedicated to the propositions and prerogatives of the antebellum South, it waged guerrilla war against the Loyal Leagues, Freedmen's Bureau, state militias, and other organizations involved in the welfare of blacks or sympathetic whites.[39]

Klan lawlessness was not only murderous—its victims numbering in the thousands—but it demoralized the North, which had to foot the expense and manpower to pacify the unruly South. Discontent over this strife grew steadily in the North, where Grant expressed the prevailing mood in 1868: "Let us have peace." The stock market crash on September 24, 1869 ("Black Friday") and economic turbulence that followed reinforced this exasperation while also focusing attention away from Southern Reconstruction. Indeed, that project seemed to hamper the new task of ending the economic crisis that in 1873 burst into full-scale depression. The interest of Northern bankers and railway entrepreneurs in having a single functioning economy also helped prepare the way for conservative-Democratic ("redemption") rule. This was established years before Rutherford Hayes withdrew (in 1877) the few army units still on occupation duty. Except in Florida, Louisiana, and South Carolina, the Klan and similar groups played a pivotal part—through intimidation and violence—in the pre-Hayes redemption victories that undid congressional Reconstruction. In 1874, for example, white violence in Mississippi claimed as many as 300 black lives as presage to redemption rule, consummated in November 1875.[40]

*   *   *   *   *

The Civil War was traumatic for the generation of Americans that lived through it. Casualties had been fearful. Destruction in the South was a long time in mending. Proposed ventures to avert calamity (Seward's seeking a foreign quarrel to kindle national unity) or erase it (war talk against French-occupied Mexico) were unavailing. Yet in a comparative framework of civil wars, the American was less devastating than most. The contemporaneous civil war in China (Taiping Rebellion, 1851–1864) spewed desolation in which millions of lives were lost.[41] The bitterest civil wars since 1865—as in Russia, Spain, Cambodia, China—have also been unbridled. The scale of atrocities, particularly against civilians, occupies a category unimaginable to a Grant or even a Sherman.

As with these twentieth-century civil wars, America's was related to a larger global conflict, the outcome of which went beyond national division. The Emancipation Proclamation was an important victory, if belated, for the antislavery cause in the nineteenth century—which had already been advanced by the French, British, and Dutch, among others. Union success doomed what remained of slavery in the New World, quickening its prohibition in such places as Cuba (1878) and Brazil (1888).

The Civil War and eradication of slavery had additional international implications, not the least of which was to maintain a lively experiment in representative government. It was not patriotic piety that caused W. E. B. Du Bois in 1935 to characterize the U.S. version of democracy as preeminent. Rather, he recognized (like Douglass before him) that the postwar United States had the potential for becoming a home of universal human rights.[42] More than he anticipated, the power of liberal example—not just preaching, bluster, or material abundance—would become a factor in the twentieth-century competition for global prestige, in which contest the totalitarian states were handicapped.

However compelling the promise of American liberty, its observance has been wildly uneven. In the period reviewed here, the moment of black freedom was fleeting. During it, universities were established (Fisk 1866, Howard 1867) to educate peoples hitherto denied by force of law from learning to read or write. Former slaves and free-born blacks were also able to assume positions of elected authority in the defunct Confederacy and to represent their states in Congress. Although this innovation depended on army bayonets, Republican control, and Democratic liability, most men elected to office acquitted themselves well. They produced a record of improvements that inspired subsequent (post-Jim Crow) black lawmakers. To the degree that some within this first generation of legislators were incompetent, venal, or corrupt—as the anti-Reconstruction catechism insists —they by no means deviated far from the prevailing standard. That not-so-innocent era was dominated by party bosses, whose low level of scruple gave notoriety to the Gilded Age. Gains in black economic life were also tangible, giving lie to the slaveowners' refrain about their wards' natural laziness. Cultivation of small plots of arable land and access to wages resulted in dramatic per-capita income rise for blacks over the days of slavery (rising in the agricultural sector from 23 percent of white income in 1857 to 52 percent by the 1870s). This *relative* gain after slavery amounted to the greatest proportionate redistribution of income in American history.[43]

None of these achievements was irreversible. Their substantial rollback in the redeemed South amounted to Confederate victory by means short of war. By the mid-1890s a rigid system of segregation had taken root in the South, concomitantly degrading black political-educational-economic life. In the despondent words of Du Bois, "The slave went free; stood a brief moment in the sun; then moved back again toward slavery."[44] Meanwhile, in the post-Reconstruction South—also to a large degree in the Northern white mind—the idea flourished that Union occupation and its works had been unspeakably cruel. The romance of the Lost Cause, already well launched by 1870, eventually assimilated the cult of Lee and projected itself into the next century with such icons as D. W. Griffith's *Birth of a Nation* and Margaret Mitchell's *Gone with the Wind*. The reality of Jim Crow was concealed in a fairy tale of chivalry and heroism against all odds.[45] Sentimentality did not allow for Fort Pillow in the past; delicacy did not protest plagues of lynching in 1900–1930.

Still, the myth of a genteel civilization tragically ruined did serve a useful function, manifest even in foreign policy. Before the establishment of an independent West Germany in 1949, the American zone of occupation was administered by General Lucius Clay. He was a Southerner whose sense of what had gone wrong during Reconstruction strengthened his determination to promote nonpunitive policies in Germany.[46] Clay was mostly successful in this aim; his administration accounts in part for West Germany's later record as an exemplar of orderly liberty and affluence. More importantly, the Confederate myth enabled the South to live with military defeat and occupation by enemy force, the only part of the United States to experience such affliction. The myth also allowed for a moral equilibrium within the nation between the competing claims of Northern liberation and unity versus Southern esprit and pathos.

Because regional reconciliation after the war had been of paramount importance to Lincoln, he eschewed revenge. He also realized, however dilatorily, that justice demanded attention be given to the plight of black men and women. His hope was that mercy and justice could be harmonized through compassion, but untimely death prevented him from devising the details.

Might he have found a workable formula? Probably not. The dilemma resided in this obvious logic: mutually exclusive claims could not be equally legitimated. Despite Radical efforts, racial justice was subsequently sacrificed to national unity. Deplorable conditions of black life in the South (and elsewhere) festered for decades until a revitalized civil rights movement began after World War II to redress the inequities.

These appreciations raise the harrowing question of whether Union victory justified the cost. Only in the long view of history can the answer be unambiguously yes. The United States was not Balkanized. Its unified power was subsequently available in the twentieth century and was implicated with justice in the contests against Nazi and Soviet tyrannies. As for the advance of human dignity in America, it may have been delayed by the post-Reconstruction reaction. Yet the partial achievement of 1863 was never repealed, nor was the force for racial equality dissipated; civil rights dormancy lasted for years but did not become a permanent condition. Nor was irrepressible American optimism—virtually a faith contrary to evidence—extinguished. No one expressed it better than the historian Bruce Catton, who having examined the war and its aftermath could still claim the following: "Like Lincoln, we are moving toward a destiny bigger than we can understand. The dark, indefinite shore is still ahead of us. Maybe we will get there some day . . . And when we get there, it is [reasonable] to suppose that instead of being dark and indefinite, that unknown continent will be lit with sunlight."[47]

The alchemy of time has transmuted the Civil War's miseries and Lincoln's ambiguous statecraft into heroic epic. The aura surrounding them permits of a few acceptable images to the national mind; a haunting one remains the tattered Army of Northern Virginia consoling its chief after surrender to Grant. As for Lincoln: his faults, as Douglass recognized, were those of his era, but his virtues were his own. The core of Lincoln's legacy is twofold: accelerating the cause of liberty in 1863 (which also allowed public utterance of his private anguish over slavery); providing a galvanizing vocabulary that has enabled generations of Americans to define themselves as a nation and steady them in a world menaced by competitions for power. Lincoln urged his compatriots, in the Second Inaugural's phrase, to do everything necessary to "achieve and cherish a just and a lasting peace, among ourselves, and with all [states]." Americans in 1865 and since could embrace this imperative, even as the Civil War lingered for decades in collective memory as an unhealed wound.

TWO

Splendid Little War

Comprehensive defeat in the 1898 war against the United States sparked a Spanish crisis of confidence. The peace treaty, signed in Paris, stripped from the once-mighty empire most of its residual holdings. Thereafter Spain's uncertain political class—divided by monarchical Catholics and secular republicans—struggled to find a common purpose. The nadir was finally reached in the civil war (1936–1939), when the rival factions became accomplices in their country's destruction. In the meantime writers and intellectuals, most significantly "the generation of 1898," sought to rediscover and rejuvenate the authentic Spain. "Miserable Castile, yesterday lording it over everybody, now wrapped in her rags," sighed the poet Antonio Machado. The similarly minded philosopher Ortega y Gasset later exclaimed: "Spain today, rather than a nation, is a cloud of dust remaining after a great people have galloped down the highway of history." Even as conflict with the United States approached, Admiral Pascual Cervera y Topete, self-conscious heir to the fleet that once tied the New World to the Old, warned that his antiquated ships and undertrained crews would be easy prey for the modernized American navy. But he was no more able than other political or military leaders in Madrid to resist the widespread feeling that preferred an honorable fight against the haughty Americans, even if predicted defeat were confirmed: better a display of Spanish courage than submission to Yankee decree in Cuba, which despite its half-century of fitful mutiny was still part of a venerable imperium.[1]

Whereas it highlighted the extent of Spain's decrepitude, the war demonstrated that the United States—despite recent trials—was not about to crack along racial or class or regional lines. Rather, it possessed ample social cohesion and sheer economic-military power. In this sense, the war heralded a restoration of U.S. morale, strained in previous decades.

Although it had seen vigorous assertions of national will—acquisition of Alaska, building of a vast railway system, admission of new states—the post-1865 era was racked with crises. They suggested that centrifugal forces were operating, which, in the litany of pessimists like Brooks Adams *(The Law of Civilization and Decay)*, foretold ultimate disaster. Even if the warnings of Cassandras were exaggerated, there was nothing imagined about those problems related to the abuse of economic power by the Rockefellers, Harrimans, and Stanfords. These were not canceled by Andrew Carnegie's extolling the social benefits of private wealth, but barely alleviated by belated exercises in philanthropy. Labor unrest meanwhile—the 1886 Haymarket affair, the 1894 Pullman strike, violence waged by the Molly Maguires in Pennsylvania's coal fields—was aggravated by market volatility and depression, exemplified by the sharp downturn of 1893–1897. Religious and ethnic tensions also quickened as a flood of immigrants from eastern and southern Europe sought to settle among citizens, still predominantly Protestant, with origins in the British isles or Germany. Eighty-six percent of the foreign-born in 1900 lived in the northeastern quadrant (above the Ohio, east of the Mississippi), typically in teeming slums, where violence and vice were bred. Pogroms would produce by 1910 slightly fewer than 2 million Russian-born Jews in the United States, whose condition of impecuniousness on arrival met alternately with anxiety or contempt. Nativist resentment on the West Coast against Asian newcomers was also high. It gave rise to incidents like the 1877 anti-Chinese riot in San Francisco and led to restrictive immigration policy (the 1882 Chinese Exclusion Act). Other social questions defied obvious answer. They stemmed from diverse sources: agrarian economy versus industrial production; free traders against the protectionist tariff; free silver advocates (led by the Great Commoner, William Jennings Bryan) pitted against the gold standard; and prairie populism opposed to the Eastern elite ("plutocracy"). Even while Henry Grady of the *Atlanta Constitution* trumpeted a new South in 1886 that was stable and safe, the finishing touches of white overlordship were being fastened onto the region's black population. Military engagements against Indians in the waning decades of the nineteenth century gave further, if unintended, meaning to what historian Bernard DeVoto called "the plundered province" of the Far West. Nor had corruption in high office ended with the departure of Grant's scandal-ridden administration. Abuse thrived at every level of government, including the main municipalities like New York, where Tammany chicanery was tradition. Against this marring of the democratic landscape, the determination of mugwumps was hardly more availing than the whine of Henry Adams. Not until the tardy arrival of the trust busters and the progressive mentality, personified by Theodore Roosevelt, did strenuous counteraction have an effect. Until then America was a splintered society, where vision of a dynamic future was further constricted by the frontier's closing, concluding—in Frederick Jackson Turner's words—"the first period of American history."[2]

Robert Dallek overly psychologized when he wrote in 1983 that the crusading Americans were "unconsciously" rescuing themselves from dreary domestic conditions by fighting to liberate Cuba from Spain. Yet he was right
to underscore the emotional release provided by the war. It gave escape from
collective malaise and created new opportunity for exertion—made more sat-
isfying as the effort was against a monarchical, Catholic, Latin nation.[3] The
"splendid little war," so dubbed by Secretary of State John Hay, impressed
contemporaries, such as Senator Henry Cabot Lodge, as just the tonic for the
country's passivity and divisions. They had been aroused to near action and
unity by the 1895 Venezuelan crisis with Britain—playing neatly into the
hands of dedicated Anglophobes—but then reverted to form following a
diplomatic solution. The exercise of martial virtues therefore struck the black
historian Edward Johnson in 1899 as a palliative to the country's aimlessness,
grown to unseemly proportion after three decades devoid of war. Even
Woodrow Wilson, yet a private citizen but an eminence at Princeton University, was not immune to the war contagion. The explosion of the *USS
Maine* in Havana harbor, throwing "a touch of fever into men's thoughts," as
he wrote, helped lead to events that sealed national unity: "It was the experience of the Mexican war repeated." Vivid memory of the struggle between
the states was at last fading, submerged in the exhilaration of conquest by
arms and the extension of American writ beyond the shoreline.[4]

For Empire

The contest against Spain was replete with usable history to a country hun-
gry for self-validation. Correspondents, including Stephen Crane *(The Red
Badge of Courage),* celebrated the war's heroes, while artists, including Fred-
eric Remington, captured their image on canvas. Former Southern officers,
notably Generals Fitzhugh Lee and Joe Wheeler, led the sons of Confederate and Union veterans, inordinately eager to prove that their mettle was also
sound. For Theodore Roosevelt the chance to fight helped remove the shame
he felt over his father's absence from service in 1861–1865. The Rough
Rider confessed with feeling in his autobiography: "If there were a serious
war I wished to be in a position to explain to my children why I did take
part in it, and not why I did not."[5] Wheeler himself served under General
Nelson Miles, who as a Union officer had held him in custody in the same
prison housing Jefferson Davis. At the moment when the battle of Las
Guasimas in Cuba (June 24, 1898) turned into Spanish rout, Wheeler for-
got himself momentarily. He shouted to his troops, of whom many were
black: "We've got the Yankees on the run!"[6]

Depictions of a brilliant war—not just those produced by conjurers working for Hearst and Pulitzer—were devoured by the public. Naval victories,

of which Commodore Dewey's in Manila Bay was the most dazzling, vindicated the expenditures recently lavished on capital ships (in which cause Assistant Secretary of the Navy Roosevelt had campaigned). Not only did the feared appearance of Spain's Atlantic fleet on the eastern seaboard never materialize, but its main force was destroyed off the coast of Cuba. Although the War Department under the incompetent Russell Alger bore responsibility for the tragicomic mess at Tampa Bay and the chaotic embarkation to Cuba, the small professional army (25,000 men in 1898) and mass of volunteers were overwhelmingly successful. Not always well led—witness the bumbling General William Shafter—or properly equipped, they nevertheless suffered light casualties. These numbered 380 fatalities from Spanish fire. Far more succumbed to malaria or yellow fever. American school children learned the names of brave men and their feats, such as Lieutenant Andrew Rowan who delivered "the message" to the insurgent General Calixto Garcia. The gallantry of Captain Philip commanding the *Texas* was taught, as when he bade his crew not to cheer as the ship's guns hit their Spanish targets: "The poor fellows are dying." No publicist outdid Roosevelt in covering himself and the Rough Riders—an assortment of Ivy League adventurers plus frontier roughnecks—with glory. By his own admission, he deserved the Medal of Honor. The satisfaction of victory was made the sweeter as most European states tilted toward Spain, thereby sharing a portion of humiliation by the New World's champion.[7]

Even its critics did not accuse the United States of haste in going to war over Cuba. President William McKinley could cite a record of diplomacy whose purpose of finding an alternative to Spanish-American violence was thwarted by Madrid's chauvinists. Their delusions of grandeur would not allow for Cuban independence. Spain's inadequate policing of the island, meanwhile, had left in jeopardy the safety of U.S.-owned plantations and sundry investments, occasionally torched by rebels. Most horrifyingly, attempts to quell native restlessness led to brutality against civilians; 100,000 died in 1896–1898. Only persistent American pressure caused the recall to Spain of General Valeriano Weyler ("the butcher") and a cessation of oppressive policies—such as the reconcentration of rural residents into squalid urban confinement. McKinley, a decorated veteran of 1861–1865, was exceedingly reluctant to take the United States into war. While the public clamor for military action grew, he delayed, citing the lessons of early experience: "I have been through one war; I have seen the dead piled up, and I do not want to see another."[8]

His hope for a diplomatic resolution had risen with the formation of a Liberal Spanish government in late summer 1897, under Praxedes Mateo Sagasta, and the tone of conciliation struck between Minister Stewart Woodford and the queen regent, Maria Cristina. It was she who reversed Weyler's policy and granted Cuba a new dispensation of autonomy under Spain's protective aegis. In December, McKinley was urging upon his countrymen—impatient ones burned him in effigy—to give Spanish officials adequate time to redeem themselves in Cuba. This course proved impossible, however, as events undermined negotiations. Madrid was simply unable to force Cuban *colons* and its soldiers to comply with reformist edicts. Certain impolitic remarks contained in a private letter by Spain's minister in Washington, Enrique Dupuy de Lome, made their way into the public prints via the *New York Journal*. As a sensation was being made about these statements, which claimed that McKinley was weak and pandered to the crowd, the *Maine* was sunk in Havana harbor; 260 of its crew were killed. The ship had been dispatched to help protect American lives and property in Cuba; the sinking in February 1898 was thought by most Americans, eager to believe the worst, to be the work of Spanish deviltry. This assumption was not dispelled by the U.S. naval board of inquiry that pronounced the ship a victim of an externally planted explosive device.[9] (This erroneous finding was reversed decades later, when investigators determined that the disaster resulted from an accidental explosion aboard the *Maine*.)[10]

The dénouement came as the Spanish waffled in response to McKinley's ultimatum on three requirements: Cuban armistice, peace parleys through his good offices between rebels and Madrid, the island's freedom. Simultaneous with this breakdown in negotiations, the drift toward war was accelerated by the oratory of Senator Redfield Proctor, who on his return from a fact-finding tour of Cuba gave a riveting account in chambers. His indictment of "the worst misgovernment" imaginable and his sympathy for suffering Cubans converted several congressional noninterventionists to action—while raising popular passions. These last had been wakened by the lobbying of Cuban insurgents in Washington, such as Evangelina Cosia y Cisneros, whose tale of woe had inspired a frenzy among American women for *Cuba libre*.[11]

The war against Spain fitted the U.S. mood exactly. It served to vent aggressive impulses while encouraging citizens to see themselves as they preferred: defenders of justice and downtrodden humanity. Spanish iniquities in Cuba, McKinley declared in his war message to Congress (April 11, 1898), "shocked the sensibilities" of Americans; they could no longer tolerate the practice of torture and atrocity near their territory. This mix of idealism and the darker side of motive was richly illustrated in Roosevelt, whose spiritedness drew him to fighting. His penchant for violence could not obliterate his conscience or intelligence, which obliged him to seek morally defensible actions. He could recite better than most contemporaries the catalogue of Spanish despotism in Cuba. He emphasized with relish the grislier details; justice dictated a war of rescue. At the same time, romantic ideas about soldiering made Roosevelt exalt and seek for himself that renown won only on battlefields. In contrast with the prating of mollycoddles, hucksters, and the lunatic fringe, as he scored the antiwar objection, true Americans welcomed the test of their manhood; for this purpose ethically primitive enemies fulfilled necessary function. He boasted of killing a Spanish soldier during the rush up San Juan Hill and in later years recollected the war as the high point of experience—for its color, camaraderie, thrill of danger. Roosevelt's British friend Cecil Spring Rice meant to be generous when he compared the Rough Rider's pleasure in battle to a six-year-old boy's demand for excitement. The skeptical philosopher William James was actually nearer to the mark in likening the mentality of Roosevelt to "the Sturm und Drang period" of adolescence. In any case, TR's gushing over the imagined glories of war caused him in 1898 to see the conflict with Spain as a vehicle of personal (plus national) deliverance from tedium and the soul-destroying softness of bourgeois life.[12]

While James condemned Roosevelt for moral obtuseness, other pundits found his outlook congenial. Under the coarsening influence of Herbert Spencer, American intellectual life was dominated by the cult of Social Darwinism. This celebrated the virtues of national muscularity, regarding its exercise as scientifically sanctioned. The purported revelations of biology also supported doctrines about race, as by Professor Pearson of Harvard (*National Life from the Standpoint of Science*). These ideas posited gradations of human excellence, with the Anglo-Teutonic occupying the top rung—the American variant of which came nearest to the future perfection ordained by evolution. The purifying qualities of war, the necessity of the fittest to assert themselves, and the laws of progress were all themes that recommended themselves to white Americans. No less than Roosevelt did his friend, naval theorist Captain Alfred Mahan, view the war against Spain as a righteous one: "on grounds of simple humanity." To this justification was joined the still finer reason: to accept manfully the competition for power, the outcome of which propelled some peoples to greatness, others—like the enervated Spaniards—to triviality.[13]

Roosevelt and Mahan were also immensely pleased when an ambivalent McKinley, after a prayerful night, later decided to place the entire Filipino archipelago under American tutelage, adding them to the other spoils of victory against Spain: suzerainty over Cuba, possession of Puerto Rico and Guam.[14] Approved by the Treaty of Paris (December 1898) ending hostilities and dignified by the purchase price of $20 million, annexation of the Philippines flung the United States headlong into Far Eastern affairs and an imperial career. Even as naysayers objected to empire in the Philippines as unconstitutional or immoral, and despite the high costs involved in subduing armed resistance in 1899–1902 (sporadically thereafter), Roosevelt and Mahan stayed intent. For them there were imperatives to surmount any doubt raised by periodic U.S. army misdeeds—the water cure, shooting prisoners—and the intensity of fighting.[15] This last outpaced that of 1898 and degenerated into unforgiving guerrilla warfare. It produced approximately two hundred thousand Filipino dead, the majority being civilian, plus an American version of "Weylerism": relocation centers for rural peasants.[16]

The Filipinos were obviously unable to govern themselves in a civilized manner, according to the Roosevelt-Mahan thesis. Their degraded condition—a combination of native barbarism and Spanish mismanagement—rendered them unfit for self-rule for years to come. These hapless people would wallow in political chaos if left to their own devices, falling victim first to themselves, then to a predator (Germany or France or Japan). Unlike the United States, it would not bother to instruct its wards in the processes of democracy with an eye to eventual independence, but would simply exploit the islands for profit. In other words, from the standpoint of long-term Filipino felicity, a singular opportunity would be lost if the United States shirked its moral duty—to uphold and protect that universal human dignity proclaimed in 1776. As president, Roosevelt congratulated (November 1902) the United States for its success in establishing improved conditions in the Philippines: "The islands have never been as orderly, as peaceful, or as prosperous as now; and in no other Oriental country, whether ruled by Asiatics or Europeans, is there anything approaching to the amount of individual liberty and of self-government which our rule has brought to the Filipinos." To this concern, Protestant missionaries of the Josiah Strong type added their voice. They hoped to undo the ill effects of Spanish Catholicism and expected that a Filipino position would aid in the spreading of Christ's truth in China, thereby fulfilling the divine commission set for the Anglo-Saxon: to be his dark brother's keeper.[17]

Businessmen involved with Far Eastern trade also viewed the Philippines as an important connecting link. Acquisition would permit a naval presence (coaling stations) that would protect maritime commerce with China while discouraging that country's exclusive orientation toward European power or Japan. No less an authority than Mahan could be cited to back this view. He asked rhetorically: "Can we without responsibility to God and man decline our aid [to China], which our respect for nationality and personality . . . will render especially disinterested, as well as especially helpful through the confidence it commands?" He professed that American maturity required a place in the archipelago as a waystation to China. To renounce it would be tantamount to repudiating a radiant American future. At the minimum, said Whitelaw Reid, editor-owner of the *New York Tribune,* possession of the Philippines would assure the conversion of the Pacific into an American lake—which would stimulate shipbuilding, industry, and commerce, all adding immeasurably to the national prosperity.[18]

Not only were the burdens imposed by democratic discipleship, the need to save souls, and to increase profits involved in the Philippines. The imperial calling also provided lessons and training for Americans in civic virtue. By tending to the needs (medical-hygenic, educational, political, economic) of those incapable of looking after themselves, Americans would foil the enemies of their own vitality: sloth and self-indulgence. Roosevelt argued in 1899 that possession of India had a salutary effect on the British character; similarly, work done well in the Philippines would improve the Americans. Senator Lodge, who had earlier worried that the United States was losing step with the leading nations, put the case succinctly: "This necessity for watching over the welfare of another people will improve our civil service, raise the tone of public life, and make broader and better all our politics."[19]

Imperial reasoning—with which McKinley went along but did not spearhead—took sparkling form in the forensic art of Albert Beveridge. This Indiana Republican (elected to the Senate in 1899) wove familiar themes into his speechifying: God's favoring of America; the sacred duty to bring enlightenment to benighted peoples, justifying suspension of government by consent for one of moral excellence; the economic reward of overseas expansion; the need for preemptive action against malevolent nations opposed to U.S. influence in Asia. Beveridge's famous lecture, "The March of the Flag," delivered to support Philippine annexation, was widely reprinted. It played a role in the Senate's ratification (by slight margin) of the acquisition provision in the Paris Treaty. "We can not fly from our world duties," Beveridge declaimed. "It is ours to execute the purpose of a fate that has driven us to be greater than our small intentions. We can not retreat from any soil where Providence has unfurled our banner; it is ours to save that soil for liberty and civilization." Nothing less than national honor was at stake in imperial custodianship.[20]

Anti-Imperialism

Among critics opposed to annexing the Philippines were people who had supported the intervention in Cuba, including black spokesmen. They originally had qualms about having black troops led (with few exceptions) by white officers and about participating in an errand of mercy while the economic-political condition of Southern blacks worsened. In 1889–1901, nearly two thousand African Americans were lynched in the former Confederacy, provoking Mark Twain to write his furious "United States of Lyncherdom." Yet by virtue of their Republican allegiance, most editorial writers in the black press endorsed the war. They also hoped that a loyal demonstration by themselves and black soldiers would win the admiration of white Americans. A war fought to liberate blacks in Cuba against a European power also had a peculiar appeal. But when the issue turned to containing Filipino nationalism in the name of establishing a U.S. outpost in Asia, most black support vanished, especially when the war produced its accretions of racialism. Frederick Douglass's son-in-law, Nathan Sprague, objected vehemently to inflicting a warped American civilization upon the unfortunate Filipinos. Omaha's *Progress* expressed this sentiment: "Every soldier in the Philippines who uses the term 'nigger' does so with hell-born contempt for the negro of the United States, and it is our one desire that he be cured of this fiendish malady by a Filipino bullet buried in the heart of such a wretch." Few editorial statements were as fiery as Sprague or the *Progress,* and some continued to support Republican foreign policy in the 1900 election. William Jennings Bryan, himself opposed to U.S. occupation in the Philippines, and his Democrats held no promise of easing black disability in the South. Still, the point stands that a substantial portion of black opinion was either lukewarm toward the Filipino war or actively against it, in which latter case young men were urged to forswear military service. As one black writer stated: "It is the plain duty of this government to remedy our own scandalous abuses rather than to extend the system under which they have arisen to other people."[21]

The scholarly fraternity was more evenly divided than the black community. Many academics favored U.S. policy in the hope that the Filipinos would be prepared for home rule in the (unspecified) future. In this group Nicholas Murray Butler, president of Columbia University, was prominent.[22] Other university presidents took the opposite position, however, notably David Starr Jordan of Stanford and Charles Eliot of Harvard. Dissenters abounded in the professoriate, including numbers of faculty at Yale and the newly founded University of Chicago. The preeminent philosopher of the day, Professor William James, also lent his prestige to the anti-imperial cause.

Uncertain in 1898 about the appropriateness of fighting Spain, he later repented of having had any doubt. It had been a "squalid war," he declared in 1910, the result of "pliant" McKinley's inability to withstand popular hysteria whipped up by the yellow press; jingoes of the Roosevelt ilk had also played a sordid part.[23] James's shift from hesitancy about 1898 to retrospective condemnation sprang from his revulsion for the battle against Emilio Aguinaldo. That conflict seemed a triple calamity to James, going well beyond his reflexive sympathy for lost causes. First, as a war of conquest, it was an infamous example of might smashing a weak nation, belonging to the category of Athens versus Melos. Second, the heedless destruction to Filipino lives and economy caused by military operations implicated the

United States in criminality. "We are cold-bloodedly, wantonly and abominably destroying a people," James protested in 1899, "who never did us an atom of harm in their lives. It is bald, brutal piracy." Third and most telling, the struggle against Aguinaldo constituted a betrayal of America's better self—*the* point of anxiety shared by James with most members of the Anti-Imperialist League, founded in Boston in November 1898. The forcible subjugation of one people by another menaced the spirit of 1776 and was disloyal to the Constitution, which extended U.S. sovereignty only to persons desirous of it. The delirium of overseas empire and war, then, undermined American institutions, threatening to destroy the national soul, nurtured through decades on the credo of liberty.[24]

As his fellow philosopher George Santayana perceived, James's previous reading of U.S. history had suffered from a patriotically induced naiveté, reinforced by his approval of the country's youthful energy. Although James was hardly a flag waver, his earlier understanding had been distorted by a commitment to American principles as superior to any in Europe (including his brother Henry's beloved Britain); these ideals had been advancing steadily since the founding. Their immanence through successive decades made the United States morally unique—an interpretation that easily slid over troubling episodes (slavery, Civil War, liquidation of Indians). This selective reading and orientation toward pre-1898 history explain the acuteness of James's anguish over policy in the Philippines. It elevated adventure above reason. Conquest in the Pacific also revealed that Americans, no less than Europeans, fell willingly to the domineering instinct (which, in "Moral Equivalent of War," James later sought to domesticate). Moreover, as he preferred to focus on tangible consequences, in keeping with pragmatism's dislike for the thin air of abstract theory, James was nonplused by the imperialist claim that U.S. beneficence would create a prosperous or serene Filipino democracy. He dismissed such a proposition as cover meant to hide the reality of coercion. This camouflage obscured the magnitude of suffering in the Philippines and allowed an atmosphere in which Filipino patriots were dehumanized—therefore objects suitable for extermination. Before the bar of justice, U.S. policy was odious, having discarded its traditional idealism: "The annexation of the Philippines, what could excuse that? What could be a more shameless betrayal of American principles? What could be a plainer symptom of greed, ambition, corruption?" A disconsolate James felt that he had "lost" his country.[25]

Because James was a prose stylist, he enjoyed a broader following than those depressingly many philosophers who have found refuge in inaccessibility. But no more than black newspapermen could it be said that he possessed a national constituency. Not so Mark Twain. His was a grand readership. After his triumphal homecoming from Europe in 1900, he threw himself into the anti-imperial crusade, taking upon himself the cause of victimized Africa (especially Belgium's Congo) and Asia. When the United States sought through the Philippines to join the colonial club—becoming "kin in sin" said Twain—he attacked his own, giving his name as a vice president to the Anti-Imperialist League. His grievances were several: he was dismayed by the discarding of Aguinaldo, one-time ally of Dewey against the Spanish; incensed by the lopsidedness of the Philippines war and the scale of casualties; upset by the treachery used by General Frederick Funston to capture Aguinaldo, whom Twain likened to George Washington and Joan of Arc.[26]

Twain excoriated in speeches and articles the suppression of the Philippines as an unjust war; it amounted to a robbing expedition. He heaped scorn upon specific officers like Funston and General Leonard Wood, the second of whom began as a medical doctor but forsook his calling by leading "Christian butchers" to kill "savages." The so-called savages included hundreds of Moro men, women, and children who had the temerity in one engagement (March 1906) to resist Wood's soldiers, dutifully bringing the blessings of democracy and civilization to the ungrateful heathens. When the reported Moro death list hit nine hundred, Twain mocked: "I was never so enthusiastically proud of the flag till now!" He was equally caustic on the subject of Protestant missionaries, Roosevelt, and the human sheep who allowed their leaders to betray national ideals. With wicked delight Twain updated the *Battle Hymn of the Republic:* "As Christ died to make men holy, let men die to make us rich." The Declaration of Independence and Constitution, he offered, should likewise be altered to reflect new truths. He also wondered aloud how a people who tolerated pandemic corruption in their public life—New York was a favorite butt of Twain's sarcasm—could presume that their model be emulated in the Philippines.[27]

Twain feared that the habits of military rule abroad would weaken popular attachment at home for democracy, thereby paving the way for tyranny. To counter this danger, he urged educators to teach their students that true patriotism resided in distinguishing between right and wrong in foreign policy and holding administrations to a high standard. The ideas of freedom, equality, and government by consent of the governed should also be imparted to the young, not a mindless obedience to political authority. For himself, he proudly bore the name of traitor applied by Funston to dissenters and for whom the penalty of hanging was advised. As for the mission of carrying North American civilization to the Philippines, Twain taught that humaneness was at the core of genuine greatness. The attempt to ply the Filipinos with bullets and Bibles was not. He asked in 1901, "Shall we go on conferring our Civilization upon the peoples that sit in darkness, or shall we give those poor things a rest?"[28]

"Favor mercy," answered Senator George Hoar. This elderly but still influential Massachusetts Republican broke from party discipline to help coordinate the fight against annexation. Proud descendant of a signer of the Declaration of Independence (Roger Sherman), Hoar took actions that led to his vilification by critics: as party defector, national traitor, abettor of Aguinaldo, accessory to the killing of U.S. soldiers in the Philippines. An ardent partisan, he countered this defamation by placing himself on the side of what he termed the historical Republican party, which had preserved U.S. unity while conferring liberty on the slaves. Dominion in the Philippines would amount to enslavement of a race of ten million souls, he protested, for which justification the United States would seek excuse in the discredited arguments of the antebellum South: backward races benefited from the supervision of a white overseer. Hoar too rejected as spurious those arguments that wanted to impose on remote peoples forms of government that bore no organic link to their history or culture. These alone were the sound pillars for future regimes in the Philippines, whose inhabitants were entirely capable of organizing their own lives.[29]

Hoar believed in common with James and Twain that the chief danger was that the United States was taking the road to perdition and would be transformed from a liberty-loving republic to a commonplace empire: the moral realm would be usurped by the logic of ruthless force. Hoar wrote (1902) this epitaph for Filipino ambition:

> We crushed the only republic in Asia. We made war on the only Christian people in the East. We converted a war of glory to a war of shame. We vulgarized the American flag. We introduced perfidy into the practice of war. We inflicted torture on unarmed men to extort confession. We put children to death. We established reconcentrado camps. We devastated provinces. We baffled the aspiration of a people for liberty.[30]

By no means exhaustive of the arguments leveled by the anti-imperialists, the foregoing synopses of James, Twain, and Hoar do illustrate the central concerns. Allowing for individual styles and emphases, Carl Schurz, E. L. Godkin, Edward Atkinson, Andrew Carnegie, and Jane Addams also subscribed. In the end, theirs was a political failure, not one of imagination. They foresaw better than most of their generation the perils of a foreign policy that would stretch from implanting American institutions onto the Philippines to nation-building in Vietnam.

* * * * *

However brief the war against Spain, April to August 1898, contemporaries remarked its momentous consequences—readily acknowledged by historians, no matter how varied their verdict on events. Implicit in the earlier career of Manifest Destiny, the idea of an imperial republic enjoyed palpability at the moment when Europe's overseas empires were at their zenith. Quest for a Chinese market and preservation of it (the Open Door notes), participation in suppression of the Boxer uprising, establishment of a naval base at Subic Bay, and designs on Central American territory to build an isthmian canal all depended on a new U.S. outlook at turn of the century.

This was the age when European statesmen like Italy's Francesco Crispi held that colonies were "a necessity of modern life." Just one year before the U.S. conflict with Spain, Great Britain had celebrated the Diamond Jubilee of Queen Victoria's reign. In honoring their aged monarch, the British also congratulated themselves on the success of their empire. In the words of the Duke of Argyll: "We could not help remembering that no Sovereign since the fall of Rome could muster subjects from so many and so distant nations all over the world." Atlases of the time were splashed with red, depicting, as the popular press boasted, an empire on which the sun never set. Ruler of the waves, guardian of India, keeper of the peace, Britain's position—only two years before the unraveling Boer War began—seemed unassailable. Pageantry and breathless patriotism met with rare exception. They were rebuked by a handful of sour dissidents, such as the socialist Beatrice Webb. (She grumbled about "Imperialism in the air—all classes drunk with sightseeing and hysterical loyalty.") To the example of British spectacle on American imagination can be added the prodding of imperial essayists, like Rudyard Kipling, who urged the United States to join the ennobling task of taming the nonwhite world.[31]

That the rewards of empire were mostly illusory and confined to a minority class composed of naval enthusiasts, missionaries, traders, lending banks, and armaments producers was evident to British anti-imperialists. According to their arguments, and detailed by John Hobson in his *Imperialism: A Study* (1902), the broader society suffered both material privation and moral compromise while privileged conspirators dragged the country from one doubtful overseas adventure to another. Naturally the American foray into empire-building—which incidentally in 1898 also included absorption of the Hawaiian islands—would inflict comparable distress on the United States. Quagmire in the Philippines (Twain's characterization) was seen as first evidence for this prediction.[32] American dissenters added that the unacceptable price of empire included the despoiling of civil life and liberties at home, from which republican life would not recover—a well-aimed but in retrospect exaggerated criticism. The anti-imperialists cited not only the fury by which their objection was denounced as traitorous but also episodes of interfering with the mails (the postmaster's interception of antiwar pamphlets sent to soldiers in the Philippines), censorship of journalists sending unfavorable reports from Manila, and violations of the rules of war, which rarely resulted in official investigation or courts-martial. Such episodes made a nonsense of McKinley's proclamation of "benevolent assimilation" of the Philippines. Instead, said Professor William Graham Sumner, despised Spain had conquered the United States "on the field of ideas and policies."[33]

That the road to hell in the Filipino war would be paved with the good intentions of alleviating Cuban misery was certainly unforeseen in 1898—as was the unguessed fatefulness for twentieth-century diplomacy of occupying the Philippines.[34] Years before pledging (1934) an end to American rule in the islands and before combat with Japan over them in World War II, the United States had replaced military rule with civilian administration (first directed by Governor General William Taft). To its latter-day apologists, this period of apprenticeship to American democracy/capitalism was remarkably successful. Among these was McGeorge Bundy, who in 1947 was as impressed as TR had been by the number and quality of American-devised improvements in the islands—economic development, schools, hospitals, impartial judiciary. Bundy observed: "The Philippine experiment may be regarded pridefully as an example of American idealism at its practical best." Fifteen years later, as national security advisor, Bundy was still confident of what Americans could do for Asians by humane intervention and state-building (armed modernization theory). By then U.S. prestige in Vietnam was becoming massively involved.[35] Yet even the record of that fiasco was not sufficient to discredit fully the eggshell-fragile theory of nation-building by outsiders—hence, those blunders in the 1990s associated with Somalia and Haiti, and stubborn defense of these actions by U.S. officials.[36]

Overall, the 1898 interventions in Cuba and the Philippines illustrate this main theme: U.S. history is a story of experience chastised by conscience.[37] At the moment of emergent American imperialism, this conscience had been shaped by the Declaration of Independence (people are created equal and endowed with inalienable rights) and the Constitution (rulers derive legitimacy from the consent of the governed), both reaffirmed by Lincoln's Gettysburg and Second Inaugural speeches. This conscience, with elaborations on it after 1898, prevented the United States in the twentieth century from surrendering completely to the imperial temptation created by its immense might. Borne by the sin of arrogance—that America is different from and above other nations—the U.S. record is stained with guilt by persecutions and aggressions of a kind familiar to students of comparative international powers. Yet the United States contains in its laws and major documents the promise of a better collective self and improving national politics. Without them and their vocabulary, the diplomatic history of the American republic—raucous and careening as it has been—would be an unrelieved story. In it, the American version of "cold monster" (Nietzsche's concept of the state) would be a huge amalgam of self-idolatrous power and wealth, without pity. Appeals to conscience by a James, Twain, or Hoar would have produced neither institutional echo nor popular stir. The same applies to TR and Mahan, whose rival ethic nonetheless shared crucial points of reference with the traditional language of U.S. democracy and uplift. Ironically, then, the transformation of America into an overseas empire, predicated on extravagant force in the Philippines, intensified the role of conscience in political discourse.[38] Woodrow Wilson's subsequent attempt to foster a semblance of world community would have been inconceivable in the absence of this moral and intellectual piece in the United States.

THREE

Safe for Democracy

Adetectable undercurrent raced in the opposite direction in the early 1900s. Yet many observers identified the crystal tide in international politics as running to peaceful resolution of conflict. Emissaries from the major powers had convened two conferences at the Hague (1899, 1907), where conventions designed to mitigate the suffering caused by war were signed; provision was also made for a permanent court of arbitration. A third such conference was tentatively scheduled for the summer of 1915. These and subsequent meetings would assure, in the words of Secretary of State Elihu Root, the steady "progress toward making the practice of civilized nations conform to their peaceful professions." The power of public opinion as a sanction for peace and the desirability of a world federation ("Parliament of Man") were also assumed by Hague devotees, such as Professor William Hull of Swarthmore College: "Nations cannot be permanently checked in their advance towards visions which their eyes have once clearly seen and their minds have begun to appreciate."[1]

Sensible people could also track the inevitability of peace in the findings of British writer Norman Angell. He argued—in his celebrated book *The Great Illusion* (1909)—that warfare in the modern context was so unprofitable for lives and property that it was obsolete. The economic interconnectedness of states meant that war could not produce an advantage to victors. Armed force would henceforth play a diminishing role in the fate of nations. The primacy of economics over politics equaled peace.[2] (A perennial optimist, Angell returned to this line in the inauspicious year 1933.) The proletarian movement also added its weight to the peace project, when in 1907 and 1910 the International approved measures pledging the workers to joint effort to prevent war. None of these actions or declarations dissipated the gloom in European chancelleries as the pace of the Anglo-German naval race increased or as periodic violence unsettled the Balkans. Still, to most people the possibility of warfare in Europe on the scale of the Napoleonic era was remote. Ornate uniforms worn by general staffs, naval displays mounted for dignitaries, and cavalry spectacles staged for drama were seen as part of colorful life—not portents of danger to Europe.³ The Irish poet W. B. Yeats later conveyed the dominant mood this way:

> All teeth were drawn, all ancient tricks unlearned,
> And a great army but a showy thing;
> What matter that no cannon had been turned
> Into a ploughshare? Parliament and king
> Thought that unless a little powder burned
> The trumpeters might burst with trumpeting
> And yet it lack all glory; and perchance
> The guardsmen's drowsy chargers would not prance.⁴

The blast of violence in August 1914 and its enthusiastic reception by throngs of Europeans stunned progressives in the United States. Historian Charles Beard wondered whether the war marked the end of civilization. The faith of social worker and reformer Jane Addams in the genius of women's "nurturing instinct" was shaken; by the twentieth century this should have cured men of the war incubus. William Haywood, radical labor leader, was incredulous that his European brothers forsook their vows of solidarity: "For weeks I could scarcely talk."⁵ Other Americans were equally bewildered, having only faint understanding of the war's immediate or deeper reasons: the rigidity of military strategy, exemplified by the Schlieffen Plan; the felt need to assert national vitality, as in Russia after its 1905 defeat by Japan; hoary grievances, like French claims on Alsace-Lorraine; vulnerable multiethnic empires, like Austria-Hungary, muddling on; unresolved imperial rivalries, as in the Balkans where Russia and Austria pecked over bits of the receding Ottoman Empire. The catalogue of causes was, in any case, purely of European province and did not impinge directly on U.S. well-being.

The assassination of Archduke Francis Ferdinand and his wife on June 28, 1914, was little discussed in Washington. The murder seemed just another of those terrorist attacks that had targeted European officialdom for decades. America itself was hardly immune to these outrages—McKinley killed in September 1901 by an anarchist—from which cataclysms had not ensued. Surely the same would obtain in Europe. The German violation of Belgian neutrality on August 4, 1914, did spark wider comment in the United States. Theodore Roosevelt among others condemned it. But the majority felt that the war, admittedly tragic for Europeans, was not a pressing concern of the United States. President Wilson's offer of mediation on August 5 was welcomed by his compatriots as a useful initiative. Beyond it the nation need not go. His urging that citizens be "neutral in fact as well as in name" was not so much an injunction as an expression of popular will. This position certainly made sense to W. E. B. Du Bois, for whom German misconduct at Louvain and Liege paled by contrast with Belgian atrocities in the Congo.[6] Secretary of State William Jennings Bryan informed J. P. Morgan in mid-August that loans made to any belligerent would cut against the grain of U.S. neutrality.

There were additional reasons for Americans to stay aloof from the struggle for mastery in Europe. Volatility in the Caribbean focused attention near to home, occasioning military interventions in Haiti (1915) and Santo Domingo (1916). Revolutionary violence in Mexico seeped over the border, resulting with the pursuit of elusive Pancho Villa by six thousand soldiers (March 1916-February 1917), led by General Pershing. Clashes between his troops and President Carranza's in Carrizal suggested that a Mexican-U.S. war was in the offing.

The administration was not only distracted by and eager to check these problems. It also continued to push enlightened legislation—in line with Wilson's *New Freedom*—in Congress, which would be jeopardized by engagement in Europe. At a time when Europeans were conducting a war that belied ideas of moral-social progress, Congress passed laws hitherto unmatched in U.S. history for liberality. They altogether reinforced Wilson's self-understanding: a preeminently domestic president through whom his generation would write its political autobiography. Child labor was discouraged with the banning in interstate commerce of goods made by youngsters (Keating-Owen Act). Congress supported an eight-hour day for railway workers and mandated protection for half a million federal employees under the Workmen's Compensation Act. Congress boosted organized labor by approving the Clayton Anti-Trust Act (labeled "labor's charter of freedom" by Samuel Gompers of the AFL), and imposed taxes on inheritance and those profits accumulated by munitions makers. Wilson sided with the underprivileged when in January 1915 he vetoed a bill that would require immigrants to demonstrate literacy.

Perhaps, by its example of decency, to say nothing of its proffered mediation, America could induce the Europeans to make peace. "The ethics of a parsimonious world" were presumably susceptible to embarrassment, to use the locution of that brilliant nonconformist Randolph S. Bourne. He warned too that the sole enemy of the United States was war itself. On this last point Bourne was seconded by the socialist Eugene Debs; he predicted that should the country be dragged into hostilities, ultranationalists would recast it into the worst military despotism on earth.[7]

Intervention

Allied to Bourne and Debs was the broadly based U.S. peace movement. It embraced Quakers, women's advocates, hyphenate Americans (principally

German and Irish), socialists of every hue, and civil rights activists. Emblematic of their effort to keep America out of the war were Jane Addams's exertions. This pioneer in professional social work was convinced by her experience with Chicago's immigrant community that diverse peoples—by extension the world's nations—could cooperate and live together. Impetus for her pacifism also came from Tolstoyan teaching (she visited the master at Yasnaya Polyana in 1896) plus a conviction that women especially abhor war and therefore are enjoined to abolish it: "Women, who have brought men into the world and nurtured them until they reach the age for fighting, must experience a peculiar revulsion when they see them destroyed, irrespective of the country in which these men have been born." Addams pleaded, in her capacity as leader of the Women's Peace Party, with Wilson to avoid steps risking war with Mexico; she won personal assurance from him on this score. She led the American delegation to the International Congress of Women at the Hague in April 1915, called to find means of ending the World War. The proceedings, which she chaired, called for an armistice, limitation on armaments, reduction of tariffs, democratization of foreign policy, self-determination of peoples, and a league of nations to replace the balance-of-power system. Thereafter she and fellow conferees visited the belligerent capitals of Europe, urging upon the heads of state and the Pope a cessation of hostilities. She also lent her prestige to the voyage of the *Oscar II,* that quixotic initiative of Henry Ford's (December 1915) to produce peace by Christmas. Addams subsequently opposed America's preparedness programs—establishing military training camps and increasing naval appropriations—and expected that in future years governments would yield to sweeping demands for disarmament. She supported Wilson's reelection in 1916 on the assumption that he would lead the United States away from war, thereby breaking with Theodore Roosevelt with whom she had previously collaborated on domestic reform.[8]

Not alone responsible for America's avoiding conflict, Addams's movement did stiffen Wilson's pacific resolve and sharpened his thought on the appropriate shape of international life and the machinery needed to ensure concord. His philosophical position on war had been earlier clarified when, as president of Princeton, he joined the American Peace Society. While governor of New Jersey, he endorsed President Taft's arbitration treaties in 1911—whose unhappy fate in Congress foreshadowed rejection of the League of Nations Covenant.[9] He publicly endorsed (May 1916) in an address to the League to Enforce Peace the idea of an international organization of states; the diplomatically inclined United States might guide it.

Wilson's peace preference was reinforced by this profound anxiety, shared by Bourne and Debs: not only would warfare derail progressive domestic programs, themselves made urgent by signs of recession in 1914, but also the material demands of war would unleash the moneyed interests. Their lust for profit would activate "a saturnalia of exploitation, profiteering, robbery" said Wilson. Still worse, the hazards of conflict would trigger intellectual-social disorder with consequences harmful to the democratic polity: the hard spirit required to win on battlefields might damage the Constitution beyond repair. Congress, courts, policemen, and the habits of ordinary citizens would be debased by the martial mentality, intolerant of anything refined or liberal. "[The] nation" Wilson stated, "couldn't put its strength into a war and keep its head level."[10]

The United States was sucked into the war's vortex long before intervention in April 1917. Wilson repeatedly floated offers of mediation. He dispatched on diplomatic errands to Europe his confidant "Colonel" Edward House, who met with principals of both sides to find common ground between them and to safeguard U.S. interests.[11] The latter were violated on the high seas, when Britain and Germany tried to disrupt U.S. maritime commerce with their respective enemies. From the war's outset Britain had seized (with partial compensation) the contraband cargo (broadly defined) of neutral vessels bound for Germany. This practice, consonant with humiliations that caused war in 1812, led Washington to make its first protest in December 1914. Others followed subsequent British depredations, including London's issuance of the "Blacklist" (July 1916) that forbade trade with U.S. firms dealing with the Central Powers. The Kaiser's government thus was not alone when it griped that Britain ruled the waves and waived the rules.[12] Berlin's naval strategy in the meantime became positively reckless—or, more accurately, desperate—as the British blockade tightened. With brief suspensions, Germany and Austria-Hungary waged submarine warfare that targeted enemy and neutral ships alike, without reference to their civilian or naval purpose. American lives and property were lost not only on British (or Italian or French) liners, like the *Falaba* (March 1915), *Lusitania* (May 1915), *Arabic* (August 1915), *Ancona* (November 1915), and *Sussex* (March 1916); but Wilson's warnings and the American flag were also insufficient to establish immunity, as when German submarines sank the tanker *Gulflight* (May 1915), the *USS Housatonic* (February 1917), and the merchantman *Algonquin* (March 1917). These sinkings infuriated Theodore Roosevelt, who called the president spineless for not declaring war. They also increased worry about long-term German intentions. Three years before the World War even started, U.S. naval strategists had begun devising ways ("Black Plan") to counter potential German incursions into the Caribbean; these might have reduced American fortifications and jeopardized trade routes.[13] In the event, Germany's declaration of unrestricted U-boat warfare in February 1917 and surge of torpedoings prompted Congress's decision for war.

Possibly the United States would have been drawn into hostilities on the Allied side without the submarine provocation. There was, after all, a geopolitical dimension to the war and related question about the integrity of the Atlantic community. To that, U.S. well-being had been pegged for decades. American security required in effect a healthy balance of power on the European continent. If Germany managed to dominate it and to overwhelm Britain—if the British fleet no longer stood between Europe and the New World—nothing could prevent an emboldened Berlin from challenging U.S. preeminence in the western hemisphere. Furthermore, the United States was intertwined with those countries bordering on the north Atlantic, forming with them a unit of culture, commerce, politics, and safety. The viability of this Atlantic community—tying the United States to Britain, France, Canada, the Low Countries—would be undone by a German victory. In this sense, U.S. survival and prosperity were linked to French and especially British victory. Prudent statecraft would sooner or later have to comply with these facts of life—so argued at varying decibels Robert Lansing, Edward House, Theodore Roosevelt, Henry Cabot Lodge, and the young essayist Walter Lippmann.

German overtures to Mexico (the Zimmermann note) plainly bode ill for any future in which Berlin held a commanding position. Not since the 1860s, when France had tried to establish an outpost in Mexico, had any power sought so flagrantly to undermine the Monroe Doctrine or the U.S. position along its southern flank. German willingness to inveigle Mexico in an anti-U.S. scheme created a level of public excitement (March 1917) that surpassed even the response to *Lusitania's* sinking with 128 American fatalities. The Zimmermann revelations also persuaded Wilson of Germany's fundamental hostility, on which subject he had been agnostic.[14]

To critics in the peace movement, not least of whom was Secretary of State Bryan, who resigned in protest (June 1915), the president had long favored Great Britain and France. Apart from his unabashed Anglophilia, they took as evidence his second and third *Lusitania* notes to Germany. These demanded reparations and warned darkly against future infringement of American rights. Wilson's failure to prevent citizens from sailing aboard Allied liners at risk of falling victim to U-boat attack was also interpreted as his baiting Germany—in contrast to the defeated Gore-McLemore resolution of 1916, which prohibited such travel. The preparedness campaigns begun in 1915 also could be read as having an anti-German twist, even as they temporarily mollified TR and appeased mounting pro-Allied sentiment. Not until later years would critics of Wilson (for example, Senator Gerald Nye in 1935) point to the putative pressure from U.S. banks to rescue the Anglo-French cause—its success being the guarantee of recovering huge loans made to London and Paris.

Wilson's request of Congress for a declaration of war did not, in the final analysis, spring from only one reason. Unrestricted submarine warfare, geopolitics, Zimmermann, and the mood for intervention had an impact on Wilson's thinking. This gathering momentum also had to overcome Wilson's reservations on the nature of Anglo-French war aims—which the president had once taught were no less rapacious than those of the Central Powers'. Additionally, Wilson believed the conflict was approaching its climax, which would be hastened by U.S. action: America's belligerent status would allow him a voice in the peace conference that he could steer in the direction of just settlement and diplomatic innovation. The reward would be a formal association of peaceful states with U.S. membership. To achieve these goals, Wilson admitted, America would have first to apply the scourge of military force "without stint or limit" to "make Right the law of the world, and cast every selfish dominion in the dust." But how, asked the inconvenient Bourne, was a war too strong to prevent going to be malleable enough to shape for liberal ends? Wilson never gave direct reply to this question, but placed his hope in reinvented nations cast in the image of New World democracy.[15]

The president's version of U.S. mission overpowered the antiwar legislators in April 1917. They had coalesced around Senator Robert La Follette and included Congress's only female representative, the redoubtable Jeanette Rankin.[16] Wilson mobilized the language of apocalypse and rebirth against the skepticism of this minority. Whereas La Follette warned of a vengeful tide of poor folk who, without influence among the rich or powerful, were being asked "to rot in the trenches," Wilson answered that freedom and righteousness were threatened by autocracy. Its ascendancy doomed the nations to unrelieved agonies. If it were successfully resisted, however, the world could be made safe for democracy; a future league of diplomatically inclined states would ensure that violence never again desolated any people, be they weak or strong. A new ethic was also emergent, superseding the grubby practice of the past: "The same standards of conduct and of responsibility for wrong done shall be observed among nations and their governments that are observed among the individual citizens of civilized states." In reiterating U.S. aims in the Fourteen Points (January 1918), Wilson also laid claim to America as upholder of universal justice in "this the culminating . . . war for human liberty."[17]

The president's depiction of U.S. objectives was undeniably eloquent while at the same time compatible with this idea flattering to Americans: theirs was a redeemer nation, again charged with a mission of mercy. The arena was far larger than Cuba; this time the world would be saved. There was a threefold problem with this presentation, however. First, it amounted to a willful distortion of the moral merits. Germany and Austria-Hungary were not the heart of darkness. Britain's naval blockade was also an indiscriminate weapon. It caused acute suffering to German children, families, and other noncombatants. Very likely Berlin's offers to halt the U-boat campaign in exchange for a less rigorous blockade (allowing food importation) would have been honored had the Allies showed interest. Second, as La Follette reminded his colleagues in Senate chambers, the Allies were not pristine democracies actuated by commitment to self-determination, as Britain's record of coercive rule in Egypt, India, and Ireland attested. Besides, no European country could match Germany for its enactment of social-industrial reforms beneficial to the toiling classes. Germany's Social Democratic Party was the largest and most influential of its kind. It had prospered for years in a robust parliamentary environment, against which background the wartime primacy of Field Marshal Hindenburg and General Ludendorff was presumably temporary, tied to the duration of emergency. As for the ramshackle Austro-Hungarian kingdom, it was indeed in need of reform. Yet it embraced in its protective paternalism a polyglot, multireligious, multiethnic population that enjoyed a level of decency in no way resembling Wilson's caricature of it. Third, the United States surely had plausible reason to intervene in April 1917. It was connected to the distribution of power in Europe and the potential threat to America's New World position should British naval supremacy cease. Wilson paid heed indirectly to these matters in his references to U-boat actions and to Zimmermann. But his couching of the issue in moral absolutism helped mislead the public about the reasons for intervention. As president, the Princeton professor failed as pedagogue. His method paved the way for that sullen American attitude toward Europe in the 1920s and disaffection in the 1930s.

Wilson's explanation was broadly persuasive in 1917, irrespective of its defects: he led a united country into the war. But there was also a sinister side. Residual doubts about the wisdom of intervention were dispelled by lurid propaganda spun by the Committee on Public Information, headed by publicist George Creel. Portraits of the enemy as merciless beast inhibited dissent while cementing wartime conformity. It promoted not only the subscription of Treasury bonds but also fostered censorship and allowed the Espionage Act of 1917. The Justice Department, enforcing the Act's provisions, prosecuted two thousand cases of individuals who allegedly interfered with recruitment/conscription or loyalty in the armed forces. Debs was sentenced to ten years under the Act for denouncing the war as a capitalist crime. The Espionage Act also gave authority to the postmaster general to exclude from the mails any literature that could be construed as producing treason or resistance to the law. In waging democratic crusade in Europe, would the United States "Prussianize" itself, asked William Borah, one of a handful of senators to vote against the Act.[18] In 1918 the Sedition Act was adopted; it made ordinary criticism of the government an offense. Pacifists in America were meanwhile reviled as a species of outlaw, whose turpitude attached to such previously esteemed figures as Jane Addams. Even Wilson set aside his scruples to condemn the war's opponents as traitorous, the willing agents or dupes of German militarism.[19]

University life also suffered as cases of curtailed academic freedom abounded. One widely remarked episode occurred at Columbia University, where the trustees fired (September 1917) two professors who had condemned U.S. intervention. Charles Beard resigned from the Columbia faculty to protest this shabbiness. Arts and culture were also affected, as when performances of Brahms and Beethoven were banished by major symphonies. A halt to the teaching of German language was recommended by militant patriots, to whose voice TR added his own. Thus the domestic side of war displayed flamboyant loyalty ("100 percent Americanism") and anti-German hysteria.[20]

In France the infusion of a fresh and seemingly inexhaustible supply of U.S. troops, entering the front lines in October 1917, helped break the stalemate. Even the redeployment of German forces from the east after Brest-Litovsk was inadequate to offset American weight. More than 4.7 million men served in the army and navy between April 1917 and November 1918. Two million of them were assigned to Pershing's expeditionary force—which included that former conscientious objector Sergeant Alvin York, marked to become one of the most decorated soldiers in U.S. history. The doughboys shone brighter than Germany's high command had imagined possible.

Losing the Peace

The Great War constituted a crisis that for decades afterward paralyzed Europe's cultural and political confidence. Europe had been a civilization persuaded that history and progress were in harmony, that science and industry would carry humanity to undreamed-of heights.[21] This optimistic faith in the future unraveled as the responsible classes proved themselves unworthy. Obtuse political leaders, unimaginative diplomats, and criminally stupid generals (how else to explain British misadventure at the Somme or Passchendaele?) had produced by November 1918 millions of dead and wounded and economies out of joint. By December, when Wilson and his entourage sailed for Europe, the continent had been further rocked by events: revolution in Germany (featuring Kaiser Wilhelm's flight to Holland); disintegration of the Habsburg empire (symbolized by the abdication of Emperor Charles); assertions of sovereignty by states (revived Poland and new Czechoslovakia) emerging from the wreckage of empires. Galloping influenza and the specter of famine added to the urgency. A conspiratorial party in Russia, the Bolsheviks, continued to exercise authority in the name of the martyred proletariat. From them the Allied governments withheld recognition while prolonging a feckless intervention to topple socialism. Wilson meanwhile worried that black soldiers serving in Europe were suckered by Marxist doctrine; they would spread it upon returning home.[22]

To construct a new world order in 1919, the president brought some admirable qualities of mind. These included convictions, above all the Kantian idea that the key to peace is the republican regime. They included recognition that a punitive settlement would fuel German resentment, thereby creating conditions for international instability: "Only a peace between equals can last." Wilson also possessed portions of shrewdness, not usually acknowledged by his critics. For example, as he assured Colonel House during the war, the Anglo-French were becoming so financially dependent on the United States that they would perforce defer to Washington's future proposals.[23] Wilson too was not oblivious to the need for organized competence in the American delegation. This appreciation was highlighted by his inclusion of leading minds from the Inquiry—that assemblage of experts commissioned by the president in September 1917 to craft war aims and plans for the peace. Among this group of men, Lippmann was prominent for having authored eight of the Fourteen Points. Even British diplomat Harold Nicolson, acerbic and weary of the "eternal inadequacy of human intelligence," approved of the Inquiry's meticulous preparation.[24] Thus Wilson, gratified by the tumultuous reception given him by European crowds (in London, Paris, Rome), had reason to think that his mission would succeed on basis sturdier than mere enthusiasm: he possessed the healing balms of power and skill.

Yet the president was hobbled from the outset by certain mental limitations and political liabilities. The former included a sentimental attachment to small nations. He assumed that they were historically less culpable; they were prone to follow nonviolent paths. He therefore overlooked the wasp sting of a Serbia (pre-1914) or Belgium (in the Congo) while acquiescing to the dissolution of Austria-Hungary and the quarrelsome little states it spawned. America's ill-advised intervention in the Russian civil war was prompted partly by Wilson's softness for the Czechs and the plight in 1918 of their troops—the Czechoslovak Legion—in Siberia.[25] Wilson's deficiency also included maladies common to the academic caste: pride of knowledge and arrogance. Perversely, given his sponsorship of the Inquiry, he ignored its members in Paris, preferring instead his own higher wisdom. (As for the U.S. diplomatic corps, Wilson viewed it with contempt and did not deign to consult.)[26] He not only denied himself the benefit of this expert counsel, he also drifted from Colonel House, "the best diplomatic brain" among the Americans, according to Nicolson.[27] The result was that as the Paris conference wore on Wilson became ever more isolated intellectually. Years later, Sigmund Freud, a lucid representative of Europe's disappointed, passed this verdict of maladroitness on Wilson: "He put himself in the deplorable position of the benefactor who wishes to restore the eyesight of a patient but does not know the construction of the eye and has neglected to learn the necessary methods of operation."[28]

Wilson's standing in Paris was weakened by the recent congressional elections that had returned Republican majorities to the Senate and House, producing in the U.S. delegation a hesitancy of manner. It was fully noticeable after the round robin (March 1919) indicated misgivings in the Senate about the projected League of Nations. This awkward political situation had arisen despite Wilson's strong appeal in the autumn for an endorsement of Democratic foreign policy. Theodore Roosevelt observed after the election that in any other democracy the administration would have stepped down. Compounding this political weakness and eroding the chance for bipartisanship, Wilson did not ask any prominent Republican to join his delegation. (Taft, Charles Evans Hughes, or Elihu Root might have proved amenable.) In contrast with Wilson's uncertain position at home, David Lloyd George had recently won a mandate in Britain. Georges Clemenceau enjoyed comfortable votes of support in the French Chamber.[29] Yet confidence in himself as an instrument of reformation in the lives of nations enabled Wilson to think himself more attuned to popular sentiment than his Anglo-French interlocutors—to say nothing of Italy's Vittorio Orlando or Japan's Baron Nobuaki Makino. Wilson's critics saw this refusal to acknowledge the narrowness of his domestic political base as evidence of megalomania: "His mind was illumined only by the incense of his own self-worship."[30]

Despite impediments to success, to Wilson the peace conference (January–June) was not devoid of solid results. The most heartening was adoption by the victorious powers of the League of Nations Covenant, formally embedded in the Versailles treaty. The League was to be organized into legislative, executive, and judicial branches. Together they would administer peace, advance international cooperation, and ensure compliance with treaty provisions. The heart of the matter was Article Ten of the Covenant, pledging League states to act—in ways unspecified—in concert against aggression.[31] The mandate system, a halfway zone between traditional imperialism and outright independence of territories, also seemed eminently wise to Wilson, who had argued against a crude parceling out of the spoils of victory; American mandate responsibility initially encompassed Armenia and Constantinople (until rejected by the Senate in 1920). As Wilson's apologists (Arthur Link, Robert Ferrell, Samuel Morison) have also shown, in the absence of his Trojan efforts, the Paris conference would have imposed even stiffer conditions on the vanquished: Italy was denied Fiume, to Orlando's chagrin, causing him to leave the meetings; Wilson prevented the Allies from inflicting the whole cost of war on Germany ($120 billion, according to Lloyd George); the Americans blocked Clemenceau from detaching all of Germany's Rhineland; they thwarted Polish designs to annex all of East Prussia.[32] Finally, in the longer view of history, as argued by scholars such as Dorothy Jones, the peace conference and Wilson's moral leadership amounted to progress in world politics. However imperfect the results or flawed the procedure (excluding German delegates), at Paris "the states began to create an ethical framework for international affairs." This was codified in resolutions on the desirability of conflict control, minimal standards of social justice, and guarantees on human rights.[33]

Nevertheless, many contemporaries viewed the conference's results with disgust. It was not just youthful impatience with imperfection that caused the young men on the U.S. and British delegations to despair. For them—Lippmann, Nicolson, William Bullitt, John Maynard Keynes—the pre-Paris Wilson had been the living promise of a vastly better world. Once negotiations were under way, they were obliged to watch as the president conceded one liberal position after another to Clemenceau and Lloyd George (ostensibly for the sake of preserving the League of Nations but in reality because Wilson was outclassed as a negotiator). The result was that Germany signed a peace peppered with Carthaginian elements: payment of steep reparations, loss of home and overseas territories, loss of population (7 million people), forced admission of guilt. The transfer to Japan of German rights in China's Shandong province highlighted for critics the conference's retreat from the spirit of the Fourteen Points.[34]

The inept performance of their prophet caused the erstwhile faithful to renounce him. Disillusionment eventually drove Lippmann to adopt a flinty position (realist) on international relations; he dismissed Wilson as a confused thinker of the "American fundamentalist" type. Nicolson echoed this sentiment when he lambasted Wilson, calling him a cross between prig and theocrat, brimming with "arid revivalism." Bullitt actually testified in Senate hearings against Versailles, in particular against the League for being toothless. Bullitt later co-authored with Freud (at least got his imprimatur) a withering biography of Wilson—revenge on the casuist whose flaw was that he could not mend Europe. (Oscar Wilde's observation is apt: "Every great man nowadays has his disciples, and it is always Judas who writes the biography.") Keynes's *The Economic Consequences of the Peace,* a polemic against the exorbitant reparations and against Wilson, fortified postwar doubts in Britain about the fairness of Versailles.[35]

The punitive terms and distribution of spoils among the victors confirmed to the extreme left the war as an imperialist exercise, and gave the lie to preachments on national self-determination, war without indemnity, an improved diplomacy. The settlement validated for Lenin his original view of Wilson as an "old hypocrite."[36] To those Asian, African, and black American activists who met in Paris—simultaneously with the conference but apart from it—the peacemakers failed utterly to lighten the burden of the oppressed. Nor was the cause of antibigotry helped when Wilson and the Europeans rejected Baron Makino's proposal to include a clause in the Covenant upholding racial equality. Requests by Du Bois that Wilson's delegation include African Americans were likewise rejected, lest their presence embarrass the Southern president. The State Department earlier erected obstacles to prevent private black citizens from going to Paris. Those who managed to make it, like Du Bois, were put under surveillance by military intelligence. As for the meetings of the Pan-African Congress, in which Du Bois was prominent, its demand that the principle of national self-determination be impartially applied everywhere was ignored by Wilson, though Clemenceau and House expressed polite interest.[37] From Zurich, where the Women's International League for Peace and Freedom had meanwhile convened, warning came that severe treatment to be meted Germany (publicized in advance treaty copy) would engender animosities; they would lead inevitably to war. Jane Addams, president of the women's league, delivered its resolutions to Colonel House in Paris. From there she and feminist colleagues visited Germany, still victimized by food blockade. They were horrified by rampant conditions of hunger and illness. Unless food aid came quickly, Addams announced, a whole generation of German children would be "doomed to early death or a handicapped life."[38]

To the newly organized government at Weimar, wobbly in the aftermath of the Spartacus rebellion (January 1919), the Versailles treaty was a shock. Among its disagreeable penalties on Germany were the administration of the industrialized and coal-producing Saar by the League (France); demilitarization of the Rhineland and its occupation by Entente forces; prohibitions on building an army in excess of one hundred thousand troops; strictures against uniting with Austria; extradition of Germans accused of war crimes. Chancellor Philipp Scheidemann resigned from office in June rather than be party to such an agreement. He was doubtless right to believe that had all of the provisions been implemented, Germany would have become a permanently stunted country. Ultimately, it was only owing to German initiatives—first under the respectable Gustav Stresemann, then Hitler—that the "Versailles Diktat" was modified. Before then, however, the Weimar regime was forced to sign, from which onus it never recovered. Thus the military practitioners of power politics—who at Brest-Litovsk imposed drastic terms on Russia—reaped payment in kind for Germany in 1919 while placing the blame on their unlucky successors. Indeed, the political genius of Ludendorff and his brother officers was to avoid implication in the humiliating

Paris peace, thereby smoothing the way for their opposition to Weimar and cooperation with resentful nationalists (first Wolfgang Kapp in 1920, then Nazi radicals). The League of Nations to them was nothing more than the institutional guarantor of an unjust status quo: to think along Wilson's hopeful lines, that the League would correct the injustices of Versailles, was to substitute reality with fairy tales.[39]

Parallel to his lost fight for a moderate peace was Wilson's inability in Washington to entwine America in the postwar order. In Paris, he had been forced to withdraw in the face of this Anglo-French imperative: resurgent German power should not again threaten Allied security or undo the balance of power. Wilson was comparably stymied in Washington, although the explanation cannot be reduced to one overarching cause. Poor judgment, partisan politics, and the counterweight of contrary philosophy were all involved.

Senate ratification of the treaty came a cropper on the president's political miscalculations. These were surely connected to his precarious physical/emotional health; battered in Paris by lengthy sessions and overwork, his condition continued to worsen in summer 1919.[40] In any case, it was Wilson who chose not to consult closely with leaders of the dominant Republican party about the Versailles treaty. Therefore, to preserve Republican integrity, Lodge, Taft, and party chairman Will Hays believed they had somehow to qualify Wilson's project—hence Lodge's fourteen amendments (reservations) to the treaty.[41] Otherwise, the peace and the League would strike the public as solely the construction of the Democratic party. The Republicans would share nothing of the credit, from which situation dire consequences were predicted for the next election. Contrariwise had Wilson taken select Republican leaders into his confidence—at least complimented them by talking with them—they should have supported the treaty and U.S. entry into the League. But the president was temperamentally unable to court partisans in Congress. To do so, let alone to barter, would have amounted to tampering with the future peace of the world; no parochial concern was worth trading for the League, whose compass held the destiny of democratic humanity. This rigid attitude effectively prevented Wilson from entering into the give-and-take necessary for statecraft to succeed.

The personal antipathy between him and Lodge reinforced the president's aversion to compromise.[42] Wilson's nationwide tour (September 1919) to muster public support for the treaty did not create the popular upsurge needed to persuade a reluctant Senate. The president only managed to ruin what remained of his health. He succumbed to severe stroke. Consequently, the Lodge reservations were neither defeated nor properly dealt with by the administration; the Senate failed repeatedly to approve Versailles. The 1920 presidential election, touted by Wilson as a referendum on the League, produced defeat for the Democrats (headed by James Cox) and enthroned a G.O.P. mediocrity, Warren G. Harding. He acclaimed the Republican landslide victory as repudiation of Democratic diplomacy.

Lodge's amendments alone would not have fatally impaired the peace treaty or U.S. involvement with the League. Britain's Sir Edward Grey and French ambassador Jusserand in fact urged Wilson to go along with the Senate. Still, the assumptions underlying the reservations and the anxieties they aroused were decisive—more crucial than Wilson's intransigence or Lodge's hostility or the rough-and-tumble of national politics. Fear that the nation would run risks if it stayed involved with Europe nourished the reservations. Americans then, as since, were reluctant to commit military or naval forces without the consent of Congress. The League, so its most determined detractors ("irreconcilables" like Borah and Senator Hiram Johnson) argued, would usurp the war-making authority of Congress. Inexorably the United States would lose its soul to crafty foreigners. American lads might be sent abroad for reasons having nothing to do with an ordinary understanding of national interest. Why discard the traditional wisdom that inveighed against entangling alliances? The large number of small countries in the League might oblige the United States to go to war at any time.[43] Would future interpretations of the Monroe Doctrine be tailored to suit European governments? These concerns also stirred ethnic Americans, notably Italians who were indignant about Fiume and Germans unhappy about the Fatherland's rough handling. Irish Americans assumed that Britain would dominate the League, becoming yet another tool of the Foreign Office. Borah discerned banks among the demons hoping for Senate passage of Versailles; through the League they could increase the returns on their foreign investments and exploitation.[44]

Other reasoning against League membership held that the treatment of Germany was so extreme that the 1919 treaty would not last. In the normal course of events, Germany could not be expected to function economically-diplomatically as though it were an oversized Denmark or Switzerland. Germany was certain to try to revise Versailles's multiple restrictions. American participation in the League would mean commitment to an unworkable and iniquitous system. Social critic Thorstein Velben labeled the Covenant an instrument of tyranny, fashioned in the likeness of nineteenth-century imperialism. John Hobson added, writing in the *Nation,* that the League's Executive Council amounted to resurrection of the reactionary Holy Alliance. The *New Republic's* editorial board urged the United States not to incriminate itself with the treaty or its agencies. Lippmann diagnosed the League as "fundamentally diseased" and worked with Borah against U.S. participation.[45]

Finally, as realpolitik indicated to Lodge, the nature of international relations in the second decade of the twentieth century was contrary to the

League idea. Balance of power, spheres of influence, and bilateral agreements embodied the essence of political possibility. Open diplomacy, universal collective security, and world assemblies—in other words, democracy in diplomacy—had no place in a fallen world, where state sovereignty and precise security requirements held sway. How much better, Lodge contended, to take as point of reference the sober understanding of John Quincy Adams or the Plymouth Pilgrims. They "faced the world as they found it, doing their best" with the material at hand. Theirs was also a wisdom that distinguished between moralism and genuine morality. The well-ordered society stood higher than the self-righteous crusader; the latter, said Lodge, was destined to squander its wealth, overextend its strength, lose its honor.[46]

Not until World War II did Wilsonian internationalism revive. It claimed that the League's failure to thrive stemmed from U.S. absence. Albeit too simplistic an interpretation, this was accepted by many Americans, notably Franklin Roosevelt. In their formula, had the United States joined the collective security system, aggressive fascism would have been checked and the world spared a second war. Internationalism had failed in 1919; by 1945 it was practically irresistible.[47]

* * * * *

Of twentieth-century intellectuals fascinated by the practical problems of power, most have been content to criticize executives and give advice from the side. Only a few have flitted around the fringes of power. In doing so, they have risked forfeiting the contemplative's virtue: detachment. Some have consequently made infamous deals (Martin Heidegger with the Nazis), assisted ridiculous causes (Max Weber briefly with Ludendorff), or dignified the untenable (Jean-Paul Sartre with communism).[48] The handful of intellectuals to occupy positions of highest authority have variously been bemused by their predicament (Václav Havel), endangered (Léon Blum), or shattered like Wilson.[49] The spectacle of this habitual writer of constitutions frustrated at Paris, humbled by Congress, deserted of friends, and broken in health testifies to the tribute exacted by office.[50] His erudition and soaring oratory were unavailing against such onslaught. Only his Calvinist thirst for martyrdom was quenched—though Clemenceau's taunting (likening him to Christ) and the French press's lampooning made him shrink further still. Wilson fared equally poorly in the antiwar literature that proliferated in the 1920s and 1930s, wherein his highly pitched ideas were ridiculed as empty sloganeering. In *Johnny Got His Gun,* young Joe Bonham lies incapacitated in a hospital ward and wonders to himself: "This was no war for you. The thing wasn't any of your business. What do you care about making the world safe for democracy? . . . You never really knew what the fight was all about."[51]

The centrality of Wilson in understanding America's response to World War I adds other poignancy. It was to him that peace advocates rallied in 1916, including Jane Addams. Her confidence in women's vocation for peace anticipated that of latter-day feminists, who have rejected what they term patriarchal politics and vocabulary, insisting that room be made for an inclusive public space allowing for women's perspective. In the spirit of Addams, muscular foreign policy productive of war and suffering must yield ground to a new outlook, rooted in the recommendations of humane feminism.[52] Yet no more than in Addams's day has this viewpoint won wide support—the difference being that she was vilified, her spiritual descendants largely ignored. Like Wilson in 1919, Addams was awarded the Nobel Peace Prize (1931), which helped draw the sting of earlier rejection but did not reverse U.S. decisions on war or internationalism.

As for the Kantian pattern that floats seductively over scholarship on Wilson, the record, alas, does not inspire hope. Kant's expectation that in the wake of a great catastrophe (World War I fits) states would be led by adversity to act rationally and cooperate went unfulfilled.[53] The formation of democratic nations into a coalition dedicated to high purpose—averting war and spreading around the globe—was dissolved by the reality of Versailles, too impractical and vague even for the U.S. Senate.[54] Wilson in 1917 had simply intensified complexity by injecting ideological crusade into a balance-of-power struggle. Furthermore, the Kantian idea that republican regimes do not make war on each other—an axiom in post–Cold War thinking—begs hard questions about U.S. democracy in Wilson's era.[55] Were its faults minor or cumulatively a disqualifying blight?

A defense of that polity has to contend with the absence of universal female suffrage (until 1920) and de facto disenfranchisement of significant numbers of black citizens. The latter was not offset by the enrollment of two hundred thousand in the armed forces—where restrictions pressed downward the number and rank of officer commissions—or by French honors bestowed on them. Wilson had earlier decreed by executive order the segregation of black federal employees and their phasing out from the civil service. A wave of lynching swept the country during this period (taking nearly one hundred blacks in 1915); NAACP protests provoked little sympathy in Washington, where proposed antilynching legislation languished. A massacre in 1917 of African Americans in East St. Louis claimed scores of lives, hundreds wounded, and extensive property damage. The Deep South experienced an eruption of antiblack pogroms and racial warfare in the first summer after the war. They dug even deeper the trench of race divide, producing fatalities and accelerating black flight northward.[56] The Ku Klux Klan also enjoyed new vitality; its influence spread beyond the traditional confine (virtually capturing Oklahoma,

Oregon, Indiana). Anti-Semitism and anti-Catholicism grew apace with racial bigotry.[57]

This misery, which took place before a wider backdrop of intolerance, fulfilled Wilson's prophecy that the country could not simultaneously wage war and maintain its moral equilibrium. War fever continued into the early 1920s, producing in Richard Hofstadter's phrase "a riot of reaction." Debs stayed in jail for his antiwar utterances until pardoned by Harding in 1921. The "Red Scare," fed by fear of Bolshevism and Bela Kun's (short-lived) regime in Hungary, allowed Attorney General A. Mitchell Palmer to dash liberties. Arrest warrants were issued to 4,450 persons. Six hundred leftist-leaning aliens were deported, while Palmer supporters cried "ship or shoot."[58] The irregular trial of Nicola Sacco and Bartolomeo Vanzetti began in 1920.

This insurgency against civil liberties was comparable in scope to that in Kaiser's Germany, said the contemporaneous philosopher John Dewey.[59] Overstated or not, Dewey's charge brings home this irony: Wilson's war to make the world safe for democracy had degraded democracy in the United States; the crusade for world revitalization had left the country more suspicious-minded than before. Additionally, the wartime pattern of eroded legal protection, discernible in the North (1861–1865) and throughout the country in 1898, was unbroken by World War I. This pattern would remain intact during World War II (internment of 120,000 Japanese Americans) and the Cold War (McCarthyism). These considerations lead to this generalization: War passion and fastidious regard for political values have not only proven incompatible in U.S. history, but wartime mentality has deflated the elevated pretension of new-world-order designs. Randolph Bourne stated the dilemma succinctly in 1917: "The optimistic mood in American thought may mean merely that American life is too terrible to face."[60]

FOUR

Freedom from Fear

Germans of conscience have long grappled with the Nazi experience. Reparations made by the Federal Republic to Israel and to Jewish survivors of Nazi persecution were one part of national expiation. The needs for collective atonement also prompted Chancellor Willy Brandt in Jerusalem in 1972 to set a wreath at Yad Vashem. There, in a memorial service to the Holocaust's victims, he read from Psalm 103: "As a father pitieth his children, so the Lord pitieth them that fear him." Two years earlier Brandt had knelt before a monument in Warsaw commemorating the 1943 ghetto uprising. He acknowledged in Moscow the "unspeakable sacrifices" forced on the Soviet people by Hitler's war against them.[1]

Soon after hostilities had ended in 1945, the philosopher Karl Jaspers sought to determine the distribution of guilt for World War II. He placed the principal powers along a spectrum of culpability according to gradations of responsibility. None was entirely innocent, neither appeaser nor aggressor. But no state shared with Hitler's the category of greatest offense: "Germany danced a . . . solo to its doom." Similar appreciation later caused the novelist-playwright Günter Grass to oppose German reunification after the Berlin Wall's collapse. Auschwitz and aggression were the legacy of previous unification, the former constituting "an irreparable tear in the history of civilization." Upon this record Germany lacked any sound basis for political reintegration.[2]

It is hard to say whether German resisters to National Socialism would have agreed with Grass's judgment. Some like Brandt in 1945 maintained that enough virtuous Germans had survived to aid Europe's "spiritual and political renewal." But many had perished in appalling circumstances. Among them was the Protestant thinker Dietrich Bonhoeffer, who described the Third Reich's godlessness and assault on Jewry as an expulsion of Christ from Europe.[3] The White Rose student circle in Munich in 1943 and the revolt by military officers in 1944 also ended catastrophically—but not before giving a testament of sacrifice to idealism, crucial for rejuvenation of German morale.

The torments of non-Aryan victims were numbing. Born into a pious Jewish family murdered by Nazis, young Elie Wiesel lost his faith in a purposeful universe ruled by a benevolent God. Only irrepressible optimism in human progress enabled the distinguished Jewish Austrian writer Stefan Zweig to affirm anything meaningful. Before committing suicide in 1942, he wrote wistfully of his single possession: the feeling of inner freedom. The dilemma for Léon Blum was that Germany had created a situation that obliged otherwise undepraved people to adopt infernal techniques. He worried that Nazi methods would remain supreme, even though he lived to see German military power obliterated: "You [Nazis] are already conquerors in this sense: you have breathed such terror all about that to master you, to prevent the return of your fury, we shall see no other way of fashioning the world save in your image, your laws, the law of Force."[4]

The career of Force in 1939–1945 has been variously explained since the war, but never satisfactorily by Marxist or other economic analysis. Such interpretive frameworks cannot adequately account for perverted science or industrialized death. Nearer to the mark has been the Catholic theologian Hans Kung, who, echoing Bonhoeffer, laid blame for the Holocaust on the history of anti-Jewish teaching and persecutions by the Church. French Nobel laureate (also Catholic) Francois Mauriac saw in the violence—specifically against Jewish children—proof of Western abandonment of the Decalogue and Sermon on the Mount; the Enlightenment's faith in inexorable advancement was simultaneously overthrown. To the Frankfurt School philosopher Theodor Adorno, the reign of Nazi iniquity meant (quite apart from the question of its origins) that poetry was henceforth not desirable or possible— a disputable proposition given Anna Akhmatova's haunting verse eulogizing Russia's wartime suffering.[5]

The internationalism of suffering was as evident in East Asia and the Pacific as in Europe during 1939–1945.[6] Indeed, Asia's war had preceded Europe's by two years, with the start of the China Incident and Japan's capture of Beijing and Shanghai. Only when the war reached its American phase was the outcome predictable, despite determined Japanese resistance and Tokyo's tireless propagandists—the latter's success manifest in the shock among Japanese when their government sued for surrender in August 1945.[7] Apparition of an almost supernatural weapon over Hiroshima and Nagasaki (Winston Churchill's imagery) climaxed the war, and gave the world yet another species of victim: the *hibakisha,* survivor of the atomic bomb. Use of this weapon caused India's Mohandas Gandhi to lament that the art of empathy was in retreat everywhere, that the United States was teetering on ethical bankruptcy.[8]

Gandhi was not infallible on the subject of empathy. His advice, for example, to European Jewry was preposterous: suicide was preferable to killing

Nazi Germans. His pronouncement too on military operations seemed irrelevant to most Americans in 1945; the overwhelming majority believed that the United States was fighting "the good war" in Europe and Asia. (Exceptions included pacifists opposed to all wars; thousands of conscientious objectors who refused to work in noncombatant service were jailed.) Certainly Americans since the war have criticized aspects of U.S. behavior; much debate has centered on Hiroshima and Nagasaki. But most citizens still endorse U.S. policy overall. Few would quibble with political theorist Michael Walzer, who characterized the Allied effort as "the paradigm of a justified struggle."[9]

President Roosevelt's stance against German-Japanese expansion sprang from the same attitude that had produced the New Deal: improvisation and jauntiness rather then systematic or deep thought. This formula was inspiring enough to sustain Americans in 1941–1945, as earlier it had helped them slog through economic crisis. Roosevelt had assured audiences in 1933 that they could surmount their problems, even though millions of people were unemployed: "The only thing we have to fear is fear itself." He was striking the same note in April 1945 as Americans looked hopefully but nervously to the posthostilities world. His last speech contained this exhortation: "The only limit to our realization of tomorrow will be our doubts of today. Let us move forward with strong and active faith."[10] Yet faith, however deep, was not sufficient by itself. A workable idea, or vision, was also required. The absence of a reliable one in 1945 invited a new season of insecurity: the Cold War.

Before Pearl Harbor

The quarter-century between Washington's two declarations of war on Germany was not as devoid of creative statesmanship as implied by the pejorative term isolationism. Its analytical usefulness is doubtful from two standpoints. First, Americans were not simply engrossed with Anglo-French repayment of World War loans and huddling behind tariff barriers, fearful lest outsiders flooded the country with cheap products. Secondly, the interwar period was not one of unrelieved intellectual aridity in the United States, as charged by interventionist critics in 1941, or many historians since. No more in America than in Britain can all the people who sought an alternative to war be dismissed as myopic or craven.[11]

Well before FDR's first inauguration, U.S. administrations had participated in efforts to increase international stability, even while avoiding intimacy with the League of Nations or its commission to explore disarmament. President Harding hosted the 1921 Washington Conference to curb the production of world arsenals. Agreement was reached on limiting the size of the five principal navies; first advantage went to the British and American (525,00 tons of capital ships), followed by the Japanese (350,000 tons), then French and Italian (175,000 tons). Understandings were also struck in support of Chinese territorial integrity and the necessity of the Pacific powers to resolve disputes diplomatically. The justifiably ridiculed Kellogg-Briand Pact (1928), outlawing war, even had its defensible side: it highlighted U.S. commitment to negotiated solutions, thus paving the way for the Hoover-Stimson censure (1931–1932) of Japanese encroachments on China. The Dawes Plan earlier had reduced the burden of German reparations, which contributed to Germany's economic revival in 1924, itself compatible with the goal of enhancing European stability. This was further advanced by Berlin's adherence to the Locarno Treaty (recognizing the inviolability of borders in western Europe) and joining the League of Nations in 1925. The London Conference in 1930 recommitted the United States and several powers—not France or Italy—to curtailing their navies' growth.

Expressions of diplomatic intent by the United States were applauded by the resurgent peace movement. It typically boasted more credit than deserved—playing down, for example, Washington's fiscal conservatism and desire to avoid lavish expense on defense. The peace leadership was nonetheless earnest and enjoyed popular backing, animated by widespread revulsion for the Great War. A growing conviction that the face of future conflict would be unrecognizably horrid, even by the standard of 1914–1918, gave added impetus (as in William Irwin's terrifying The Next War). Prominent among antiwar crusaders was Carrie Chapman Catt, suffragette leader, founder of the League of Women Voters. She decried militarism as inimical to both justice and genuine security. Catt's attitude translated into practical support for the League of Nations and calls for U.S. commitment to the World Court. She also rallied her sex at the time of the Washington Conference to "compel" right action: "Let us consecrate ourselves to put war out of this world. God is giving a call to the women to come forward, to stay the hand of men, to say, 'No, you shall no longer kill your fellow men!'" Catt later organized the annual conferences of the Committee on the Cause and Cure of War, which in its first meeting (1925) identified 257 causes of war. She hailed the Kellogg-Briand Pact as a preventative of war and worked for its Senate ratification. Catt was labeled a subversive for this (plus other) activity by the Daughters of the American Revolution, which conducted an investigation into her putative Bolshevik connections.[12]

Professor James Shotwell was every bit as devoted to peaceful resolution of conflicts as Catt. He also had greater impact on foreign policy through his connection with the Kellogg-Briand treaty. A medievalist-turned-activist, Shotwell (a veteran of Woodrow Wilson's Inquiry) emphasized international institutions and law to end world anarchy. French foreign minister Aristide

Briand offered the outlawry of war on the basis of conversations with him. Secretary of State Frank Kellogg, not wishing to get caught in a purely bilateral arrangement with France, countered with a proposed multilateral agreement. Its final form, signed by sixty-two nations, lacked any enforcement mechanism to punish perpetrators of aggressive war or protect victims. No nation had to supply troops, money, or military equipment. To its critics, such as the Democratic gubernatorial candidate of New York, Franklin Roosevelt, the treaty made Americans "feel self-righteous by a general declaration abjuring war" without paying the costs to ensure peace. Shotwell and company were not blind to the treaty's defects but argued that Kellogg-Briand was a necessary step in the direction of sanity. Only the danger posed by Hitler in the late 1930s caused Shotwell to alter, if grudgingly, his Kellogg-Briand enthusiasm.[13]

Soon after installation as president, Roosevelt took two steps that enjoyed the support of progressive-activists of the Catt-Shotwell ilk: elaboration of the Good Neighbor policy (begun by Herbert Hoover) and recognition of the USSR in 1933. The Good Neighbor initiative was viewed by the peace movement as a welcome departure from traditional policy. Its gunboats and meddling had not only marred U.S.-Latin American relations but had also exposed the hypocrisy of Washington's rhetoric on self-determination. Roosevelt's improvements amounted to a corrective: support of the nonintervention resolution at the Seventh Pan-American Conference (Montevideo, 1933); lower tariff policy (repairing damage to Latin exports caused by Smoot-Hawley); repeal of the Platt Amendment; renegotiation of the Panama Canal treaty. The resulting reduction in tensions yielded further benefit not necessarily foreseen by peace activists. Implementation of the Good Neighbor led to unprecedented levels of hemispheric security cooperation in 1939–1945, notwithstanding Argentine obstreperousness or Washington's fuming over Mexican confiscations.[14]

Supporters of Soviet recognition were a diverse lot. They included businessmen (Armand Hammer, Walter Arnold Rukeyser), who hoped that formal relations would ease access to the socialist market, thereby also promoting America's economic recovery. Equally unsentimental people (Roosevelt himself) understood that increased Soviet-U.S. cooperation might have a sobering effect on the mischief-making Japanese and impress the Nazis, just recently come to power in Berlin. Leftist intellectuals and artists (Theodore Dreiser, Paul Robeson) also favored normalization with the first socialist republic, where proletarian success as they conceived it presaged justice elsewhere. The establishment of Moscow-Washington relations was to the peace movement an example of cooperation and communication that could strengthen international brotherhood. Unfortunately, representatives from these groups did not make a fuss about the raging famine in the

Ukraine and north Caucasus. This disaster was intertwined with Stalin's ter-
roristic collectivization, aimed at breaking the peasants' resistance. No
protest was whispered on the American side during discussions with Soviet
negotiators (headed by Maxim Litvinov). No mention was made of possible
aid, along the lines of the American Relief Administration in 1921–1923.
Despite accumulating evidence from travelers to the stricken zone, journalists, and diplomats, FDR's government kept silent while approximately six
million people died.[15]

If an excuse for U.S. obliviousness is possible, it is related to America's introverted outlook in the Great Depression. This crisis left little intellectual
imagination or resources to deal with the plight of faraway peoples, whose
needs, the power of wishful thinking held, were being met by their own
leaders: Americans had to concentrate on restoring plenty at home, where
dust bowls, failed banks, and joblessness posed the worst threat to national
cohesion since Southern secessionism. Neither the flurry of Roosevelt's first
hundred days—with its instant agencies to protect farmers, workers, and in-
vestors from the market's fluctuations—nor later measures to loosen the grip
of monopolies on economic life bore lasting results. After Roosevelt's landslide reelection in 1936, with Democratic majorities in the House and Senate, the New Deal still could not find or apply the right formula, as shown
by the economic downturn of 1937–1938. Nor could the administration
deflect the intensity of anti-Roosevelt critics. Their invective against the
president (that he was a traitor to his class, a would-be tyrant) combined
with his own blunders (the court-packing scheme) to weaken the New Deal.
It could not in the end eradicate poverty or narrow glaring gaps in the distribution of wealth. By late 1938 the New Deal was low on prestige as Republicans scored congressional gains during midterm elections for the first
time in ten years. Roosevelt meanwhile was jeered by the primitive-minded,
such as Father Charles Coughlin. To him the New Deal amounted to a conspiracy of Jews ("the Jew Deal") and communists, all of whom were bent on
creating a dictatorship in Washington and making war abroad.

Powerless to reinvigorate the New Deal in 1938, FDR was equally unable
to reverse the disintegration of international order. This sorry condition was
already manifest in Italy's conquest of Ethiopia, Japan's China incursion,
Hitler's remilitarization of the Rhineland and dismissal of Versailles limits on
the size of German armed forces, and the Berlin-Rome intervention in
Spain's civil war. German territory and population grew at a leap in March
1938 with the Austrian *Anschluss*. At Munich in September the status quo
powers—cautious Britain, divided France—delivered a small country to the
mercies of Nazi expansionism. Chamberlain and Daladier also reconfirmed
by their surrender of protection to Czechoslovakia earlier signals of their
countries' military unpreparedness.[16] Henceforth French obsession with

sécurité—which had dictated Paris's diplomatic maneuvering for two decades—latched onto an obsolete defensive mentality, exemplified by the Maginot line. Germany's continuing dynamism, by contrast, was demonstrated less than a year after Munich: Hitler concluded the nonaggression pact with his supposed arch foe, the USSR.[17]

Roosevelt's margin for maneuver, as Germany completed preparations of war, was reduced not only by the Depression's exigencies. Pacifist sentiment was at its crest in the United States, compared to which admirers of German daring and efficiency (Charles Lindbergh, Coughlin, the Bund) represented an eccentric minority. Responsible politicians, distinguished historians, leading educators, and mainstream clergymen joined activists to keep the country away from the hazards of war. The peace movement at its height commanded the sympathies of millions of people. Fully three-quarters of those voters polled in August 1941 opposed U.S. military intervention in Europe on behalf of the beleaguered Anglo-Soviets or in Asia for China.[18]

Among wary senators—Robert Taft, George Norris, Burton Wheeler, William Borah, Hiram Johnson—none was more vehement than the Republican progressive, Gerald Nye of North Dakota. He had headed (1934–1935) the select Senate committee charged with investigating allegations that financiers and munitions makers had tricked the country into declaring war on Germany in 1917. Nye concluded with fanfare that the redemption of large loans to the Anglo-French plus the prospect of profits had excited the captains of usurious banking and heavy industry. They pressed Woodrow Wilson, whose false neutrality and desire for war had been plain from 1914 onward. Wall Street was the villain (tempting target in the midst of economic turmoil), ordinary Americans the losers. Nye sounded this tocsin in May 1935: "It is sales and shipments of munitions and contraband, and the lure of profits in them, that will get us into another war."[19]

Congress passed the Neutrality Act in late August with provisions recommended by Nye: ban on travel by Americans to war zones, prohibition of loans to belligerents, impartial embargo on weapons to combatants. Observance of this last article in 1936 rankled the Spanish republic as it fought Franco, whose Italian and German patrons supplied generous amounts of materiel. Renewal of the Neutrality Act in 1936 and 1937 (with minor adjustment) underlined the depth of feeling against anything suggesting interventionism.

Revisionist historians added to the antiwar sentiment by agitating the feeling of people bothered by Versailles's punitiveness. These historians, enjoying a popular following normally withheld from their number, adopted the line of earlier German scholars, who had argued that the Kaiser's government deserved a share of guilt for the World War; but France, Russia, and

Britain were not exonerated, bearing at least as much blame (or more, depending on the individual scholar) as Germany. Harry Elmer Barnes, Sidney Bradshaw Fay, Walter Millis, and Bernadotte Schmitt also criticized President Wilson for taking the country into a war whose outcome could not have decisively affected U.S. well-being. The story of clever Anglo-French propaganda, duplicitous Allied diplomats, and gullible Americans read like a cautionary tale in the late 1930s: the United States should cleave to George Washington's wisdom that warned against quitting North American safety for risks in Europe's shifting rivalries and coalitions. Renewed entanglement with Europeans might fatally compromise the nation. The doyen of revisionists, Charles Beard, also warned that an activist foreign policy with its "palaver" about dangers abroad diverted people from attending to pressing domestic issues. In any case, the United States lacked the technical and ethical competence to cure political ailments coursing through Asia and Europe. Besides, there was relatively little to choose from between traditional Anglo-French imperialism and the upstart Axis powers, said Beard. As signs of war appeared in Europe he advised in 1939:

> Not until some formidable European power comes into the western Atlantic, breathing the fire of aggression and conquest, need the United States become alarmed about the ups and downs of European conflicts, intrigues, aggressions, and wars. And this peril is slight at worst. To take on worries is to add useless burdens, to breed distempers at home, and to discover, in the course of time, how foolish and vain it all has been. The destiny of Europe and Asia has not been committed, under God, to the keeping of the United States; and only conceit, dreams of grandeur, vain imaginings, lust for power, or a desire to escape from our domestic perils and obligations could possibly make us suppose that Providence has appointed us his chosen people for the pacification of the earth.[20]

The University of Chicago's respected president, Robert Maynard Hutchins, added his authority to Beard's when in 1940–1941 he spoke against FDR's rearmament policies. They would not, he testified, give dignity or employment to the downtrodden, be they slum-dwellers or the rural poor. The New Deal was unfinished business. Until ill-fed, ill-clothed, and ill-housed citizens found relief, until the American way of life was restored to pride, the government should resist taking the easy way out: fixing other peoples' problems as a substitute for action at home.[21]

The bulk of church organizations and student associations were no less resolute before Pearl Harbor, even after the fall of France in June 1940 gave Germany mastery over Europe. Charles Clayton Morrison, editor of the *Christian Century,* wrote persuasively on the heartbreak of war. The ecumenical Federal Council of Churches counseled Americans against the evils of militarism and, borrowing from the historic peace churches, approved as absolute the commandment against killing. A proper American role would be to mediate among the aggrieved parties, not add to the suffering. University students echoed the sentiment of the Oxford Union, when earlier it had voted (1933) never to fight for king or country. Delegates of the American Youth Council in 1940, opposed to the "rash" administration, booed FDR during his address to them. The America First committee, best known of the isolationist collection, was founded by a Princeton graduate at Yale Law School in September 1940—from which base it expanded its membership to more than 800,000 with chapters nationwide. Figures admired by college students, like the social democrat Norman Thomas, also assumed pacifist positions. And Catt, though she abhorred fascism, remained true to her peace calling. Under her editorial direction the Committee on the Cause and Cure of War published a lauded book in 1935, *Why Wars Must Cease*— a primer for the antiwar movement.[22]

Peace activists could cite an impressive body of evidence, showing that FDR was one of their own. Beginning with his first presidential election bid, he often stated that he despised war; he would not let the country slide off a neutralist path. FDR gave this emotional witness at Chautauqua in 1936:

> I have seen war on land and sea. I have seen blood running from the wounded. I have seen men coughing out their gassed lungs. I have seen the dead in the mud. I have seen cities destroyed. I have seen two hundred limping, exhausted men come out of line—the survivors of a regiment of one thousand that went forward forty-eight hours before. I have seen children starving. I have seen the agony of mothers and wives. I hate war.

Four years later FDR promised parents that their sons would not be sent to fight in distant lands. When earlier Prime Minister Chamberlain had returned from Munich with his respite from European war, FDR exclaimed: "Good man." That Roosevelt proved to be a renegade from the isolationist faith explains Charles Beard's subsequent judgment of him: betrayer of the Constitution.[23] But FDR was not so much a lapsed believer as he was disingenuous about his intentions. In no other area of his responsibility, in fact, was the elusiveness of his mind more apparent than in foreign policy.

Roosevelt's problem—acute after France's defeat—was to coax his reluctant countrymen into a war that he perceived as grim necessity. The imperative arose from three concerns. In ascending order of importance, they were for him: to save representative democracy and the tradition of tolerance, exemplified by west European parliamentary practice; to preserve a domestic order in the United States that could not weather indefinitely the economic or cultural-political strain of a Fortress American concept; to ensure U.S.

security, at odds with German control of the North Atlantic or dominion in Europe—inviting future collaboration with Japan against the New World. Roosevelt therefore took actions designed to hasten American engagement while protesting that his administration would do everything possible to avoid war. Increased naval procurements, passage of the Selective Service Act (first peacetime draft in U.S. history), the destroyers-for-bases swap with Britain, plenteous Lend-Lease aid, undeclared naval war against Germany as of mid-1941, appointment to cabinet position of Republican interventionists (Henry Stimson, Frank Knox), and muzzling of dissenting ambassadors (Joseph Kennedy in London) were measures that had a dual purpose. They helped wean Americans from the illusion of security through noninvolvement and buttressed countries resisting Axis conquest.

Yet the urgent question for interventionists remained whether the United States would take enough action in a timely fashion to avert disaster. It would eventually engulf not only America but also broader civilization, warned the theologian Reinhold Niebuhr. He charged in his 1940 rebuttal to pacifism that "Christian perfectionism and bourgeois love of ease" had sapped the fortitude of the United States. Smug liberals and safe suburbanites were deliberately ignorant; they denied "the depth to which human malevolence may sink and the heights to which malignant power may rise," preferring instead escape from hardship. Niebuhr doubted whether comfort-loving Americans could be useful in creating a world society sturdy enough to check totalitarianism; the time for constructive action was perhaps already past.[24]

Such gloom did not fit the effervescent FDR, however. He sketched a version of posthostilities life even before Japan and America slipped into war, followed obligingly by Hitler's declaration against the "mongrelized" United States.[25]

World Orders

Each belligerent framed its aims in language to appeal to the largest possible population, both domestic and international. Even the Nazis, whose ideology was based on the claim of Nordic superiority, were able to broaden their base by portraying Germany as the shield against European enemies: communism, Jewry, sterile modernity. Although Hitler's New Order quickly revealed itself as no more than a looting operation to benefit Germany, foreign individuals and governments still worked on Berlin's behalf, expecting that Nazi victory would reward junior partners (Vidkun Quisling, the Vichy regime).[26] The coercive nature of Japan's Greater East Asia Co-Prosperity Sphere was dignified by references to onerous European imperialism and the promise of pan-Asian cooperation. Japanese neonationalists to this day extol the co-prosperity idea; they claim that its realization would have delivered Asia from Anglo-U.S. domination into abundance and liberation.[27] The mild treatment of collaborators after the war reflected the degree to which non-Japanese nationalists forgave the antiwhite side of Tokyo's war. Emilio Aguinaldo of 1898 fame, for example, who cooperated with Japanese authority in the Philippines, was never tried. Thus Tokyo's conception of new order enjoyed a type of success after 1945. This was no small feat, given the brutality with which Japan ruled abroad: slaughter in China of which atrocities in Nanjing were only one chapter, experiments on prisoners, impressment of women into sexual slavery.[28] The government's inability to win wide Asian support—per the lackluster Greater East Asia Conference in Tokyo, November 1943—has also been curiously overlooked by Japan's postwar apologists.

Popular feeling in Great Britain was mobilized longer than in any other Allied power. Hope was sustained by the gathering commitment to an equitable future society, traced in Sir William Beveridge's 1942 report. Its recommendations anticipated social legislation adopted by Clement Attlee in 1945–1951 with provisions for "cradle to grave" security. In the Soviet Union, partial lifting of totalitarian controls suggested a postwar life justifying the huge cost—25 to 27 million fatalities. Traditional loyalty and institutions, notably Christian Orthodoxy, were also invoked by Stalin, reinforcing the notion that communist dogma might play a lesser role in coming years. As for their international goals, both the British and Soviet governments let themselves be associated during the war—at least on the level of public rhetoric—with U.S. preferences. This identification with Washington did not impede Churchill or Stalin from energetically pursuing their respective interests, however. These were in the case of Britain retention of imperial prerogative and the resurrection of a balance of power on the continent harmonious with island safety.[29] Stalin wanted border arrangements in Eastern Europe tailored to defense-in-depth requirements and local regimes that would not lend themselves to anti-Soviet causes (as had Finland, Hungary, Romania, Bulgaria, Slovakia); extending Soviet-style socialism as opportunity arose was also a goal.[30]

Professed American aims melded Wilsonian precepts with conventional regard for power realities. Between these opposite points of reference there was room for overlap, as in FDR's four-policemen concept (UK, USA, USSR, China). This would advance exalted purpose on the one hand (namely the United Nations) but would on the other employ traditional methods: force and great power condominium. The Atlantic Charter of August 1941 and subsequent reaffirmations, like the declaration on liberated Europe, also blended liberal internationalism with Roosevelt's practical sense. Thus national aggrandizement was eschewed; the idea that people everywhere might enjoy "lives in freedom from fear and want" was trumpeted.[31] Principles of self-determination, fair trade, equal access to natural resources, economic-social advancement, freedom of the seas, and arms reduction were also confirmed in the Atlantic Charter. Yet the Charter's qualified language about "existing obligations" backed Churchill's contention that the British empire was exempt from the document's more fanciful bits on self-determination outside of Europe. (The prime minister's clarification galled the Quit India movement in 1941, whose protests culminated in thousands of imprisonments.) Roosevelt's own thought on the colonial question was not purely high-minded. Cooperation with the British, French, and Dutch compromised the United States in Asia, where feeling was grounded in bitter experience of white rule. Distance from it, Roosevelt held, served operational ends and encouraged prospects of a widened Open Door. Subsequent plans for international monetary reform were likewise slanted to American advantage. Enactment of liberal conceptions of free trade and economy would undeniably profit all peoples, as Secretary of State Cordell Hull cooed. Still, the United Nations, the International Monetary Fund, and World Bank would all depend on Washington's leadership, from which corresponding benefit would accrue to the United States. FDR averred that upon this foundation of institutions the ancient quest for "peace on earth" would be realized. Linkage to them would also slow Congress's isolationist reflexes, whose exercise was antithetical to U.S. security.[32]

The Rooseveltian theme was readily refrained by administration officials. They invariably amplified the president's words, giving them a more utopian cast than he had originally intended. This he permitted as a spur to the public: to concentrate its attention, to quicken its faith. Undersecretary of State Sumner Welles, an FDR favorite, spread the good news in his paeans to Wilsonian universalism: "We shall win this war, and in Victory, we shall seek not vengeance, but the establishment of an international order in which the spirit of Christ shall rule the hearts of men and of nations." Vice President Henry Wallace, darling of the Democratic party's left wing, was rapturous in depicting a new world where "the common man" would at last flourish. The welfare of all people would replace warfare as the first concern of governments and lead to conditions of unmatched freedom and plenty. The latter was symbolized by Wallace's famous remark that "The object of this war is to make sure everybody in the world has the privilege of drinking a quart of milk a day." Paradoxically, then, the blood-letting was destined to produce the kingdom of humaneness, Wallace predicted. Disappointed by the lack of specificity in FDR's planning, Wallace did not hesitate to call for a future United Nations organization equipped with its own army and air force. Every state, including America, would subordinate itself to the United Nations. Its supremacy would hasten the day of global government (an idea not unlike that entertained by world federalists, such as Grenville Clark and Louis Sohn).[33] Wallace dreamed of a commercial-cultural-transportation network set in the northern Pacific, tying Alaska, Siberia, Mongolia, and China in unprecedented unity. A system of highway and airway should also be constructed to connect South America, North America, Siberia, China, India, the Middle East, and Europe. He welcomed what he saw as the inevitable convergence of the Soviet Union and United States: "Both are striving for the education, the productivity and enduring happiness of the common man."[34]

Eleanor Roosevelt also advanced ideas not fully shared by her husband. She did so as part of this couple's liberal commitment, testing notions—in her syndicated column *My Day*—that she thought worthwhile but knew FDR would not publicly endorse. The First Lady particularly admired Wallace and during his vice presidency aligned herself with his stripe of internationalism. Catt and Shotwell also shared parts of Wallace's outlook. The former pushed the idea of a Department of Peace, whose director would occupy a cabinet position. Shotwell devised plans to curtail national sovereignty, although he rejected imminent world government as unfeasible.[35]

Whereas several Republicans dismissed the administration's ideas—Clare Boothe Luce chided Wallace for his "globaloney"—others supported them. Chief in this second group was Wendell Willkie, the G.O.P.'s failed 1940 presidential candidate. He blunted the G.O.P.'s isolationist edge; he also boosted bipartisan policy by his endorsement of Lend-Lease and his well publicized tours on FDR's behalf to the Middle East, China, and the USSR. Willkie's best-selling book, *One World,* which chronicled his travels, was suffused with this faith: U.S. primacy would "help [establish] a new society in which men and women the world around can live and grow invigorated by independence and freedom."[36]

Not all thoughtful Americans during the war were convinced that FDR was going to lead the world into sunlit uplands. Niebhur did think that the United States—in its stumbling way—was acting in accordance with divine intention directed toward life, spirit, and order. Perhaps the big powers would also act honorably after the war while the lesser ones were granted rights. But he doubted that the sacrifice of millions of people would bear fruit in the foreseeable future. True security, like true justice, could never be realized on earth. In trying to achieve them, the United States might conflate a zeal for righteousness with a subconscious hegemonial ambition. In this respect Henry Luce's "American Century" was worrisome, with its breezy chauvinism and unwillingness to probe the grittier side of motive. Niebuhr espoused vigilance to fend off egoistic corruption by power: "We must seek to maintain a critical attitude toward our own power impulses; our self-criticism must be informed by the humble realization of the fact that the possession of great power is a temptation to injustice for any nation."[37]

Walter Lippmann shared Niebuhr's concern about the possible debauching by power of U.S. philosophical commitments. Unlike Niebuhr, he invested less in injunctions against national pride. In their place, Lippmann urged upon his readers a line that stoically accepted the verities of realpolitik. They indicated in FDR's day (just as in 1917) that aggressive German power should not be allowed to impair the north Atlantic community on whose resilience U.S. security depended. Balance of power and spheres of influence, moreover, were not a priori immoral; they were the proven devices by which states down through the ages had organized their security and collective peace. Lippmann doubted that international law or any version of world parliament could preserve peace after the war. Only sovereign Britain, America, and Russia, acting in concert, could achieve this goal. An American diplomacy premised on enlightened self-interest would prevent the country from embarking on endless and debilitating crusades. Lippmann also advised that Washington not object to the Soviets' organizing their sphere of influence in Eastern Europe—no more reprehensible than what the United States assumed for itself in Latin America.[38]

Lippmann's and Niebuhr's skepticism was not calculated to reassure the majority of Americans. A few, like George Kennan (then serving in Embassy Moscow), did feel that revived Wilsonianism was as delusory as when first articulated. Senator Taft also attacked the international pretentiousness of FDR, Welles, Wallace, and Willkie. Yet the public at large placed its hope in a drastically improved postwar order, onto which prospect FDR shined the New Deal's optimism. Willkie's *One World* sold a million copies. Welles's book on the need for a resuscitated League of Nations (*Time for Decision*) was heralded by critics as an outstanding work, just the inspiration to steady an Allied world in arms.[39]

Still, Americans in 1941–1945 were generally cooler than during the Great War, when many had expected their efforts to succeed in inaugurating an era without strife and safe for democratic idealism. Citizens were less inclined during the Second World War to accept propagandistic depiction of the enemy as ogre, indulged in less sloganeering, and had fewer illusions about the dawning of perpetual peace.[40] This more serious mood actually paralleled the difference between FDR's attitude in World War I and World War II. War's mercilessness was simply beyond anyone's control, Roosevelt as president admitted. Only deluded people could expect that war's destructive energy might be harnessed for productive purposes, he said (even as he tried to persuade Americans that they participate fully in the posthostilities world). The G.I. Bill, passed by Congress in 1944, probably did more to persuade troops of a bright future than did litanies of Axis evils or Allied virtues. Additionally, military leaders, notably General George Marshall, worried about the nation's willingness to maintain a war with heavy U.S. casualties—ultimately four hundred thousand dead, one million wounded. Economic planners wondered whether the end of wartime production would snap the country back into depression and redundancy. Sixteen million people in uniform, millions on the assembly line in the "arsenal of democracy," a GNP in 1945 that had more than doubled (to 211.9 billion dollars) since 1939, and talk about an economic bill of rights could not guarantee future prosperity. The war had accomplished what the New Deal could not by putting America back to work. But what would rescue a peacetime economy from the market's plunging again?[41]

Critics concerned with civil liberties were also unhappy with the war's impact on Roosevelt's vaunted Four Freedoms: freedom of speech and worship, freedom from want and fear. Senator Taft, for example, citing the World War I record as reference, announced in 1940 that another conflict would wreck American democracy. He was the only senator who later protested the relocation and internment of Japanese Americans during 1942–1944. California's attorney general, Earl Warren, by contrast pressed for the deportation, belatedly repenting as Supreme Court justice for the misdeed.[42] (Several thousand German and Italian Americans, only a fraction of whom proved politically unreliable, were also incarcerated.) The suspicion sown by Congressman Martin Dies's bullying Committee on Un-American Activities as it tried to ferret out communists made Eleanor Roosevelt liken it to the Gestapo. Henry Wallace charged: "The effect on our morale would be less damaging if Mr. Dies were on the Hitler payroll." Surveillance by the FBI and military intelligence of suspect groups and individuals surpassed that of World War I, though memory of that earlier repression inhibited a free-for-all. Investigations of right-wingers, use of wire-tapping, mail tampering, and employment of "special operations" surely foiled some Nazi knavery. At the same time, these devices damaged precisely the democratic practices whose preservation FDR sought. Approximately one hundred publications were closed on federal authority.[43]

Labor freedom was not completely stifled during the war, despite FDR's denouncing of strikes as unpatriotic. Factory shutdowns and slowdowns were staged in nearly every industry, including those directly involved with military production. The most dramatic action occurred in 1943, when thousands of coal miners went on strike. Eleanor Roosevelt, otherwise sympathetic to workers, asked union leader John L. Lewis whether he was making life rough for U.S. soldiers and sailors.[44]

The condition of one million African American servicemen was rougher still. Secretary of War Henry Stimson was mindful of this situation, linked to "the original crime of slavery," as he confided in his diary. He pushed reforms on the army to make better use of what he called America's "great asset of the colored men," despite his nagging doubts about the competence of black officers and troops. He depended increasingly on the advice of Dr. Frederick Patterson of Tuskegee Institute and Truman Gibson, the secretary's black aide for "Negro affairs." These men resolved to create training programs to eliminate illiteracy and increase the combat effectiveness of black soldiers. Stimson was also willing to confront segregation in the South (where many military camps were located) on behalf of soldiers angered by multifarious discrimination. As opposed to hidebound officials in the navy department, Stimson's staff was also willing to hear grievances from black recruits against mistreatment by white officers or to investigate incidents of fighting—occasionally fatal—between black and white soldiers. To counter this last problem, the army sponsored educational programs to encourage troops of both races "to live up to our American promises." These efforts were supported warmly by Eleanor Roosevelt, who had earlier associated herself with the contralto Marian Anderson against bigoted concert organizers, and the 1937 antilynching legislation. Although segregation in the armed forces was still intact in 1945, support for it was crumbling, as black soldiers had distinguished themselves in combat beside white comrades, notably in the Battle of the Bulge. Yet as black soldiers told Walter White of the NAACP during his Pacific islands inspection, much work remained: "We know that our battle for democracy will begin when we reach San Francisco on our way home."[45]

Insofar as World War II was a fight for racial justice, civil rights activists in America were enlivened: their cause was joined to the colossal effort overseas. Recruitment posters featuring boxing champion Joe Louis in uniform suggested a hopeful future. Yet existing segregation in the armed forces amounted to "a stab in the back of democracy," said Walter White. Adam Clayton Powell, elected to Congress in 1944 from Harlem, also attacked segregation in the services. Adopting one of the themes in Gunnar Myrdal's 1944 study of race in society *(An American Dilemma),* Powell fastened onto the contradiction between U.S. pledges and domestic reality: "Abroad the United States was preaching 'the century of the common man' and the 'Four Freedoms,' yet it was denying these freedoms at home . . . America was talking about the creation of a new world while its conscience was filled with guilt."[46] Powell preached double victory—against Axis power and the social-legal liabilities that lamed African Americans. Of those whites who upheld discrimination in the United States, he declared: "It is just as important to see that these people and their brand of Americanism be crushed as it is to recapture Singapore." He vowed that there would be no return to the pre-Pearl Harbor pseudodemocracy.[47]

Leading white personalities also saw a connection between the war and America's racial condition. Eleanor Roosevelt equated home-grown racism with Nazism, while condemning the indignities visited upon blacks, Indians, and Hispanics. Earlier she had quit the select Colony Club over its policy of excluding Jews. Willkie and Welles were exceedingly lucid on the need to combat racism and anti-Semitism domestically as well as abroad. Henry Wallace's outspokenness on behalf of blacks antagonized many white Southern Democrats; their opposition was rewarded in the 1944 election when FDR dropped Wallace as vice president.[48]

Contradicting Myrdal's expectation, World War II did not redefine the status of blacks in America any more than it did that of women, who filled millions of vacancies on factory assembly lines ("Rosie the riveter"). But as with women, so for African Americans, the war triggered a train of events that led to improved conditions—despite the spate of race riots (Detroit, Harlem, Beaumont, Los Angeles) that occurred in 1943. The dispersal of blacks beyond the former Confederacy, begun in World War I, increased as workers followed industrial jobs to the north and west, leading to overall strides in black income. Under threat of a massive protest march on Washington, the executive branch banned racial discrimination in war plants that produced goods on federal contract. Membership in the NAACP soared from fifty-four thousand in 1939 to half a million by 1945. Registration drives in Dixie yielded a 10-percent rise in voters after the Supreme Court ruled in 1944 against all-white primaries *(Smith* v. *Allwright).* Life expectancy for African Americans lengthened during the war, though the gap between white and black hovered around ten years. Congressman Powell appointed the first black man to graduate from the U.S. Naval Academy. Still, Axis propaganda took advantage of opportunities (such as the vicious Detroit race riots) to illustrate the evils of American life to Arabs and Asians. Yet this point also stands: the contradiction between fighting fascism in Europe while condoning discrimination at home embarrassed white America; it lurched in directions indicated by its liberal professions, no matter the opposition of Eugene Talmadge, John Rankin, Theodore Bilbo, or other segregationists. Walter White could write affirmatively after the war: "All the failures of the democratic ideal when it encountered the color line had not destroyed my belief in government of, by, and for the people, or caused me to wish in exchange any form of totalitarianism, however . . . roseate its promises."[49]

Legacy of War

Victorious Allied arms could not generate the new order yearned for by people whose doctrinal passion was Wilsonian internationalism. The shaky Anglo-U.S.-Soviet coalition lay in shreds by late 1945, despite desultory attempts thereafter to mend it. The idea of continued great power cooperation to brace the United Nations and police the peace also proved evanescent. A new balance of power was created in Europe instead—with the victors bickering over the trophies there and in Asia. Efforts to impart redemptive meaning, in which the Nuremberg trials played a part, had also been nullified: the Holocaust and use of atomic weaponry were the war's enduring legacy.

The Big Three partnership, dubbed the Grand Alliance by Churchill, was an expediency, its sole purpose being defeat of Axis power. The bonhomie shown at conferences—Teheran, Yalta, Potsdam—and flashes of optimism in Allied societies did not cancel underlying suspicions or diverging ambitions. Chances of future concord came apart because the essential contrariness of allies once again predominated. Within the Anglo-U.S. camp tensions arose from FDR's anti-imperialism and chastisement of the British empire. These were even delivered to Churchill in the presence of Stalin, who could barely restrain his glee. The president suggested at Teheran that India might benefit from reforms along the Soviet model. Churchill's hope to return the monarchies to Italy, Greece, and Belgium likewise ruffled FDR, who did not hesitate to remind his colleague of America's traditional Anglophobia. FDR's sponsorship of China as a great power, capable of sharing police duties, struck Churchill (and Stalin) as quixotic. The prime minister reluctantly endorsed FDR's demand at Casablanca for the enemy's unconditional surrender. The president's contempt for French military prowess and his suspicion that General de Gaulle was a would-be dictator chafed against British plans to refloat France as a player in Europe's balance of power. General Marshall's preference for an early massive assault on German power in Europe (cross-Channel invasion) competed with Churchill's desire to weaken the enemy with attacks on the periphery (North Africa, Sicily, the southern Balkans), which incidentally also served British interests in the Mediterranean. The shifting tide of power—Britain's ebb versus America's flow—added to Churchill's apprehension and that querulousness that occasionally broke the smooth surface of Anglo-U.S. partnership. In 1943 U.S. factories produced 37.5 billion dollars worth of armaments, compared with 11.1 billion dollars in Britain. The American Joint Chiefs were not above buying Britain's acquiescence by threatening to modify their Europe-first strategy in favor of concentrating on Japan.[50]

More unsettling for the future peace than Anglo-U.S. squabbling were those problems that dogged Western collaboration with Stalin. While never admitting that he had contributed to Britain's precariousness in 1939–1941 by cooperating with Hitler, Stalin upbraided Britain and the United States for their delays in opening a land offensive in Europe. Until June 1944 his country bore the brunt of fighting Germany, defeating it at a cost that dwarfed all previous military experience; FDR's 1943 declaration of unconditional surrender might have stiffened Stalin against the temptation of a separate peace, but it could also be read as a stratagem to fight Hitler to the last Red Army soldier. Pre-Pearl Harbor comments by Senator Harry Truman that it was in Western interests to let Germany and the USSR hack each other to pieces raised further doubts about Anglo-U.S. intentions—to say nothing of Senator Taft's remark that a Soviet triumph would be more dangerous than Germany's.[51] Western willingness in 1942 to treat with Vichy officialdom in North Africa, in the person of Admiral Jean Darlan, suggested a continuing softness on fascism. Lack of Anglo-U.S. good faith was also apparent to Stalin in the Manhattan project that excluded the Soviet Union, albeit not its spies.[52]

To the English-speaking powers the titanic Soviet contribution to Axis defeat did not erase disappointments or alarms. Among them was Soviet callousness toward the Polish government in London exile—to say nothing of discoveries made at Katyn Forest. This attitude was underscored by the Kremlin's withholding of aid to General Bor-Komorowski's Home Army in Warsaw in 1944 and Stalin's refusal to cooperate with Anglo-U.S. air power to relieve the Polish fighters. Soviet wishes to keep territorial advantage in Eastern Europe acquired during 1939–1941 (at the expense of Poland, the Baltic states, Romania, Finland) also bode ill for the Grand Alliance's future. Virulent Soviet words against the West in previous years and the hostility of the Comintern—until its dissolution in 1943—also weighed on the Anglo-U.S. governments, though they assured their publics that Russia was an ally deserving of Lend-Lease and other consideration. Soviet versus Anglo-U.S. grievances ultimately overwhelmed oaths of fealty made under the duress of coalition warfare.

The last instance of important Allied concert occurred in late 1945, when the International Military Tribunal (composed of British, American, Soviet, French jurists) convened in Nuremberg. That city, once host to spectacular Nazi party rallies, was linked to the promulgation of laws on "race hygiene" and restrictions on German Jews. The Allies helped to purge Nazi mentality from the national life of Germany by meeting in Nuremberg. Even more important to the tribunal's proponents, such as Supreme Court Justice Robert Jackson, the Nuremberg proceedings upheld standards of civilized conduct based on law and morality.[53]

Violations of these had been committed by both sides during the war. The Americans, for their part, had waged unrestricted submarine warfare in the Pacific and even before dropping atomic weapons had employed population bombing, which used incendiary devices and napalm. Roosevelt too had displayed a vindictiveness at odds with the Four Freedoms and restoration of right conduct to international life: making light of Stalin's proposal for a summary execution of fifty thousand German officers; pressing unconditional surrender to a point that discouraged anti-Nazi Germans, thereby helping prolong the war; endorsing for a while Henry Morgenthau's plan to keep postwar Germany crippled; toying with ideas of crossbreeding docile Pacific islanders with the Japanese to expunge the enemy's "barbarian" makeup.[54] Moreover, critics of Nuremberg have argued, the tribunal had an inescapable taint of victors' justice; naturally, the vanquished were found guilty of heinousness. Senator Taft protested in 1946 that only the appearance of legality was being observed: the trial was an over determined exercise where men were tried under *ex post facto* statute (a view later endorsed by Justice William O. Douglas). Robert Hutchins was too conscious of U.S. deficiencies to favor the Nuremberg trials. He issued this reservation: "I should feel better about having Americans judge the anti-Semitism and the concentration camps of Germany if I could forget the anti-Semitism and lynchings in the United States . . . We are sufficiently vulnerable to lay ourselves open to some embarrassment if we set ourselves to pass judgment on the domestic conduct of other nations." The presence of judges and lawyers representing the Soviet Union also added to the discomfort of various observers, including George Kennan. Annexation of the Baltic republics, the suspected truth about Katyn Forest, the Winter War against Finland, and Stalin's cooperation with Hitler in the destruction of Poland meant that Soviet misconduct equaled that of Germany's in critical categories of guilt.[55]

Despite these objections, the tribunal enjoyed broad support in the Allied nations as it sifted through evidence related to four areas of indictment: conspiracy, crimes against peace, war crimes, crimes against humanity. The tribunal eventually sentenced twelve Nazi leaders to death, including Hitler's foreign minister Joachim von Ribbentrop. The vainglorious Hermann Goering cheated the gallows by committing suicide hours before his scheduled execution. Other Nazi defendants were given prison sentences ranging from life—in the case of demented Rudolf Hess—to lesser terms, as with Hitler's beetley ambitious architect, Albert Speer. Three men were acquitted, including the pre-Hitler German chancellor, Franz von Papen.[56]

Objections that justice applied unevenly was no justice at all and that a regime with a gruesome record itself was represented on the bench were serious. But they were less important in the long view than the symbolic significance of holding an international court trial. The proceedings admittedly might have been fairer and less open to criticism if the International Court of Justice at The Hague had gotten authority to judge German leaders.[57] But after the carnage of total war precipitated by aggressive states, after the German policies of genocide, after the deliberate mistreatment and enslavement of millions of P.O.W.s and civilians by German authorities, it was necessary to reaffirm the norms of uprightness—however imperfect the procedures. Furthermore, the spectacle of high-ranking civilian and military officials of the Nazi Reich brought to task for their cruelty and then punished focused public attention on the chief culprits, thereby deflecting charges—as after World War I—that the entire German people were guilty.[58] Organized retribution of this sort also helped prevent acts of revenge against German nationals (of the kind that has soured Armenian-Turkish relations for decades), and prepared the way for Germany's reentry into a peaceful Europe. To Karl Jaspers at the time, Nuremberg was nothing less than a harbinger of an era wherein German salvation was possible. Willy Brandt and Günter Grass also gratefully acknowledged Nuremberg—as political medicine to inoculate German youth against future totalitarian temptations.[59]

The most spellbinding moments at Nuremberg related to Germany's extermination war against European Jewry. Eyewitnesses, piles of documentary evidence, and pictures of ovens and corpses placed the Third Reich squarely in the annals of inhumanity. Most Americans (and Britons) were unaware of the muderousness of Germany's anti-Jewish (also anti-Gypsy, anti-Slavic) actions until the liberation of the death camps in the final months of warfare. No doubt Grass was correct metaphysically when he said that "Auschwitz can never be grasped."[60] But his statement does not explain why Jewish agony was largely unnoticed by the U.S. public during the crucial time. That resulted mainly from Washington's policy, inexplicable it its own way: first indifference, then tardy and ineffective rescue.

Part of the American failure was connected to Assistant Secretary of State Breckinridge Long, notorious for his evasions and procrastination in assisting the rescue of Europe's Jews. His administration of immigration policy serves as useful reminder that even in the routine of the bureaucratic office there is such a thing as dereliction of duty to conscience. Under his authority the United States prevented fewer Jewish refugees from entering than were actually allowed by none-too-lenient law. The saga of the *St. Louis* was a case in point, in which a shipload of persecuted people was forbidden haven in U.S. ports and forced to return to Europe. Earlier the United States was complicit in Europe's abdication of responsibility at the Evian-les-Bains conference (1938), which declared itself opposed to Nazi racialism but did nothing to help Jews fleeing Germany. Once the "final solution" was under way and known in the administration's highest reaches (as of August 1942), the United States could have taken steps then recommended by such people as Rabbi Stephen Wise, Niebuhr, and Catt: ease visa restrictions; bomb the extermination camps and train tracks leading to them; tell Nazi leaders that they would be held accountable after the war; publicly denounce the genocide; challenge the British on their exclusion of Jews from Palestine, where the Grand Mufti of Jerusalem spread hatred of Jews (along with sedition against British mandate authority). None of these proposals was adopted at the time because, said officialdom, they were impractical. They would consume finite resources. Such measures would boomerang, making life even worse for Jews (how?, one wonders) in German-occupied Europe. "Favoritism" would fuel resentment among non-Jewish Americans, of whom 55 percent held anti-Semitic opinions, according to a 1945 poll. Despite FDR's conveying sympathy for European Jewry in private conversations, it was not until 1944 that the president created the War Refugee Board, in whose founding Secretary of the Treasury Morgenthau was influential. (He had outmaneuvered the State Department whose negligence was detailed in a Treasury report, *On the Acquiescence of This Government in the Murder of the Jews*.) The War Refugee Board saved 200,000 Jewish and 20,000 gentile lives. Yet by the time the board was established, the Germans had already committed villainy on a scale that, in Eleanor Roosevelt's words, "makes one ashamed" of the "civilized race." To that indictment can be added this conclusion: indifference to the annihilation of European Jewry and mediocre policy were the outstanding failures of FDR's government.[61]

Use of the atomic bombs impinges as vividly on contemporary American imagination as does the Holocaust.[62] The two are occasionally compared. German and U.S. racism are equated and Germany's methodical attempt to exterminate a people is likened to that destruction rained upon Japan in August 1945. Such comparisons are misleading, however. They overlook both the radicalism of Nazi policy and the more circumscribed aim of the United States: Japan's unconditional surrender. Such comparison also trivializes Nazi means and objectives. It is abetted by so-called revisionist history—the Holocaust did not happen; the gas chambers were a mere detail—and less malicious but still-telling phenomena: President Ronald Reagan's memorial visit to Bitburg cemetery (containing the remains of Waffen SS), proposals by entrepreneurs to build a supermarket and fast-food restaurant near the main gate to Auschwitz.[63]

Notwithstanding its analytical weakness, the Holocaust-atomic bomb comparison does serve one useful purpose: underscoring the gratuitous harm inflicted on Hiroshima and Nagasaki. Undoubtedly this conclusion is clearer today than it was in the summer of 1945 to war-weary Americans, whose desire was to end the war speedily at low cost. To most the alternative to using the bombs was to launch a full-scale invasion of the Japanese home islands—meaning a prolonged war, whose ghastly outline was visible in the recently finished fighting on Okinawa. (American casualties numbered 11,300 dead, 34,000 wounded, 36 ships sunk, 760 planes lost; Japanese officials counted on their side 120,000 military and 42,000 civilian casualties.) Yet inasmuch as judgment of the evidence and contentious interpretations is possible here, it seems fair to say that the two atomic attacks were unwarranted.[64]

Japan stood on the brink of surrender in midsummer 1945. The Imperial foreign ministry was hoping to enlist Moscow to broker a peace, or at least make the Americans realize that in Tokyo a peace party (by no means dominant) was looking for ways to end the war. President Truman knew about the foreign ministry's communication with Soviet officials.[65] It was a matter of comparatively short time before U.S. goals were won, probably in November.[66] The strangling naval blockade around Japan had merely to be tightened. The terrifically destructive conventional bombing of Japan's cities and military installations could have been increased. In other words, the existing air and naval campaigns—producing high numbers of civilian casualties—were enough to finish the job. Neither a land invasion nor the atomic bombs were needed, in which latter case even the proposed atomic demonstration (Franck Report) for Japanese leaders makes little retrospective sense.

Nonuse of the atomic bomb would have been hard to justify to those families of American servicemen who would have died in a continuing naval and air war. Nonuse would also have been difficult to defend to taxpayers once the Manhattan Project's price tag (2 billion dollars) was known, playing to anti-administration partisans in later elections. Finally, nonuse would have invited a larger Soviet role in the East Asia-Pacific war, which would have strengthened Stalin's claim to a share of occupation in Japan (an objectionable idea—strategically, economically, and politically—as the Grand Alliance dissolved). Yet had Washington been able to muster slightly more patience, the combat would still have ended on terms favorable to the United States, unencumbered by these lingering doubts: perhaps America had resorted to means that were extravagant even by total war's lack of restraint; perhaps Gandhi was closer to the truth than Truman, who claimed too emphatically that he never lost sleep over the Hiroshima-Nagasaki decision. In their distinctive ways, Generals Marshall and Eisenhower and atomic scientists Leo Szilard and James Franck also had misgivings about instantly incinerating thousands of people at a time when the war's obvious finale was near. A young California woman was typical of many Americans when she allowed herself this confusion on learning the news: "It sank in. Seventy thousand or a hundred thousand or two hundred thousand civilians? It came as a shock . . . to see women, children, and old innocent civilians burned. And Nagasaki! Two of them?" Years later Arthur Schlesinger, Jr., an impeccably mainstream scholar, judged the decision to use the atomic bombs as the most tragic in U.S. history.[67]

* * * * *

Within the span of only eighty-five years (1861–1945), the United States had been involved in three major wars. Combined American fatalities exceeded one million. The Civil War determined whether the nation would survive as a single entity, devoted to a credo of equality, and predominantly industrial. The First World War landed the country in the center of international affairs, from which position Americans voluntarily retreated. The immediate aftermath of the Second World War constituted a unipolar moment in history, as the United States emerged with a preponderance of power. The country's economic productivity, in whose wake followed the 1944 Bretton Woods agreement on open trade, overshadowed what survived in Europe and Asia—to say nothing of U.S. military prowess, augmented by atomic monopoly.[68] Yet no more than in 1865 or 1919 was the moment of victory pliable enough to allow U.S. strength to forge a durable order according to wartime ideals. The Grand Alliance was coming apart and with it that structure of peace envisaged in the Atlantic Charter and at Teheran and Yalta. The surpassing quality of American power then gradually faded: the Soviet Union acquired atomic weaponry (1949); the founding of the Warsaw Pact evened somewhat the distribution of power in Europe (1955); the devastated surged to become economic giants (West Germany, Japan); clients consumed inordinate attention and resources (Korea, Vietnam).

Part of the problem resided in FDR's irresolution on the desirable shape of postwar life. The president's blueprint, such as it was, fell short of any rigorous standard of thought: too provincial for liberal internationalism (failure in the Holocaust, foreshadowed by unresponsiveness to the Ukrainian famine); too blind to the danger of unreflecting hegemonial purpose (per Niebuhr's warnings); too indifferent to the requirements of future balance of power (eliminating Japan and Germany as military players). Roosevelt's eclecticism—combining elements of realpolitik, Wilsonianism, tactical fluidity with strategic vagueness—was inherently unstable. This approach may have been in keeping with the national preference for flexibility over longterm planning. But Roosevelt's ways and aims occasionally flummoxed the British, offended the Free French, elevated Chiang beyond reason, did not allay Stalin's most cherished suspicions, and proved impossible of implementation by FDR's successors. A keener focus on postwar goals plus consistency would not have cured the world, but they would have reduced that bewilderment and rush to advantage that followed Axis defeat: the Cold War and congealing of the security state.[69]

The chief problem as of late 1945 was not political, however. It was existential and by definition not solvable by statecraft's remedy. No country, not even the powerful United States, could have put right a world that killed 60 million people (the majority civilian), produced 30 million displaced Europeans, and mocked Kant's cosmopolitanism in death camps where Nazism swept victims from all Europe.[70] The prospect of another unleashing of demonic fury seemed implicit in the atomic bombings, against which the United Nations Charter with its condemnation of "the scourge of war" seemed a fragile vessel indeed. In this context, too, FDR's pep talks on nothing to fear were fatuous. The attack on Pearl Harbor had forever destroyed America's sense of impregnability. Hitler's totalitarianism and the means used to subdue it had set the political-military universe trembling, as the *New York Herald Tribune* editorialized. That the foreseeable future would likewise be saturated with fear was grasped by Robert Hutchins, as he remarked the demise of a promising world order. In a spirit reminiscent of Blum on Hitler and Force, Hutchins said (June 1945): "The words *peace, justice, cooperation, community,* and *charity* have fallen out of our vocabulary. They are, in fact, regarded as signs of weakness and as showing that one who uses them is guilty of the capital crime of modern times, lack of realism . . . The new realism is nothing but the old Realpolitik. It represents the conquest of the United States by Hitler." Earlier Norman Thomas had foretold the dangers likely to follow Axis vanquishment: "The method of modern [total] warfare is self-defeating in terms of ideal ends. War itself is the only victor." As if glimpsing East Europe's Stalinist future, Thomas continued: "Intolerance, dictatorship, brutality are [war's] inevitable accompaniments and they live on even when exhaustion . . . stills the guns."[71]

That the world was not transformed after the defeat of Hitler had less to do with the intrinsic value of wartime idealism than with the unyielding nature of world politics: competitive, insecure, barely domesticated by law or diplomatic tradition. Nuremberg represented a rear-guard action to uphold meaningfulness in international life.

Yet the existence of worlds worse than that of post–World War II is obvious in Nazi-conquered Europe, against which nihilism the United States made a crucial contribution. Thenceforth, innovative minds had to reconcile the wish for limited sovereign powers cooperating together with this reality: the state system was not about to disappear, not even in Western Europe where the dreams of Jean Monnet and Robert Schuman found partial expression. The 1942 prayer of poet Stephen Vincent Benet could stand reasonably for a point of destination: "We can make if we choose, a planet unvexed by war, untroubled by hunger or fear, undivided by senseless distinctions of race, color or theory . . . Grant us a common faith that man shall know bread and peace—that he shall know justice and righteousness, freedom and security, an equal opportunity and an equal chance to do his best . . . throughout the world."[72] But until this millennium arrived, the counsel of Niebuhr was more cogent. Insecurity, he taught, was the abiding condition of modern men and women. Against it the United Nations might helpfully make a small difference; therefore, the United States should lend its support. Yet as long as the pride of nations persisted and tribal loyalties obtained, the best one could hope for was that great states would involve justice in the manipulation of power. Whether the United States would play its part satisfactorily, Niebuhr realized, only the unfathomable future could tell.

Unleavened realism would lead to the "abyss of cynicism," unadulterated idealism to "the fog of sentimentality." The classical wisdom also still applied in international politics: each solution leads to fresh problems. The United States would need elements of everyday shrewdness and uncommon purpose to assure security for itself and a semblance of safety for others. World community, à la Henry Wallace or FDR at his most flamboyant, should remain the objective, Niebuhr allowed.[73] But the ancient record of broken human achievements augured for more of the same even after the demolition of Nazi Germany.[74]

FIVE

Evil Empire

Treatment of the Cold War lies awkwardly in this book's schema. A case can be made that Soviet-U.S. rivalry from the end of World War II to 1991 amounted to a coherent international system defined by bipolarity, self-regulation, and clearly delineated spheres of influence. These properties allowed for a basic stability.[1] Within it the major antagonists never came to direct blows, preferring instead that relative safety derived from proxy combat. Washington's and Moscow's monitoring, moreover, of the diplomatic-military equilibrium prevented its disruption by ongoing threats: competition in the margins (i.e., the Third World), ideological struggle, arms race. Admittedly, the resultant peace was imperfect from the standpoint of purists or people living in vulnerable zones, as in Eastern Europe and Southeast Asia. But this proximate peace, however troubled, was superior to the preceding era (blighted by 1914, 1939) and in ways preferable to that of post-1991, with its peculiar scourges: rampant ethnic strife, religious fanaticisms, failed states. With such concerns in mind, a respected political scientist, John Mearsheimer, warned in 1990 that "a complete end to the Cold War would create more problems than it would solve."[2]

Thus the span of years during which the Soviet Union and United States organized world affairs might be regarded by future historians as a golden age, at least in contrast with the turmoil on either side of its existence. The great powers spun a set of rules by which they usually abided. Lesser powers occupied reasonably defined niches in diplomatic-military blocs. Even the weakest states—allowing for exceptions like Cuba or Afghanistan—were left with some room for maneuvering to play the main rivals against each other, reaping benefit from both, per the nonaligned movement's stratagem. Viewed in this context, then, American claims of victory in the Cold War were as irrelevant as Mikhail Gorbachev's contention that everyone lost. Rather, an international system, satisfactory from various standpoints (stability, predictability, keeping a lid on tribalism in the Balkans), passed from the scene in 1989–1991 along with the Soviet Union, thereby introducing a new cycle of permutation.[3]

Yet the period of Soviet-U.S. antagonism can be examined profitably here, even if the Cold War is properly understood as a discrete system (or "long peace") in the history of international politics. Like the other conflicts reviewed in this book, the Cold War was a time of testing for the United States. Exacting payments came in blood—33,650 battle deaths in the so-called Korean police action; 58,000 dead in Vietnam—and treasure for weaponry. Washington expended 11 trillion dollars altogether on Cold War defense, according to one responsible analyst.[4] The strain of Cold War also quickened discussion in the United States about America's role in the world. Certainly the diffuse nature and duration of the Cold War discouraged the crisper debate on future order seen in previous conflicts. Nevertheless the Cold War did repeatedly oblige a range of Americans to grapple with questions of national purpose and world design.

Animating all the talk, giving it urgency, was the manifest danger of nuclear extermination. William Faulkner in 1950 conveyed the anxiety of his compatriots: "When will I be blown up?" The predicament for Reinhold Niebuhr was that reliance on atomic defense might disqualify the United States as an ethical society; willingness to commit extreme evil in the name of containment could nullify whatever moral imperative was mobilized against Stalin.[5]

Relations between the United States and USSR in the forty-five years of their antagonism alternated between tension and détente. For analytical purposes, in fact, three separate Cold Wars are distinguishable. The first began with the victorious Allies bickering over their shares of Axis assets, achieved clarity in 1946 with Churchill's "iron curtain" speech and Stalin's declaration that the world was divided into two camps, and was fully joined in 1947 with the unveiling of Truman's doctrine. Events following in rapid succession pushed Soviet-U.S. relations near the point of rupture. These included the 1948 crisis over Berlin, when the Soviet-imposed blockade endangered that city's goods from and access to the West. The Anglo-U.S. airlift and implied resort to war, should the Soviets interdict the air bridge, subsequently defeated the communist action—though Berlin remained for decades a flashpoint in the East-West contest of wills. Also in 1948 a coup by Czechoslovak Marxists brought communism to power in Prague. That same year Tito's Yugoslavia was expelled from the Stalinist fold; Belgrade retained its independence thereafter by economic-security arrangements with the West. To prevent similar deviations, the Soviet leadership enforced draconian measures in the rest of Eastern Europe; loyalty to Moscow and to its satraps was assured by omnipresent terror, exemplified by that distorted justice administered by peoples' courts.[6] The founding of NATO in 1949, whose explicit purpose was to deter Soviet aggression against the West, dug deeper Europe's political-military division.[7] Truman responded to Soviet acquisition of the atomic bomb in 1949 by approving plans that sped the arms race; an even more destructive thing, the fusion—or hydrogen—bomb should be developed.

In the Far East, Mao's 1949 conquest of mainland China and alignment with the Soviet Union ("leaning to one side") suggested to observers on both sides of the ideological line that the Asian balance of power had swung against the West. Evidence to support this thesis was available in the North Korean invasion of the South in 1950, the idea being that Stalin and his Chinese comrades felt so emboldened that they inspired the North Koreans to unify their country on communist terms. The West presumably was on the defensive and could not respond forcefully.[8]

The first Cold War began to thaw in 1953. Stalin, viewed by Americans as responsible for causing post-1945 tensions, died in March. His immediate successor, Georgi Malenkov, promoted a "new course" premised on the need for Soviet-U.S. coexistence, increased East-West trade, and other economic cooperation. The Korean War also ended in 1953 in a compromise, which has held since despite moments of danger. In Geneva, the next year, delegates from East and West negotiated a settlement to stop the fighting in Vietnam. The first post–World War II conference of Soviet and U.S. leaders convened in 1955 to resolve—or at least review—the main problems: Germany, Austria, Eastern Europe, nuclear arms race. Despite crises in 1956 (Soviet suppression of the Hungarian rebellion, the Suez Canal war), relations between Moscow and Washington did not completely deteriorate for which credit Khrushchev deserves mention. He was wedded to the anti-Stalin campaign—inaugurated with his "Secret Speech" at the Twentieth Communist Party Congress—and embraced the notion of competitive but peaceful coexistence.

The second Cold War started in late 1958, when Khrushchev delivered his ultimatum on Berlin, and culminated with the 1962 Cuban missile crisis. Signs of improvement after this close call were apparent in 1963, when the limited test ban treaty was signed.[9] Thenceforth, nuclear arms control was an object of Soviet and U.S. concentration, even as recriminations flew between the powers over the Vietnam War and the Warsaw Pact's 1968 invasion of Czechoslovakia. In the early 1970s Soviet-U.S. détente was fully under way, its centerpiece being strategic arms control, signified by the SALT I and ABM treaties of 1972.

Détente frayed in the mid-1970s as critics in both Moscow and Washington charged their adversary with enjoying unilateral advantages—in Middle East diplomacy, arms production, plays for influence in Africa and Latin America. The Senate suspended deliberations on SALT II following the 1979 Soviet invasion of Afghanistan. Détente became moribund as the treaty languished, remaining so through the first Reagan administration. Wheat embargo, Olympics boycott, renewed arms race, and choleric rhetoric embodied yet another U.S. Cold War effort. Warnings of an evil empire everywhere on the march and research on a comprehensive defense shield (SDI) also marked U.S. policy in Cold War three. Only as the USSR shambled to its demise—with a reformist government headed by Gorbachev and in step with a faltering economy—did the competitive-cooperative cycle in Soviet-U.S. history cease.

Conflict

Scholarship on the first Cold War continues to improve with better access (hardly perfect) to archives in countries of the former Warsaw Pact and declassification (annoyingly slow) of previously confidential Western records. Eventually this process might produce a rough consensus among American historians on the origins and conduct of the Cold War, or at least refine the competing schools of interpretation: the orthodox, justifying Washington's policy as reacting to alleged Soviet provocation (Herbert Feis, John Spanier) versus revisionist and corporatist assumptions about the putative capitalist mainsprings of U.S. policy (Gabriel Kolko, Lloyd Gardner, Michael Hogan) versus postrevisionist attempts to find common ground between left and right (John Gaddis).[10] Irrespective of the outcome of this historiographical debate, it runs parallel to arguments by Americans during the Cold War over world orders.

The USSR bore responsibility for beginning the Cold War, according to Truman government broadcasts. Stalin was said to pursue a policy that defied his earlier pledges—made at Yalta, for instance—to permit the spreading of democracy in Eastern Europe; his malevolence was visible in Soviet domination of Poland and attempts to sow trouble in Italy and France through the local communist parties. The Soviets waged unfriendly diplomacy against Turkey and Iran. Stalinist dictate in Eastern Europe proceeded apace with the establishment of communism; the people living therein had to cope with smothering foreign subjugation no less excruciating than that of Hitler's. In short, the Soviet Union was militant and aggressive. Western policy was defensive, as implied in the word containment. Except for the U.S. response, Soviet armies would have sprawled over Europe right up to the English Channel. The Marshall Plan and founding of NATO confined Soviet influence in Europe to the poorer zone, but these measures could not reverse Stalin's manipulation of so-called free elections in the East. Eventually, the administration wagered, Soviet power would recede from Eastern Europe by means short of war; the USSR might then cooperate with Western powers to uphold an order based on freely elected governments, open markets, and a healthy regard for international law. This hoped-for pattern constituted a return to the World War II vision of future world politics. The United States in the meantime had to retain a preponderance of economic-military might and police those areas where Soviet power—direct or pushed by surrogates—could reach beyond desirable boundaries. The most vivid statement by Washington along these lines was the Truman Doctrine.

Occasioned by the felt need via economic aid to shore up Turkey (resisting Soviet pressure on the frontier's placement) and help the Greek government (fighting communist insurrection), the Truman Doctrine associated U.S. aims with democratic universalism. The president told Congress in March 1947: "We shall not realize our objectives . . . unless we are willing to help free peoples to maintain their free institutions and their national integrity against aggressive movements that seek to impose upon them totalitarian regimes. This is no more than a frank recognition that totalitarian regimes imposed upon free peoples, by direct or indirect aggression, undermine the foundations of international peace and hence the security of the United States." In effect, as Woodrow Wilson had taught, U.S. security was intimately involved with enlightened forces abroad struggling against tyranny. In a Manichean world the stakes were absolute. The USSR's nefarious designs contrasted sharply with American goals. "It must be the policy of the United States to support free peoples who are resisting attempted subjugation by armed minorities or by outside pressures," declared Truman.[11]

Skeptics, such as Senator Taft and Walter Lippmann, objected to what they regarded as the president's hyperbole; if accepted, it would encourage the United States to adopt policies that outstripped resources, causing national impoverishment, or provoke an otherwise avoidable war with Russia. Both Taft and Lippmann wound up supporting the Greek-Turkish assistance package but not before castigating Truman's language. In their view, it smacked of subterfuge, whereby Soviet intentions and capabilities were exaggerated to persuade Congress of the wisdom of granting aid. George Kennan privately warned Dean Acheson—influential proponent of the hard sell—that the decision not to discriminate explicitly among dilemmas overseas according to a hierarchy of interests would confuse the public's understanding of foreign policy.[12]

Secretary George Marshall was senior among those State Department officials unhappy with the Truman Doctrine's stridency.[13] He tried afterwards indirectly to qualify it. When it fell upon him to draw an outline for European recovery (June 1947), he employed a text cooler in tone, albeit still pitched to win adherents. The result, a product of Charles Bohlen's pen, was a decided improvement over Truman's explanation of issues. Marshall's speech dispensed with anti-Soviet flourishes, merely hinting that the USSR was cooperating with mischievous forces, against which the United States was prepared to act. The main point was that Washington stood ready to provide resources to help the Europeans (in East and West) repair their war-ravaged societies. Such recovery, said Marshall, emphasizing the pragmatic over the moralistic, was in America's economic-political interest. To achieve it, Marshall called on the "foresight" and "willingness" of the American people "to face up to the responsibility which history [had] clearly placed upon [them]." Except for this lapse, he eschewed loftiness.[14]

Kennan's seminal "X article" in *Foreign Affairs* (July 1947) on Soviet behavior also rejected Truman's language. Kennan, then director of the State Department's Policy Planning Staff, portrayed the "challenge" posed by Moscow as a "test" of the nation's "quality."[15] He claimed too that American mettle would be proven if the country came together in single purpose to bear the responsibilities of Western leadership. But he refrained—in contrast with Truman—from pronouncing lugubriously on freedom's fate in an unstable age or on the gloom cast worldwide by totalitarianism.

Because the chief executive is the main educator in the United States on foreign policy, not State Department functionaries, it was Truman's analysis—plus idiom—that became the yardstick by which success and failure were evaluated in the early Cold War. Congress's passage of aid—valued at $400 million—to Greece and Turkey dignified Truman's approach, setting the stage for that greatly more ambitious program of assistance envisaged in the Marshall Plan. Subsequent speeches by the president naturally reinforced his version of events. At Berkeley in 1948, for example, he exclaimed that the only type of expansion sought by the United States was one that advanced "human freedom and the wider enjoyment of the good things of the earth in all countries." As outgoing president in January 1953, he reiterated this theme: the Cold War pitted "those who love freedom [against] those who would lead the world back into slavery and darkness."[16]

Unforeseen by Truman in 1947, the right wing of the Republican party soon appropriated his vocabulary—interpreting it literally to excoriate him, his cabinet, and the Democratic party for not doing enough to defend liberty against communism. McCarthyism, shorthand for zanier anticommunism, was intellectually grounded in the emotionalism of the Truman Doctrine. The doctrine itself exemplified one of the harmful tendencies in American life: to mix short-term and limited objectives with grand formula, thereby blurring political vision in the United States. Thus arose the country's difficulty in conducting a calibrated or subtle policy, such as trying in 1949–1950 to coax China away from the Soviet Union to foster an Asian balance of power conducive to Western security.[17]

Henry Wallace, commerce secretary following his removal from the vice presidency, was a choice target of anticommunist fundamentalists. They were as unforgiving of his foreign policy recommendations in the late 1940s as of his earlier New Deal activity. The former also drew the president's contempt. Truman perceived Wallace, whom he fired from the cabinet (September 1946), as a silly pacifist, "parlor pink," and member of that guild of dupes that constituted "a sabotage front for Stalin." Lingering questions about Wallace's previous experiments in varieties of mysticism added to Truman's skepticism. Wallace held the president's personal integrity and mental acuity in comparably low regard.[18] The political duel between the two men in the 1948 campaign threatened to drive enough liberal voters away from the Democrats to Wallace's Progressive party to ensure Thomas Dewey's election. In the event, Wallace's showing was weak, poorer even than Strom Thurmond's independent candidacy that year. Wallace won only 1.2 million votes—none in the electoral college—while Truman, against expectations, outdistanced Dewey and the Republicans. However unimpressive the tally of Wallace's presidential run, the Progressive candidate's criticism of Truman in 1946–1948 represented an alternative account of the United States and its world role.

Wallace accused Truman of casually forsaking cooperation with Stalin, pursuing instead expensive preparedness programs and an excessively ideological approach—repudiating diplomacy to prevent war. Only Wall Street tycoons, big cartels, the British empire, and militarists would profit from such a stance, Wallace charged. Of the Truman Doctrine, he gave this prediction, itself not a wholly inaccurate reading of future events: "Once American loans are given to the undemocratic governments of Greece and Turkey, every reactionary government and every strutting dictator will be able to hoist the anti-Communist skull and bones, and demand that the American people rush to his aid. . . . American dollars will be the first demand, then American army officers and technicians, then American G.I.s." Yet Washington could reverse the drift toward trouble by taking timely initiatives. Ideally, Wallace believed, these would redeem the principles of one world and the common man's welfare. He urged that Washington share information on atomic science with Moscow (in ways more generous than the Baruch or Acheson-Lilienthal plans), the idea being to calm Soviet jitters about U.S. intentions. He advised that Truman make substantial financial aid available to Moscow to boost postwar reconstruction—without the conditions of the Marshall Plan, whose rejection by the Kremlin made sense to Wallace. He also advocated a recognition of great-power equivalence (not fully in line with his one-world notion): the United States should not object to the Soviets organizing Eastern Europe according to their tastes, just as the United States reigned preeminent in Latin America and Western Europe. In this light Wallace saw the communist coup in Prague as an understandable, if regrettable, response to U.S. support of local conservatives, egged on by

Washington's ambassador, Laurence Steinhardt. For Stalin's part in realizing "the century of peace," Wallace suggested (in an open letter) that the USSR cooperate with the West in such key areas as reducing armaments, allowing free trade and movement of citizens, permitting exchange of scientific findings—all while concluding peace treaties with Germany and Japan. Stalin's reply was polite but noncommittal. Anticommunist liberals, such as Arthur Schlesinger and Hubert Humphrey of the Americans for Democratic Action (ADA), were astonished by Wallace's naiveté, holding in their view the false promise of appeasement. "Poor Henry is really a prisoner of the Commies," sighed ADA activist Reinhold Niebuhr.[19]

However dubious his judgment on the nature of Stalinism, Wallace was a discerning critic of the home front. He spoke defiantly against Truman's 1947 executive order that instituted a regime of loyalty investigation of federal employees—which cleared the way for the firing of thousands of people on flimsy charges. That same year, Wallace decried as absurd J. Edgar Hoover's statement that communists were everywhere boring into the organs and tissue of U.S. society. Albeit committed to representative democracy and free enterprise (with provisos to help the needy and check the greedy), Wallace did not rebuff the support he received from individual American communists. He feared that to shun such people would encourage red-baiting and the atmosphere of mounting hysteria. He suffered dearly for this principled stand in the 1948 campaign: he was smeared by opponents as a Soviet sympathizer—or worse—and attracted FBI scrutiny. Wallace's election bid was further weakened by his contention that U.S. preachments on world liberty should beget practical changes in the segregated South. His civil rights advocacy and addresses to integrated audiences during his Southern campaign tour upset local customs. He was greeted by furious white crowds in North Carolina and Alabama. They assaulted him with eggs and tomatoes; he was forced to cut short prepared remarks or cancel them entirely. Protesters also hurled epithets: "Go back to Russia, you nigger-lover."[20]

Among African-American supporters of Wallace, none was more visible than Paul Robeson. He served as a co-chairman of Wallace's election committee and was considered briefly by Progressives as a possible vice presidential running mate. As star of stage, film, concert hall, and college athletic field, Robeson—son of a former slave—had won a wider acceptance by white America than any other person of his race. His had been a charmed career, although most of his audiences had sniffed at his civil rights activity and defense of the Soviet Union as racial paradise. This skepticism of Robeson's politics was transformed in the excited late 1940s into vilification. The eventual object of congressional investigation, Robeson was also blacklisted, his passport revoked, and his safety threatened. His emotional well-being was finally rattled, his physical health impaired. This fall from favor, triggered by close association with Wallace, was assured by Robeson's equating Hitler with Southern segregationists and comparing U.S. foreign policy to that of the Third Reich—both standing "for counterrevolution all over the world." American racism and imperialism, Robeson asserted, would conspire to start a war against communism unless firmly opposed. Additionally, Robeson's goodwill tours of Eastern bloc countries in the late 1940s and his prediction that blacks would not participate in any war against the USSR discomfited mainstream African-American leaders. The NAACP repudiated him. Jackie Robinson (baseball player) snubbed him. Sugar Ray Robinson (boxer), Adam Clayton Powell, and Walter White attacked him for raising doubts concerning the patriotism of black citizens. Later, during the Korean War, Robeson denounced U.S. intervention. He opined that troops would be better used to fight the Ku Klux Klan than dispatched abroad. As the war sputtered to stalemate, Robeson charged: "No one has yet explained to my satisfaction what business a black lad from a Mississippi or Georgia sharecropping farm has in Asia shooting down the yellow or brown son of an impoverished rice farmer." The Soviets had named a mountain in the Urals for Robeson by the time he delivered this utterance (1953) and had awarded him the Stalin Peace Prize.[21]

Arms Race

Korean combat halted in 1953 and Stalin, "genius leader of communism," departed this earth. In that year Republicans also occupied the White House for the first time in two decades. One of the early questions facing President Eisenhower arose from the demarche made by Stalin's successors. They advertised the plausibility of peaceful coexistence, which also entailed benefits of increased Soviet-Western trade. Britain's Prime Minister Churchill and Foreign Minister Eden were eager to explore this Soviet initiative. But Eisenhower responded cautiously. He rejected Churchill's proposal for an immediate meeting with the new Kremlin leadership as premature. Still, lest he appeared too stubborn, thereby falling victim to the Soviet peace offensive, Eisenhower replied with his "Chance for Peace" speech (April 16, 1953). It put forward reasonable-sounding proposals that he knew in advance Moscow must reject. These concerned Germany's reunification and the Red Army's withdrawing from Eastern Europe.[22] Soviet intransigence plus opposition to national self-determination were thus reemphasized; public criticism of the administration for not exploring an avenue out of the Cold War was muted.

The "Chance for Peace" statement was more than just cleverly phrased propaganda, however. This speech was also a serious recital of aims for the post–Cold War world, delivered by a leader hoping to avoid open conflict. He characterized the Cold War as exhausting:

> A life of . . . fear and tension; a burden of arms draining the wealth and the labor of all peoples; a wasting of strength that defies the American system or the Soviet system or any system to achieve true abundance and happiness for the peoples of this earth. Every gun that is made, every warship launched, every rocket fired signifies, in the final sense, a theft from those who hunger and are not fed, those who are cold and are not clothed.

As examples of extreme cost, Eisenhower named specific items, including a modern bomber as equal to thirty new school buildings, a fighter plane as equal to half a million bushels of wheat, a destroyer as equal to eight thousand new houses. The goal of statecraft in these circumstances was to negotiate an end to the East-West confrontation, after which mankind's ancient nemesis, poverty, could then be tackled in "a declared total war." Here Eisenhower, sounding like Henry Wallace circa 1948, taught that trust among nations would be fortified by the production of abundance with its fair distribution to all people.[23] Eisenhower listed in this connection such essentials as food, shelter, hospitals, and schools, all of which might be underwritten—in allowable anachronism—by the peace dividend. He also made a vow: "This Government is ready to ask its people to join with all nations in devoting a substantial percentage of the savings achieved by disarmament to a fund for world aid and reconstruction." Extension of this aid—roughly modeled on the Marshall Plan—would help poor nations to develop their economies and participate in profitable multilateral trade.[24]

Eight years after Eisenhower delivered the "Chance for Peace," the Cold War was still a stubborn fact of life, postponing indefinitely any version of world order based on economic cooperation. Inability to end the stalemate or cap the arms race constituted Eisenhower's main disappointment on leaving office. Cancellation of the Paris summit conference (May 1960) and testing in the late 1950s by both sides of nuclear bombs, sparking worldwide concern about the health effects of fallout, were legacies of the seemingly interminable Soviet-U.S. rivalry. Fundamentally, Eisenhower's farewell address (January 17, 1961) was a public meditation on the consequences of continuing the Cold War. He alerted his countrymen to the pernicious influence of what he termed the "military-industrial complex." It could by its sheer size corrupt civil liberties, usurp the democratic procedures of U.S. government, and damage the economy by forcing it to become addicted to military technology and costly weapons. University research and free inquiry might also become captive to federal contracts shaped to narrowly defined security needs. Maybe, Eisenhower added, a scientific-technological elite would gradually persuade citizens to substitute its expertise for the wisdom of elected officials. Apart from these dangers spawned by the Cold War, he perceived another, no less baleful for the future: moral impoverishment and the squandering of finite capital. The Cold War generation, as custodian of U.S. liberty and wealth, had to resist the impulse of spending everything in one burst of effort: "We . . . must [not] live only for today, plundering, for our own ease and convenience, the precious resources of tomorrow. We cannot mortgage the material assets of our grandchildren without risking the loss also of their political and spiritual heritage. We want democracy to survive for all generations to come, not to become the insolvent phantom of tomorrow." Disarmament reached through comprehensive diplomacy was, for the outgoing president, the realistic alternative to American collapse or world war.[25]

Notwithstanding his dire forecasts, Eisenhower never lost faith in the ability of U.S. statecraft to navigate safely between the Scylla of Western breakdown and the Charybdis of thermonuclear exchange. Other national figures shared this optimism, even though in cases—Governor Adlai Stevenson or Senator John Kennedy—they believed themselves better equipped to lead the United States through these perils.

Such confidence was less evident outside the political class, however—especially as the dangers of the second Cold War became more pronounced. Unabated testing of bombs confirmed antiwar activists, of whom the Christian pacifist A. J. Muste was prominent, in their fear that nations in modern arms would not survive. In other words, there might be no post–Cold War politics whatsoever. Muste wrote in 1957: "The world is all too obviously confronted with the threat of mass annihilation, the poisoning of its air, water, soil and food supplies, perhaps the initiation of mutations which will produce repulsive physical and mental deformations in our children's children, if there be any such."[26]

Muste denounced the production by both sides of weapons of mass destruction: they exemplified the debauched state of modern civilization. Muste pressed for unilateral American disarmament. He lobbied famous scientists, including Albert Einstein, to place their names on the side of universal disarmament. Muste warned of nuclear war by technical accident. An older man whose pacifist counsel dated back to World War I, he participated in "peace walks" (including one from San Francisco to Moscow), demonstrations (on the White House lawn and in Red Square), and civil disobedience at military sites, for which he was jailed. He and his colleagues on the Committee for Nonviolent Action scored the United States and USSR during the Cuban missile crisis for pursuing policies from which nothing resembling victory could follow. The only way out of the Cold War, Muste said, was for the United States to support democratic revolutions in the decolonizing world and to abide by the ideals of democracy and racial justice at home; this example of uprightness should also convert the communist bloc to decency, even friendship with the West.[27]

The shape of future world order was also addressed by people politically opposite to Muste. To the philosopher Sidney Hook, once an associate of Muste's (during their infatuation with Trotsky in the 1930s), the pacifist and his allies abroad (notably Lord Bertrand Russell) entirely missed the point: the Cold War featured freedom opposed to unalloyed, immutable, merciless tyranny. Pacifist teachings, moreover, were corrosive, weakening as they did the faith of Western publics in their national policies and the capacity of Western governments to persevere. Neither disarmament nor the demonstrable superiority of Western life could win the Cold War or save humanity. Hook believed that the key question raised by Soviet technological achievements (Sputnik, huge H-bombs) was whether the West would be willing to resist by all possible means. Nuclear deterrence, he averred, required the heroic will to use doomsday weapons and to suffer the ultimate consequences. In the absence of this determination, the human future might surpass for wickedness anything imaginable, even a third world war. Bluntly put, some worlds—Hitler's, the USSR's—were worse than none at all: "Those who are prepared to sacrifice freedom for peace and for mere life will find after such sacrifice no genuine peace and a life unfit for man. Paradoxical as it may sound, life itself is not a value. What gives life value is not its mere existence but its quality. Whoever proclaims that life is worth living under any circumstances has already written for himself an epitaph of infamy."[28]

Not oblivious to Soviet domestic reforms after 1953 or Moscow's ballyhooed foreign policy reorientation, Hook still maintained—against objections from critics like Russell and Kennan—that the USSR amounted to a permanent pathology; it was immune to improvement, implacably hostile to the West.[29] The fruits of sinister science and totalitarian controls in the hands of a police state, synchronized with Western pusillanimity, could trigger a dark age of limitless years. Neither intellectual enlightenment nor the conversion of evil to a higher moral plane would ever follow. Better *in extremis* to die bravely than to enter a nightmare future populated by demoralized creatures who would curse the cowardice of the last free generation. In 1962, just months before the Cuban missile episode, Hook wrote: "Six million Jews went to their death submissively without humanizing their tormentors. The Jews who went down fighting in the Warsaw Ghetto in a desperate resistance died more nobly. I therefore deny that our situation is absolutely unique."[30]

Yet Hook doubted whether Western choice would ever be so grim as to decide between death or slavery. He therefore urged the commencement of full-fledged East-West negotiations. He devised plans for the phased retreat of Soviet and U.S. troops from Europe—differing in detail from contemporaneous schemes by British Laborites and German Social Democrats but not in the central thrust. As the Cold War wore on, and its focus shifted to Asian and African countries breaking from European empires, Hook hoped that America would place itself forthrightly on the anticolonialist side. To whatever degree Washington was implicated in the sins of the Anglo-French or other fading empires, U.S. prestige was diminished. Underwriting the French in Indochina, for example, he said in 1958, had only earned for Americans the disdain of free people everywhere.[31]

Vietnam

Hook was not easily persuaded in the early 1960s of the merits of U.S. intervention in Vietnam. He defended the large-scale military commitment only after it was made, warning thereafter that communist victory would plunge Southeast Asia into bloodbaths, prison camps, and purges. History after 1975—the plight of the boat people, Pol Pot's Cambodian killing fields, the fate of people incarcerated in re-education camps—proved to his satisfaction the validity of LBJ's policy. Hook ascribed blame for the final debacle to Congress, which withheld aid from South Vietnam in 1975 as the North marched, and to the demoralization inflicted on the American polity by sensationalist journalism, subversive professors, and rebellious college students. Against all this misfortune the real or imagined defects of the Saigon regime had been mild, Hook contended. Presumably, had it prevailed against North Vietnamese invasion and Viet Cong insurrection, the regime would have—with outside assistance—corrected its shortcomings by adopting democratic-economic reforms. Essayist Norman Podhoretz, writing in similar heat after the fall of Saigon, added that by abandoning the Vietnamese, the United States sacrificed its honor.[32]

Aid to Saigon had not been niggardly. Military outlays exceeding $150 billion fueled inflation in the 1970s. Roughly 3 million U.S. servicemen had been assigned to the long war. Thousands had been killed, many thousands more wounded. Veterans returning home often faced scorn rather than gratitude.[33] Not since Abraham Lincoln had America been so bitterly divided as in the late 1960s.

This division added a burden of palpable cost that surpassed anything imagined by Lyndon Johnson when, after the 1964 Gulf of Tonkin escapade, he multiplied support for South Vietnam. That its cause had been America's ever since Truman, Johnson ardently believed. The hypnotic power of the domino theory also influenced his thinking. This concept obscured the realities of Sino-Soviet rivalry, overlooked ancient Chinese-Vietnamese antipathy, and misread the nationalist appeal of Ho Chi Minh. Encouraging arguments by policy advisors (excluding George Ball) and concern over the repercussions for the Democratic party of "losing" Vietnam also combined to sway Johnson, otherwise fretful that an Asian war would sabotage his cherished Great Society. Johnson believed (or at least contained his doubts) in 1964–1965 that his government could wage war abroad while eradicating poverty and the effects of racial prejudice in America. Massive diversions of time, energy, and wealth were inconceivable to the president, who later rued that he had ignored intimations of the Great Society's demise: "That bitch of a war killed the lady I really loved—the Great Society."[34]

Johnson was never more hopeful of a good outcome in Southeast Asia than in the spring of 1965, when he outlined for audiences his Vietnam policy. His words echoed JFK's purpose—bravado might be a better term—to pay any price to assure the success of liberty overseas. Johnson restated the presumed lessons of Munich. He upheld the sanctity of U.S. reputation as a guarantor of Western security. He raised the alarm against that dread emanating from China. In phrases brimming with the liberal tenant that all peoples are alike, he said that every Vietnamese, communist and noncommunist, wanted the same things: food, health, education, national progress. As such, Vietnam's goal was America's. And Johnson promised aid to solidify any fair peace settlement. The Mekong River area might be transformed into a productive region on the model of the Tennessee Valley Authority. Other projects, akin to America's own attack on poverty, could be introduced to squelch illiteracy, disease, and hunger. Not only did Johnson invite his audiences to imagine an Indochina laden with plenty, he also asked them to contemplate a post–Cold War world. Law, reason, and negotiation should replace the violent settlement of international disputes. Good faith among nations and cooperation would displace fear and destitution. Soviets and Americans, Chinese and Indians, North and South Vietnamese might yet collaborate to rid their lands of despair and the danger of total destruction. As had Eisenhower, Johnson also deplored the waste exacted by Cold War. He told a Johns Hopkins University audience: "The guns and the bombs, the rockets and the warships, are symbols of human failure." By discarding them, by emphasizing universal ambitions, humanity would decide on life over death: "This generation of the world must choose: destroy or build, kill or aid, hate or understand."[35]

Johnson's dream of a bright future was smashed by communist Vietnamese resistance, invariably disparaged by U.S. leaders as "fanatical." South Vietnamese officialdom meanwhile did not produce a popular or effectual alternative to Ho. Body bags, controversial bombing, and the shock of the Tet offensive shook America's confidence and broke the war consensus. An anguished President Johnson forswore reelection in March 1968, the same month that a unit of U.S. soldiers shot three hundred unarmed civilians in My Lai. The Nixon-Kissinger government subsequently liquidated American participation in the war but not before expanding the scope of operations (Cambodia incursion), intensifying the bombing (Christmas 1972), and compounding the human cost. This last included more than a third of all American fatalities in the war, nearly 110,000 South Vietnamese dead, and more than half a million communists killed. On learning that Kissinger would receive the 1973 Nobel Peace Prize (with North Vietnam's Le Duc Tho), George Ball quipped "the Norwegians must have a sense of humor."[36]

Ball is best remembered of "establishment" dissenters for his proximity to executive authority (LBJ's undersecretary of state) and the persistence of his warnings. He argued even before 1965 that the United States might become mired in a hopeless guerrilla war in an area inconsequential to the global balance of power; the war would consume inordinate amounts of materiel and manpower; the United States and its purpose were compromised by ties to a Saigon regime commanding scant respect.[37] No more than Ball did Kennan, Lippmann, Niebuhr, or University of Chicago political scientist Hans Morgenthau harbor romantic ideas about the Viet Cong or the government in Hanoi: they were hostile to Western interests, heartless to enemies. Still, none of these dissenters—respected in foreign policy circles as practitioners or commentators—believed that any vital concern was at stake in Vietnam. Whatever the war's outcome, no matter how tragic for people living in Indochina, nothing that happened there could decisively affect the economic well-being or security of the United States and its major allies. The spectacle meanwhile of a military Goliath pummeling a peasant nation, the ongoing crisis of political legitimacy in Saigon, and the deepening of divisions in U.S. society hurt national standing abroad—all of which played directly to Soviet advantage. Richard Nixon once worried aloud, as the war dragged on, that the United States was in danger of becoming "a pitiful, helpless giant."[38] Secretary of Defense Robert McNamara, a tardy convert to the antiwar position, ultimately held that intervention had been an egregious error. He confessed even earlier: "The picture of the world's greatest superpower killing or seriously injuring a thousand noncombatants a week, while trying to pound a tiny backward nation into submission on an issue whose merits are hotly disputed, is not a pretty one."[39]

Other intellectuals, artists, clergymen, and civil rights leaders—many normally uninvolved in foreign policy debates—also expressed dismay at America's Vietnam venture. These included renowned pediatrician Benjamin Spock, Nobel Prize-winning chemist Linus Pauling, folksinger Joan Baez, actress Jane Fonda, linguist Noam Chomsky, the Reverend William Sloane Coffin, writer Susan Sontag. Indicative of their thinking was that of novelist Mary McCarthy. Although married to a Foreign Service officer, she visited Hanoi in 1968 to express solidarity with the victims of the bombing. She also wrote passionately about this experience, hardly crediting that the United States "would actually attack from the air a small poor country that had not attacked us." Rabbi Abraham Feinberg was equally distraught that his beloved United States "wallowed" in the "cesspool" of Vietnam. He too traveled to Hanoi to register sympathy for those who suffered. For political theorist Hannah Arendt, aghast that the war was rending U.S. society, Vietnam policy cast doubt on the judgment of leaders in Washington. The war, she maintained, "was an unbelievable example of using excessive means to achieve minor aims in a region of marginal interest."[40]

Martin Luther King at one time thought of visiting North Vietnam. Appreciative of Johnson's support of civil rights legislation—aware too of that revenge LBJ visited on those who crossed him—King nevertheless broke ranks with cautious black activists (in the NAACP and the Southern Christian Leadership Conference) to condemn the war. It hobbled the campaign against poverty, King complained. The war claimed a disproportionately high number of casualties among African American soldiers; U.S. weapons harmed countless innocent people in Vietnam, of whom children burned by napalm were the most pitiable. Realization of an integrated American society was also being delayed, King brooded: "We [are in 1967] taking the black young men who [have] been crippled by our society and sending them 8,000 miles away to guarantee liberties in Southeast Asia which they [have] not found in Southwest Georgia and East Harlem. So we [are] repeatedly faced with the cruel irony of watching Negro and white boys on TV screens as they kill and die together for a nation that has been unable to seat them together in the same schools." The militant Black Panther organization went further than King. It held that African Americans should not be inducted into the army; if fighting were necessary, better to conduct it in Mississippi.[41]

Senator J. William Fulbright was not a friend of the civil rights movement, but along with King he recoiled from Johnson's Vietnam policy. As chairman of the Senate foreign relations committee, Fulbright opened hearings in 1966 to publicize the folly of fighting the war along LBJ's lines. The war was doubly wrong, Fulbright said, quite apart from its imbalance between costs and potential benefits or from instances of official mendacity on the nature of military operations. First, the insatiable war devoured limited resources that should be committed to alleviating domestic problems, signaled by urban unrest, beginning in Watts in 1965. Second, the war was symptom and cause of that arrogance of power that had felled great empires in the past. As it was, Fulbright scolded, few Americans understood their record of imperialist transgression—against Indians, Mexico, Spain—or realized that their vaunted "way of life" had little appeal to poverty-stricken people in the Third World. Surely the Vietnamese would like to create their own world unassisted by Americans, whose presumptuousness about what is best promised humiliation rather than dignity for Southeast Asia. Johnson's policy meanwhile would render the United States indistinguishable from previous empires: vacant of principle, devoid of meaning, a vapid imperium of no particular virtue. The Vietnam War, Fulbright feared, would rob America of its uniqueness, culminating "in our becoming an empire of the traditional kind, ordained to rule for a time over an empty system of power and then to fade or fall, leaving like its predecessors, a legacy of dust." The post–Cold War world might having nothing to recommend, any imaginable U.S. victory being morally neutral or simply loathsome.[42]

Ending the Cold War

Only sixteen years elapsed between the collapse of America's forlorn Saigon client in 1975 and the dissolution of the USSR into its national component parts. Conclusive evidence may never be available, but very likely an effect of détente in the early 1970s was to prolong the life of the USSR. In this respect, the dissident Andrei Amalrik's "Will the Soviet Union Survive Until 1984?" remains tantalizing.[43] He published his essay in 1969, just as Leonid Brezhnev's administration was looking for ways to curb the Cold War. Unchecked, it threatened to cause the USSR's nuclear destruction. Short of this, the Cold War involved a crushing load of military expenditure that undermined the Soviet economy and kept its revival hostage into the distant future. Alternatively, improved relations with the United States would permit the funneling of resources into the neglected consumer sector. Infusions of Western capital/technology and joint ventures could also help invigorate the ailing economy. Viewed from this angle, then, other Soviet aims of détente—better relations with West Germany and leverage for managing the obstreperous Chinese, or consolidation of Brezhnev's domestic preeminence—may have been important, but they were decidedly secondary.[44]

Détente no more represented an end to the Cold War for Nixon and Kissinger than it did for Brezhnev or his foreign minister, Andrei Gromyko. Like their Soviet counterparts, U.S. policymakers pursued détente as a means to regularize the power competition and rein in its most unstable element: a potentially careening arms race. An economic web tying the USSR to the West (credits, most-favored-nation status, investments) plus cooperation on technical-cultural matters (from ecology to outer space) could also strengthen Kremlin commitment to the international status quo. This still served American advantage circa 1972, notwithstanding Soviet boasting that the "correlation of forces" had shifted in favor of Marxism-Leninism. At the same time, officials hoped that détente would encourage the Soviets to press the North Vietnamese to be more accommodating in Paris peace talks. Renewed U.S. relations with mainland China might also produce pressures on Hanoi's negotiators while having a salutary effect on Soviet leaders: reminding them that America still enjoyed prestige and ability for adroit maneuver. In this last sense, détente was both a pause in the Cold War and a foreshadowing of its outcome on American terms. Yet ironically the Nixon-Kissinger conception of détente, as publicly enunciated, posited a world order radically different from the unipolarity marking the Cold War's finale.

Nixon and Kissinger asserted that a pentagonal power pattern was emerging. It encompassed not only the two great nuclear powers (or "superpowers" in the language of a courteous fiction that placed the economically lame USSR on a par with the robust United States). Japan, communist China, and an increasingly coherent Western Europe were also said to be players of importance. In coming years, the United States would not have to bear so much of the weight of balancing Soviet power. China and Japan could share in this task in East Asia. In Europe, the community and the European members of NATO could shoulder larger parts, thereby ushering in a new era of cooperation with the United States. The USSR's economic integration with the West ("interdependence") would meanwhile proceed, encouraging good—as defined in Washington—Soviet behavior. Thus the foundation would be set for a stable structure of peace (Nixon's terminology), ensuring freedom from world war for future generations of Americans, Soviets, Europeans, and Asians.

The Basic Principles agreement of 1972 codified, if vaguely, Nixon's and Brezhnev's several commitments. The most important of these were to noninterference in each other's internal affairs, consultation on issues of mutual concern, renunciation of unilateral advantage, reciprocity in things great and small, negotiated solution of disputes, and promotion of peaceful settlement to third-party conflicts.[45] Edgy observers in Beijing derided the Basic Principles and subsequent pledges (on prevention of nuclear war in 1973, Vladivostok agreement in 1974) as the establishment of a Soviet-U.S. condominium intended to run the world. The most celebrated Soviet dissenter, Alexander Solzhenitsyn, also disliked détente, saying that it amounted to a betrayal of Western safety and values. "Relations between the Soviet Union and the United States," he told an AFL-CIO audience in 1975, "should be such that there would be no deceit in the question of armaments, that there would be no concentration camps, no psychiatric wards for healthy people. Relations should be such that the throats of our women would no longer be constricted with tears, that there would be an end to the incessant ideological warfare." The Committee on the Present Danger, founded by skeptics of détente in 1976 (Paul Nitze, Eugene Rostow, Max Kampelman), also campaigned against what it saw as a looming Soviet menace. This was apparent in Kremlin violations of arms treaties, elaborate civil defense efforts, harassment of nonconformists, and incitement of communist insurrection in corners of the Third World.[46]

The administration, especially in the person of Kissinger, responded with a mix of sooth and reassurance: détente was better than unrestrained Soviet-U.S. rivalry; Western vigilance was still intact. Détente itself was an ongoing process, not a permanent condition, argued Kissinger. The goal was to bolster certainty in international life, which was inescapably bound to a Soviet-U.S. *modus vivendi*. From this, each power stood to gain in the critical categories—in descending order of importance—of security, improved bilateral economic relations, defense savings, and cultural-technical life.

The Soviet and U.S. governments during the détente years entered into numerous solemn agreements. Among them were treaties to advance nuclear nonproliferation (1969, 1977), prohibit the installation of nuclear weapons on the seabed (1971), limit the production of strategic arms (1972), recognize the inviolability of post–World War II European borders (1975), and reduce underground nuclear testing (1976). Efforts to find an exit from the Cold War impasse also energized East-West trade (for example, Soviet purchase of U.S. wheat, U.S. credits to Moscow to buy technology-machinery) and produced thrilling cooperation, as in the 1975 Apollo-Soyuz docking in outer space.

Even as the edifice of détente was being erected, its foundation was starting to crack, the point of vulnerability being Kremlin violation of human rights norms. The introduction of legislation in April 1973, by Senator Henry Jackson and Representative Charles Vanik, made Nixon's granting of credits to the USSR and conferring of most favored nation (MFN) trading status dependent on the liberalization of Soviet emigration policy. In the ensuing battle in Congress, the Jackson-Vanik side enlisted more than just those people anxious about the plight of Soviet Jewry and the condition of persecuted dissidents, Solzhenitsyn to Andrei Sakharov. The proposed legislation (eventually passed) also drew critics such as Hans Morgenthau, who felt that the Soviet Union's internal order had to be altered. Otherwise the existing political structure—a despotism—would manifest itself aggressively in international relations. The Jackson-Vanik idea therefore deserved support as a step toward regime modification in an open direction, leading to a reliable détente partner for the West. Other critics spoke against the risks to U.S. investment of helping Russia develop Siberian energy resources and the imprudence of programs to improve the economic viability of a longtime adversary. The impact of Watergate investigations on the administration's ability to govern, along with Congress's attempt to reclaim its constitutionally ordained voice in foreign policy, further combined to aid Jackson-Vanik. The Nixon-Kissinger defense of credits and MFN for the USSR, in which cause Soviet leaders joined (assailing outside interference and America's own moral failings), was alas unavailing. Détente never fully recovered.

As the decade of the 1970s progressed, other issues contrived to weaken great-power cooperation. Lack of early consultation or cooperation during the 1973 Yom Kippur War struck at the core of promises to enhance mutuality—climaxing in Nixon's putting U.S. military forces on high alert, lest the Kremlin sent "peace-keeping" troops into the Middle East. Later the presence of Soviet-sponsored Cubans in Angola and Ethiopia impressed skeptics as contrary to the spirit of détente, to say nothing of Soviet propaganda blasts against American "imperialism" in Iran during the anti-Shah revolution and embassy hostage crisis. The invasion of Afghanistan, midwife to the Carter Doctrine (protecting the Persian Gulf), Soviet threats against Poland, and unabated persecution of dissidents reduced what remained of American tolerance for détente. For their part, Soviet leaders were equally uneasy. Their grievances included Kissinger's squeezing the USSR out of Middle East diplomacy, constant Western harping on human rights, Washington's playing of the "China card," and—after Afghanistan—the Olympics boycott, grain embargo, MX missile, neutron bomb, assistance to the mujahedeen, and Senate shelving of SALT II. In 1980, the U.S. electorate chose a vociferous critic of détente for the presidency, Ronald Reagan. His first administration was marked by a brisk arms buildup and a return to the charged rhetoric of early Cold War. Reagan was deranged, his actions dangerous, according to Soviet leader Yuri Andropov; they could easily trigger a Soviet-U.S. war.[47]

Hardline rhetoric in Washington and deployment of such weapons as Pershing and cruise missiles alarmed some Western observers too, giving renewed impetus to the antinuclear movement. Its 1980s incarnation was loosely defined, broadly popular, unabashedly internationalist, and convinced that the nuclear powers were behaving like lemmings dashing to the sea (George Kennan's imagery); the future possessed a world order of unspeakable bleakness. Subsumed in the antinuclear movement were the Physicians for Social Responsibility, one of whose leaders was the outspoken Helen Caldicott. Pediatrician and feminist, she was propelled by a sense of overriding urgency to assume a front rank among activists. Her books, statements to the press, and public addresses emphasized the material costs of arms race and, more chilling, the medical consequences of nuclear war. Her crusade once took her to the White House, where she tried to win President Reagan to her cause. She subsequently labeled him the Pied Piper of Armageddon, whose complacency was exceeded only by his ignorance of imminent dangers. With other audiences, Caldicott enjoyed greater success. She focused their attention on graphic descriptions of destruction:

[A nuclear bomb dropped on New York] if it explodes at ground level on a clear day . . . will release heat equivalent to that of the sun—several million degrees Celsius—in a fraction of a second. It will dig a hole three-quarters of a mile wide and eight hundred feet deep, converting all the people, buildings, and earth and rocks below to radioactive fallout particles which will be shot up into the atmosphere in a mushroom cloud . . . Anyone who watches the flash without being vaporized will have his or her eyes melted by the intense heat, other people will be turned into charcoal.

In 1985 the International Physicians for the Prevention of Nuclear War (IPPNW), with which Caldicott was also affiliated, won the Nobel Peace Prize for its work in heightening popular awareness of the arms race. That the East-West standoff ended without nuclear mishap later impressed Caldicott as a miracle of deliverance for which organized mothers and internationalized medicine deserved praise, no less than Gorbachev, whom she credited with mustering the courage to dismantle the Berlin Wall (1989) and conclude the Cold War.[48]

The White House's comment on antinuclear activists during the waning years of Cold War was skeptical. Officials questioned the genuineness of concern and insinuated that movement leaders were unwitting tools of Soviet power. When Dr. Bernard Lown, American co-chairman of the IPPNW, appeared in Oslo with his Soviet counterpart, Dr. E. Chazov, to receive the Nobel award, several journalists joined the chorus of criticism. They wondered about the lack of integrity that allowed an American doctor to lend himself to a regime that still entombed dissidents in psychiatric hospitals and hijacked humanitarian forums to mislead guileless people.[49]

According to the Reagan-Bush line, it was only American steadfastness and willingness to press hard—covertly in Afghanistan, overtly with SDI, steadily through NATO—that caused the Kremlin leadership to surrender its East European allies and disgorge the USSR's non-Russian peoples. Such an interpretation of the Cold War's climax in fact is scarcely more convincing than that credit taken by Caldicott and company. What the Reagan-Bush government did to confound the USSR paled in comparison with the history of the Soviet Union's self-inflicted wounds. These were created during seventy years of rule by leaders whose policies maimed the nation and debilitated the regime. Purges, terror, forced collectivization in the 1930s, plus continued injuries from an overly-planned economy, police state, and imperial grasping, achieved what no Western strategy could: a loss of confidence by the Soviet political class in its vision and legitimacy.

Thus was also created a novel problem for the United States after 1991, one for which it was unprepared: to forge a concept of world order for a situation in which the Soviet Union no longer existed. As Helmut Sonnenfeldt, formerly of the National Security Council, later reflected, successive administrations had spent practically no time in imagining a post–Cold War order. Such systematic thinking had seemed somehow frivolous against the day-to-day rush of events.[50] Hence that series of improvisations by Washington—discussed in the next chapter—that followed in the aftermath of Soviet implosion.

* * * * *

Inasmuch as the Cold War was a competition between powers, it differed little from the Peloponnesian War or Rome versus Carthage or Elizabethan England vying with Philip's Spain. Equivalent policing in spheres of influence—the Caribbean and Central America for the United States, Eastern Europe for the USSR—and the conducting of brutal combat in poor countries (Korea, Vietnam, Afghanistan) also underscored the power dimension of Cold War.

Viewed as another round between totalitarianism and twentieth-century democracy, the Cold War shared traits with the Anglo-U.S. struggle against Nazi Germany: elimination of the adversary's regime coincided with the end of hostilities; the ideological dimension gave the conflict an aura of transcendence.

The Cold War can also be seen as a test of American quality, per the familiar formulation by Kennan. He had warned his compatriots (in the Long Telegram, 1946) against "the greatest danger that can befall us . . . that we shall allow ourselves to become like those with whom we are coping." To avoid this grotesqueness, he wrote (in the 1947 "X article") the United States had to "measure up to its own best traditions."[51] From this angle, the Cold War bore mixed results, with particular disappointment in three categories of national life: intellectual imagination, domestic society, security strategy.

Of the first, one has only to reflect upon that zeal depicted in Graham Green's novel *The Quiet American*. Therein no alternative mode of life to the West's was allowed, paving the way for a host of measures antagonistic to the original commitment to national rights of self-determination in sundry Third World settings. In this same vein, Senator Fulbright aptly identified the conflating of vast means with extravagant purpose as an arrogance of power that could not tolerate departure from American preference. Stirring rhetoric, such as JFK's pledge to "support any friend, oppose any foe to assure the survival and success of liberty," did not cancel the counterweight of Truman's simplifications or Dulles's preachiness or Reagan's bombast—which cumulatively exaggerated the imminence of Soviet military danger. Moreover, as any believer in the democratic faith must hold, sensible talk about national interest and balance of power (advocated by Kennan, Marshall, Lippmann among others) should have met with success—preempting then that infantilizing of public thought for which executive branch officers bear partial blame. Dean Acheson later admitted that under the pressure of crises "we made our points clearer than truth."[52] A result of this bludgeon approach to public education was to mislead many Americans into thinking that vital interests were at stake everywhere, even in such so unlikely a spot as Vietnam. There foreign policy came a cropper on the substitution of platitudes for analysis; the purported universal applicability of the Western model was rejected by Asian peasants who were not enamored of America's Cold War ideology.

As for domestic politics and economy: The Cold War allowed an elaborate internal security apparatus to grow whose threat to civil liberties was most immediately felt during the Joseph McCarthy season of hysteria but lingered well beyond. Paul Robeson's contemporaneous Soviet apology was also striking, and not merely for its misplaced idealism or naiveté. His sympathy for the USSR was above all a rebuke to that racial injustice which underut U.S. professions of devotion to liberty, mortifying also to politically moderate African Americans, such as the eminent diplomat Ralph Bunche. (He declined Truman's offer of assistant secretary of state because he did not want to subject his family to defiled life in segregated Washington.) The price paid for political nonconformity by Robeson further underscored the limits of tolerance in Cold War America. Backdrop to all this dreariness were those economic distortions caused by what Eisenhower labeled as the military-industrial complex. These reached hefty proportions in the 1980s, giving substance to Kennan's charge that the U.S. economy had become dependent on outlandishly expensive arms programs.[53]

Worse still was American willingness in case of supreme emergency to cause suffering to countless children, families, and other noncombatants in the USSR (and elsewhere in the communist zone). The American side of the nuclear balance of terror—no less than its adversary's—amounted to a repudiation of the Nuremberg standard of decency in international life. In other words, Churchill's hopeful irony that safety in the nuclear era is the "sturdy child of terror and survival the twin brother of annihilation" did not obviate this uncomfortable truth: the moral worth of a nation is also determined by the threats it wields.[54] Nuclear deterrence may have prevented a third world war, allowing for the Cold War's finish favoring the West. True or not, this same strategy, resting as it did on premeditated indiscriminate slaughter on a huge scale, eroded America's just cause: a resort to unjust means trumping the ends.

None of this critique means that the United States came to resemble Stalin's Soviet Union—a place of unsurpassed weirdness and horror—or any of the milder variants of tyranny that followed 1953. But Kennan's original point of comparison was not the appropriate one. The valid measure of U.S. failure and success, domestically and internationally, was based on American conscience and standards. Their articulation—from 1776 to subsequent refinements in the Bill of Rights, Nuremberg, and support of the UN declaration of human rights—was incompatible with Cold War strategies and internal security excesses. Preparations to incinerate millions of innocent people equaled a monumental corruption. In this sense French philosopher Bernard-Henri Levy's severity applies to America, as well as to Russia: "Never before has the will to death been so nakedly and cynically unleashed."[55] Vengeful as he was, Stalin would doubtless have savored the unexpected bonus of Soviet demise in 1991: the United States had so stooped to conquer that the price of Cold War victory was the whittling away of America's better self.

This sorry character in political guise was incapable of vigorous or uplifting thought on the desirable contours of a post–Cold War world. Most presidents (Truman onward) had suggested worthwhile directions, but occasional remarks did not constitute sustained discourse on how to organize the international future. Such as it was, discourse on this topic was fragmentary and brief. The Cold War had immobilized political imagination by making it think that Soviet-U.S. rivalry was a permanent condition.

Was there an alternative to this and other Cold War sterility? As exercise in counterfactual history, the answer must draw on imaginary achievements: internationalizing atomic energy, speaking plainly to the American public, not drawing the Chinese into Korea by sending troops toward the Yalu River (after Inchon, September 1950), responding creatively to Soviet overtures in 1953, detecting early the pitfalls of Vietnam, and clinging more tightly at home to U.S. definitions of fairness. (Even so, contra Robeson, Cold War anxiety actually helped to advance racial justice in America. Truman and Eleanor Roosevelt were among the advocates of change who agreed with— also acted on—this logic of Acheson: "Discrimination against minority groups in this country has an adverse effect on our relations with other countries.")[56] What was the alternative to the West's prevailing in the Cold War? Perhaps, a permanent relaxation of tensions might have eventually superseded the Cold War contest, corresponding roughly to the Nixon-Kissinger idea of détente. Or some third-party conflict might finally have emerged to eclipse, wholly or in part, the East-West rivalry. The most plausible alternative to ending the Cold War on terms favorable to America was something worse: either an intensely sinister world order made protracted by the demands of the uninhibited Leninist state or the continuation of a dizzying arms race. If not leading directly to oblivion, either outcome points to a type of limbo: a cross between George Orwell's *1984* and the depressing Cold War history of Eastern Europe or that "life of perpetual fear" prophesied by Eisenhower. As for the nuclear dilemma in the late 1940s: During the years of its atomic monopoly, the United States exercised restraint toward the Soviet Union, at the minimum overcoming the crudest temptations of atomic diplomacy.[57] One shudders to think how Stalin would have behaved had the USSR enjoyed comparable military advantage.

SIX

New World Order

Americanan diplomacy was disconcerted in 1989–1991 by the shadows of peace that gathered as communist regimes in Eastern Europe were expunged, the Warsaw Pact was eradicated, and Soviet power collapsed. Even while German youths danced atop the breached Berlin Wall and George Bush announced the Cold War's end, praising God's mercy and U.S. perseverance, sterner voices warned of confusing times ahead: the verities of international life had faded along with bipolarity and the vocation of containment.[1] At the same time, contra the philosophical musings of commentator Francis Fukuyama, history was as disobliging as ever. It had not stopped. Nor had the United States achieved a Hegelian apotheosis, wherein future problems would be of a mundane sort, barely worth noticing after the heroic exertions of two world wars and the Cold War.[2] Observers as diverse as Georgi Arbatov (for years with the USA/Canada Institute in Moscow), former secretary of state Lawrence Eagleburger, and leftist scholar Noam Chomsky remarked that the assumptions underlying U.S. policy for nearly fifty years no longer obtained. How now would the United States define its purpose? Arbatov warned that Americans would miss having a focal point of hostile reference as Moscow converted from foe to friend. Eagleburger challenged his compatriots to grasp the magnitude of world changes and to respond appropriately—philosophically and practically. Chomsky detected a frantic search by the foreign policy elite for enemies to replace the absent Soviet rival, in which case radical Islam might prove useful.[3]

Official Washington reacted to fast-paced change with a declaration of intent, first announced by President Bush, then elaborated upon by Bill Clinton: the United States would henceforth assume the role of benevolent hegemon, dispensing favors and justice according to the dictates of prudence, based on conventional security and economic desiderata. Multilateralism would be the preferred vehicle of action. Unilateralism as a last resort was not eschewed. This formula, never so baldly stated as above, was grandly christened the new world order.[4] Its proponents saw therein a revival of

Wilsonian liberalism but with crucial emendations. The new variant was anchored in this twofold awareness: U.S. might is not unlimited; all international dilemmas are not of equal importance but correspond to a hierarchy of American interests and values.[5]

Critics schooled in *realpolitik* have seen too much emphasis on unrealizable perfection in this formula, plus a lack of fluency about power politics. Leftist skeptics have perceived nothing but a verbal inanity to distract world attention from the enormity of U.S. power, which doggedly pursues still more privilege and wealth. (Evidence for this thesis was said to be found in a leaked confidential government study, "Defense Planning Guidance for the Fiscal Years 1994–1999." This mostly ignored the United Nations and stressed Washington's need to prevent the emergence of any superconcentration of power beyond U.S. control.) American rapaciousness has meant that the prerogative of lesser states must contract. The chance of the poorest to cope will dwindle to a point of vanishing, consigning entire human populations to misery. Their desperation, the indignant Samir Amin (African Marxist) has predicted, will lead to violent resistance against domination.[6]

Before that distant reckoning, Bush, otherwise uncomfortable with the "vision thing," mobilized the United States and its allies (militarized multilateralism) against Iraq on behalf of an embryonic new world order.

Supremacy

The lessons of World War II and the Cold War had taught Bush that tyrants perpetrate aggression unless checked by determined counterforce. He read the effortless Iraqi invasion of Kuwait in August 1990 accordingly: it positioned Iraq for future action against Saudi Arabia while whetting the appetite of Saddam Hussein for further foul play. This too-familiar situation placed key interests in jeopardy. First, and most important, the abundant oil reserves of the Arabian peninsula might soon fall into the hands of a regime unsympathetic to Western concern with moderately priced petroleum. An Iraqi stranglehold on supplies and prices would leave the United States and its major allies at the mercy of a despot. Second, the logic of brute force would continue to prevail in international relations even after the Cold War, an especially odious prospect in light of America's economic interests scattered around the globe. Therefore to maintain access to Persian Gulf oil on acceptable terms and to uphold the status quo as legitimate—whilst extolling the principle of collective security against aggressors—Bush initiated Desert Shield, then Desert Storm.

A more lopsided contest than that which ensued would be hard to imagine, unless one were to include the U.S. assaults on puny Grenada (1983) or impoverished Panama (1989). Iraq at the time had a population of approximately 18 million people. The country's gross national product was roughly the size of Kentucky's. Hussein's most demonstrative allies were the dispossessed Palestinians, whose resentment of rich Kuwait—however deeply felt—could not translate into militarily useful contribution. Added to these deficiencies were the continuing costs borne by Iraq from its inconclusive war against Iran (1980–1988), and the fragility of a state where minority claims (for example, by the Kurds) provoked punishing reprisal. Poorly educated peasant conscripts, not hardened veterans in the widely touted Republican Guards, constituted the army's main manpower. Pitted against this weakness was a Washington-led coalition that counted military, air, and naval forces from the preeminent post–Cold War powers—not the least of which was British and French supplement to American immensity (470,000 troops). Financing of this operation came from the affluent, among which were Germany, Japan, and exiled Kuwaitis. The result was stunning: one hundred thousand Iraqi soldiers may have been killed (perhaps three hundred thousand wounded) versus American/coalition battlefield deaths numbering two hundred (fewer than one thousand wounded).[7] Surviving Iraqi forces staggered out of Kuwait in late February 1991. In the first flush of victory, Bush pronounced that the United States had "kicked the Vietnam syndrome once and for all."[8] Decisive steps had been taken toward building a better world order. Wisely, from its standpoint, the administration did not dwell on the extensive damage done to civilian lives and infrastructure in Baghdad. Disinterested analysts later reported that the destruction of sanitation facilities led to epidemics of water-borne disease that took a high toll among children. Continuation of the embargo after 1991 also affected the quantity and quality of foods and medicines available in Iraq. Susceptibility to disease and malnutrition fell disproportionately on the vulnerable: old people, youngsters, the poor. But the embargo made little dent on Hussein's popularity—he adroitly played the martyr—or the regime's ability to govern.

Insofar as the new-world-order idea was not mere sloganeering to legitimize Gulf policy to an anxious public, inasmuch as the war was not just about oil (or "jobs," in Secretary James Baker's forthright infelicity), Bush extemporized. His message, makeshift at first, rested on this premise: the end of Cold War tensions meant that an occasion had arisen that was favorable to harmonious world politics. This would be fostered by the intensification of free markets; the strengthening of international laws and institutions, notably the United Nations (which blessed U.S. actions in the Gulf); and the proliferation of democracies presiding over capitalist economies. In this design, regional balances of power should be maintained. The sovereign state remained inviolate. (Thus Bush's warning to non-Russian Soviet audiences against "suicidal nationalism" and Washington's support of Iraq's territorial integrity after the Gulf War against Kurdish importunities.) The democratic state was exalted. Collective security to repel aggression, particularly that practiced by the strong against the weak, was depicted as a paramount idea. Finally, the primacy of U.S. leadership to safeguard the expanding zone of peace and liberty was assumed. The neo-isolationist temptation and the siren song of America first—as hymned by Bush's fellow Republican Patrick Buchanan—had to be rejected. American leadership could, incidentally, involve the use of financial aid to help fledgling democracies, as in rapidly changing Russia. The alternative to this U.S.-led order was a mayhem of terrorists, renegade states, and megalomaniac dictators. The enthronement of caprice or violence would shame Cold War victory. Belatedly, without much apparent enthusiasm, Bush added a humanitarian element to his emphasis on stability and order. This secondary concern was manifest in American protection of Iraqi Kurds and Shiites subject to Hussein's postwar wrath. Later, the humanitarian idea was expanded to include rescue in starving Somalia (December 1992), a botched operation that was ended by President Clinton as too costly after the death of eighteen army rangers.[9]

Even as he employed it, Bush was never enthusiastic about the terminology of new world order. It smacked too much of innovation, had a faintly utopian ring, and implied the attainability of an immutable perfect condition. All these notions ran counter to Bush's understanding and practice of diplomacy. Therein fluid situations, nimble maneuver, and a premium on give-and-take predominated over strict adherence to script or rigid commitment to blueprint. These qualities of mind enabled Bush to respond helpfully with financial aid (after delay, admittedly) to Yeltsin's reforms, and to assemble a coalition of disparate states against Hussein. After the Gulf War, Bush rarely invoked the new world order.[10]

This omission must have been welcomed by President Clinton, who, wanting to imprint his own stamp on national policy, has sought to concentrate primarily on domestic matters: broadening the scope of health care coverage, raising educational levels, healing the race divide, reversing environmental degradation. He pursued a minimalist foreign policy during his first term. When world problems intruded on his attention, the first post–Cold War president and his advisors—Warren Christopher, Anthony Lake, Madeleine Albright—cleaved to the substance of Bush's internationalism. Faltering Russia remained an object of concern and a recipient of aid. The viability of NATO (also its expansion) was still seen as crucial to the continuance of a pacific Europe. Trade imbalance with Japan, Israeli-Palestinian feuding, the postcommunist transition of Eastern Europe, the spread of nuclear weapons, and chaos in former Yugoslavia were among the unresolved issues inherited by Clinton, for whom answers were no more obvious than they had been to Bush. At the same time, Clinton had to confront a burgeoning anti-internationalism, evidenced by congressional reductions in State Department funding, delays in Senate ratification of ambassadorial appointments, popular antipathy (at least sourness) toward the United Nations, and Washington's failure to honor U.S. financial obligations to that organization. Arrears amounted to about a billion dollars by late 1995. Clinton and Christopher rallied against this introverted outlook, and said, in words hardly different from Bush's, that the United States had to bear the responsibilities of global leadership.[11]

The Clinton version of U.S. leadership has showcased "engagement" in world affairs. Its aim is to safeguard security-prosperity and ensure the success of representative governments, the latter presumed to be more peacefully inclined than other regime types. "Enlargement" of the community of free market democracies has become the explicit goal. Human rights as a concern of foreign policy has won slightly more attention than from Bush, at least rhetorically, in the avowedly neo-Wilsonian administration. *Idealpolitik* became a watchword employed hopefully by Clinton's Oxford classmate, Deputy Secretary of State Strobe Talbott.[12] In the China test, however, commerce parading in the costume of "constructive engagement" soon prevailed over a blunt human rights diplomacy—witness President Clinton's retreat from candidate Clinton's position on the advisability of revoking MFN and the hoopla in Washington when (October 1997) President Jiang Zemin visited.[13] As for mass slaughter in Rwanda, U.S. officials sermonized but refrained from taking significant action.

Sluggishness in human rights has not constituted the whole story of foreign policy since the Cold War, according to observers sympathetic to the U.S. design. Professors James Chace and John Ruggie, for example, have cheered a number of initiatives. By early 1997 these included low-risk military interventions that pacified volatile zones: Haiti (Operation Uphold Democracy), the Taiwan Straits (dispatching two aircraft carriers to warn Beijing away from launching an offensive against Taipei), Macedonia, and Bosnia. Regarding this last, negotiation of the Dayton accords and deployment of thousands of U.S. troops have helped check the worst violence in Europe since World War II and preempted its spread through the Balkans. Additional, if fragile, progress is tangible in other domains too, Chace and Ruggie have noted. Policy toward Moscow—mutual arms cuts, aid—has helped Yeltsin's government retain power against resurgent communists and national extremists whilst keeping Russian-American relations on an even keel. Timely economic assistance saved Mexico from bankruptcy and secured America's southern border from concomitant chaos. Clinton presided over the signing of a peace accord between Israel's Yitzhak Rabin and the PLO's Yasir Arafat, thus improving the possibility of normality in a wounded region. Ratification of the North American Free Trade treaty and pressure on Japan to open its markets have helped steady the U.S. economy. The threatened use of sanctions and pledges of modest help (food, fuel, finance) from South Korea, the United States, and Japan caused North Korea to curb further work on its nuclear weapons program. All of these actions fit into the Chace-Ruggie brief for the new world order and this assumption pervasive in Washington: America's experience already is, or is inexorably becoming, the universal human one.[14]

Criticism

Yet the new order as outlined by Bush and Clinton has hardly drawn overwhelming support from the U.S. public. Nearly 40 percent of voters, according to a 1995 opinion poll, had deep reservations about the government's pursuing an activist foreign policy.[15]

Selling the world order to international specialists has also been tough, notwithstanding able defenders such as Chace and Ruggie. Henry Kissinger's first response was to recoil from what he saw as the reemergence of American religious revivalism, cloaked in the new-world-order idea, wherein a perfected political universe was alleged to be within grasp. He warned that such nonsense would substitute the utopia of ultimate solutions for the only authentic possibility: politics as amelioration in a world of flux.[16] Kissinger also scoffed at the rush toward what he viewed as trendy ideas, centered on the supposed importance of integrating economic and security strands into a seamless weave. Strategic thinking still requires a geopolitical outlook. Economic globalization, communication in cyberspace, and the rise of postmodernism do not obviate this plain fact: America is an island off the shores of the Eurasian landmass. Domination by a single power of principal European or Asian areas would pose a grave danger to the United States, Cold War or no. American thought and practice must therefore remain fixed on the requirements of supple balance-of-power diplomacy, concludes the former secretary of state.[17]

George Kennan has questioned the need for any overarching concept. Such things, he has told the public, typically become shibboleths, as illustrated by the career of his own containment idea. By definition they discourage careful attention to the details and complexity of specific problems. Only a few principles ought to guide Washington. The foremost should be an injunction against intervening in the messy affairs, however horrid, of faraway peoples—with exception made for those instances of breakdown that impinge on key U.S. interests. More often than not, Kennan has said, the United States cannot muster the technical or other wherewithal to provide lasting solutions for distant nations. Besides, as the record of intervention shows, the introduction of American armed force invariably, if inadvertently, makes bad situations worse: a case in point is Somalia. Kennan's preferred

wisdom was encapsulated by John Quincy Adams, who advised his generation against democratic crusading. Just as Kennan first quoted these words
of Adams (delivered in 1821) as authority against LBJ's Vietnam venture, so
he repeated them in the mid-1990s: Should the United States enlist under
banners other than her own "were they even the banners of foreign independence, she would involve herself beyond the power of extrications, in all
the wars of interest and intrigue, of individual avarice, envy and ambition,
which assume the colors and usurp the standard of freedom." To this teaching Kennan has added that mainly by example, not by precept, does one
country influence another. A justly ordered and tranquil United States is
likelier to have a wholesome touch abroad than one that yammers on about
the defects of others or sends armies to apply remedy: "It is very difficult for
one country to help another by intervening directly in its domestic affairs or
in its conflicts with its neighbors. It is particularly difficult to do this without creating new and unwelcome embarrassments . . . for the country en-
deavoring to help. The best way for a larger country to help a smaller one is
surely by the power of example."[18]

Professor Ronald Steel has complemented the Kennan critique by concentrating on America's domestic condition. This requires prompt attention,
as indicated by too-high rates of illiteracy, drug abuse, infant mortality, violent crime, homelessness, poverty, imprisonment, and a widening gap between poor and rich. Until these problems are adequately addressed, the
United States should master its hubris (trying to remake the world in America's image) and spend its limited assets on correcting internal problems. Left
unchecked, these will cause the country permanent harm. Gaseous utopi-
anism of the new-world-order variety amounts to evading confrontation
with home-grown emergencies. Albeit in words less urgent than Steel's,
William Hyland, former editor of *Foreign Relations,* agrees that the time has
come to "shift resources to the domestic account." James Schlesinger, previously secretary of defense, likewise has emphasized the imperative of hus-
banding national strength after the Cold War. He has also expressed
misgivings on democratic proselytizing: anti-Western Islamic fundamentalists might easily win power through electoral means in places like Algeria or
Egypt.[19]

Professor Samuel Huntington is equally hard-boiled about the supposed
universality of human rights as conceived in America and western Europe or
the applicability of democratic gospel in a world riven by clashing civilizations: "What is universalism to the West is imperialism to the rest." Wisdom
argues for the United States-Atlantic Europe unit to maintain its own clearly
delineated sphere; Washington ought not meddle in the affairs of other peoples (Moslems, Hindus, Chinese, etc.). Their traditional conceptions of society are not connected to, or even compatible with, the West's. A fatuous

cosmopolitanism bandied about in Washington will quicken suspicion and discord, possibly resulting in a military showdown for which the West, according to Huntington, is not fully prepared.[20]

Professor Paul Kennedy, who has cautioned against imperial overreach, has also established common ground with Huntington insofar as both scholars perceive yawning gaps between the Western and non-Western worlds. Kennedy's emphasis, however, is on economic disparity rather than the cultural differences: "Perhaps the global problem of the early twenty-first century is basically this: that across our planet a number of what might be termed demographic-technological fault lines are emerging, between fast-growing, adolescent, resource-poor, undercapitalized, and undereducated populations on the one side and technologically inventive, demographically moribund, and increasingly nervous rich societies on the other." Unless political leaders take meaningful action, demographic and environmental pressures could combine to make a hash of world order, resulting in dismalness for all humankind by 2025: plagues of violence, waves of emigration from poor to rich states, irreparable ecological damage. The alternative to this scenario, says Kennedy, is for the representatives of rich northern countries and poor southern poor ones to craft a comprehensive economic-diplomatic deal—a rebirth of the new international economic order fashioned by Third World theorists in the 1970s. This deal might involve the prosperous nations of the Organization for Economic Cooperation and Development contributing one percent of their GDP to development aid. (In 1994 the stingy United States was contributing less than 0.2 percent of its GDP, one of the worst records among industrialized states.) Thousands of scientists and engineers released from Cold War-related research could concentrate their minds on devising solutions to air and water pollution in Africa and Asia—by finding economical and efficient ways, for example, to employ solar energy in lieu of fossil fuels. Other measures might promote the status of women in Third World countries, the proper use by southern governments of aid allocated, and the deployment of appropriate technologies. Campaigns should also be initiated to reduce Third World fertility rates, enhance the United Nations's peacekeeping powers, and teach tolerance of cultural diversity. It is not naive or unrealistic to hope for such a north-south package of reforms, says Kennedy, given the alternative: international anarchy. Whether American political imagination after the Cold War can rise to this task remains an open question, Kennedy admits in less than sanguine tone.[21]

Neither has the new world order inspired wide confidence abroad. Professor Lawrence Freedman (University of London) has wondered about the sustainability of the U.S. concept in the absence of a profound strategic imperative. To Alain Lamassoure (French government spokesman), the program is saturated with American ambition. This is a woeful thing, even if

U.S. officialdom phrases its aims naively and only vaguely comprehends the full extent of their practical meaning. It is, in any case, incumbent upon France and its European allies to accelerate their progress toward union: "So as not to leave U.S. power alone like some kind of gendarme or judge over the affairs of the world."[22]

Andrei Kozyrev, Russia's first postcommunist foreign minister, has expressed misgiving over "obsessive" proclamations of American leadership in every sphere of international life. Russia, he has warned, cannot be relegated to the minor role of faithful follower. Reactionaries, such as Vladimir Zhirinovsky, will point to "chauvinistic new banners flap[ping] in the Washington wind" to needle Russia's beleaguered democrats. NATO's proposed push eastward (Czech Republic, Hungary, Poland) in particular will only fulfill the macabre suspicions and prophecies of the worst element in Russian society. Sober U.S. realism should imply equality with Russia, otherwise "both countries will surely lose." As if to underscore Kozyrev's points, Gennadi Zyuganov, Russian communist party chief, has called the new world order "alien" to Moscow's interests. "Any policy that counts on Russia's remaining in its humiliating position," he wrote in 1996, "following in the American wake, is doomed to defeat." He was also emphatic that Americans respectfully recognize that Russian customs and conditions will prevent his country from developing in ways congruent with U.S. experience. Yeltsin himself, though beholden to Washington, has played with the idea of doing what he can to further a multipolar world (involving China, Iran, India) to offset U.S. preponderance.[23]

Officials in the People's Republic of China too have been unenchanted with Washington's version of world order. The human rights aspect specifically has raised hackles. Beijing's diplomats have cited the flawlessly democratic Chinese constitution and its many provisions protecting civil liberties—speech, assembly, and so forth. Access to food is also a human right, in which case the communist regime's feeding of 1.2 billion people is no mean achievement, say publicists—conveniently overlooking the approximately 30 million deaths that occurred during the state-made famine in the Great Leap Forward, 1959–1962. (The magnitude of that food disaster places it in the same category as the 1937–1945 war against Japan, when between 10 and 35 million Chinese died).[24] Official media such as the *New China News Agency* have meanwhile admonished the U.S. for its failings, ranging from racial discrimination ("the darkest abyss in American society") to the mangling of the electoral process by big-money contributors. Washington should put its own affairs in order before lecturing others or preening as the paragon of all righteousness: "The U.S. Government, posing as the human rights judge of the world, turn[s] a blind eye [repeatedly] to the serious human rights problems in its own country."[25]

Perhaps the angriest rejection of new-world-order thinking to date has come from Samir Amin and Noam Chomsky. Writing immediately after the Gulf War, Amin blasted what he sees as the false universalism and tawdry values of American-organized international capital. It practices piracy under the cloak of morality, law, and justice. World unification by the market, backed by Western military force, he argues, will solidify the existing class system, whereby wealthy states grow richer and the impoverished sink deeper into despair. Enlightened social movements in the north (labor, civil rights organizations, progressive intellectuals) and genuine southern governments (not military juntas or one-man dictatorships) must focus their energies on achieving a viable polycentrism in the world. The objective is to create political space for the weak, who can then shed the yoke of subordination and devise workable economic-political strategies against the hypocritical world order. Running parallel to international economic disparities is the enormous military imbalance between north and south. This continues to worsen—witness the weak against the domineering in the Gulf, says Amin—thereby enhancing the overall position of privilege. Against growing talk in the north, particularly in the United States, about the criteria for humane interventions (as in Rwanda or Bosnia), Amin asserts: "Never have the armies of the north brought peace, prosperity, or democracy to the peoples of Asia, Africa, or Latin America. In the future, as in the past five centuries, they can only bring to these peoples further servitude, the exploitation of their labor, the expropriation of their riches, and the denial of their rights."[26]

Chomsky has also reproved in searing language the military dimension of the post–Cold War order. Therein the collapse of the USSR has resulted in freedom for the United States from any countering power. Chomsky has damned the "racist frenzy" that swept the West during the Gulf conflict (as did, incidentally, various editorial writers in Third World newspapers). The war against Iraq was assuredly a test case for the world order, he maintains, in which this lesson was highlighted: "The United States remains a violent and lawless state, a stance that is fully endorsed by its allies and clients, who understand that international law is a fraud to which the powerful appeal when they seek some veil, however transparent, for whatever they choose to do." As for the world order, it is run by the rich for their sole benefit. This arrangement is sanctioned by mainstream academics who spin a smooth technocratic yarn that in the end signifies only their defection from the ranks of intellectual integrity. A de facto system of governance by transnational capital—institutionalized in the IMF, World Bank, G-7, GATT—constitutes a multilateralism not envisaged by the UN General Assembly or admitted by the tricksters and cognoscenti in Washington. The task of decent people in the north and south, then, is to combine their efforts to unmask illegitimate authority and to fight, by whatever means necessary, for true freedom and justice. Until then, any order celebrated by Washington and lauding morality and economic fairness must be seen for what it is: a grand illusion to fool people into thinking that injustice is justice, cruelty is mercy, the jungle is civilization. Chomsky must necessarily agree with this judgment of Libya's Muammer El-Qadhafi: The only visible difference between the old and the new order is that the latter has even less inhibition in pursuing lustful self-aggrandizement and evil.[27]

* * * * *

What has the new world order added up to? As an idea, it is meager. It lacks insight comparable to Lincoln's on the needs of posthostilities healing. The moral intensity of Wilson's internationalist reforms is also absent. Equally wanting is FDR's finesse at marrying higher principle to the realities of force. Clarity of purpose, as in Kissinger's balancing powers against powers to shore up stability, is also missing. Bland and devoid of conviction, the new-world-order idea blossomed briefly. It enjoys ever-less currency in official and popular usage.

Bush might reasonably be saddled with the blame. He was miscast in the role of imaginative leader, let alone designer of any international order. Intellectual boldness was not his forte. Solidity, reliability, and predictability (the Somalia intervention aside) were his strengths and those of his cabinet officers. Clinton's relative indifference to foreign policy has also helped to frustrate lively discussion in the years since Bush.

Champions of these two administrations can take modest solace in the observation made at the beginning of this book. American versions of order have never taken hold in the way intended by their authors. Indeed, narrowly conceived, the tale told in these chapters is a melancholy one. Supremely talented presidents (Lincoln, Wilson, FDR) have fared no better than lesser mortals (Bush, Clinton). In a sense, this book is a history of good ideas that failed after the passing of national security crises. The hopefulness of malice toward none and charity for all yielded to postwar violence in the former Confederacy; the practical effect was to retard social progress, culminating in the reaction of the Jim Crow regime. The 1898 war of rescue and liberation in Cuba led to harsh campaigns to suppress Filipino independence. The war to make the world safe for democracy led to sulky aloofness from European affairs, retained even after they assumed a shape hostile to U.S. interests. The promise of future concord implicit in the World War II Grand Alliance dissolved when faced with post-1945 suspicions. The Cold War compromised meaningful standards of conduct confirmed at Nuremberg by giving rise to the nuclear arms race and the inherent possibility of annihilation.

Seen in this context, then, it is unsurprising that elevated talk about a new world order has amounted to little. Nearly overwhelming whatever exists of international stability, furies from the post–Cold War Pandora's box abound: ethnic strife, religious conflicts, numerous states from Africa to Asia to southeastern Europe so near to disintegrating that they cannot satisfy the minimal needs of their citizens or play useful diplomatic roles. Meanwhile the Bush-Clinton administrations have not kept faith with their own professions of commitment to international law and organizations and the primacy of negotiated settlement. The invasion of Panama and kidnapping of a trivial thug, Manuel Noriega, is one example. The Gulf War is harder still to defend, given the scope of suffering inflicted on Iraq. Examples of more recent vintage include: the hounding of UN Secretary-General Boutros Boutros-Ghali and American refusal to participate in proceedings under the World Trade Organization to judge European objections to Washington's embargo of Cuba (Helms-Burton Act).[28]

What accounts for this pattern of failure stretching from the Civil War onward? Much of the answer lies in the political nature—undisciplined or democratic, call it what you will—and the codified fragmentation of power in American life. This condition has sustained a cacophony of ideas during moments of crisis. The effect has been to dilute the executive branch's preferred concepts so that they have lost zest. Lincoln's hope was thus drowned out in the din produced by a truculent Thaddeus Stevens and the Radical Republicans versus the likes of Nathan Bedford Forrest. Woodrow Wilson foundered as progressives (Jane Addams, William Bullitt, Walter Lippmann) criticized him and as both he and they were taxed by Henry Cabot Lodge and company. This phenomenon of intellectual dilution has been compounded since World War II by the felt need in Washington to embellish the truth to gain popular support for policy—leading to distortions, credibility gap, and widespread distrust of national leaders.

Indeed, a connecting skein runs from Acheson's cavalier approach to public education, to widespread disillusionment with LBJ circa 1968, to the subsequent Watergate crisis of confidence in government. Jaundiced public perceptions of and wavering support for Bush-Clinton policy flow, at least in part, from residual skepticism dating to the Vietnam-Watergate era. Furthermore, the continuously recombining coalitions of power in American politics and the opposing tugs of caution ("isolationism") and confidence ("internationalism") are antithetical to constancy. Thus containment and anticommunism during the Cold War were convenient shorthand definitions of the national interest but they could not be integrated with any larger view of U.S. aims or purpose. Twentieth-century American democracy in foreign affairs, in short, has suffered from the same handicap identified by Alexis de

Tocqueville in 1835: "[the inability] to regulate the details of an important undertaking, to persevere in a design."[29]

The failure of U.S. versions of order is also connected to the gladiatorial arena created by force and power that leave little room for sturdy or respectable ideals. Those put forth by governments—not least by the United States—have often been no more than fig leaves to dignify the will to dominate. In the words of one unbending realist, Kenneth Waltz: "England claimed to bear the white man's burden; France spoke of her *mission civilisatrice.* In like spirit, we [Americans] say that we act to maintain world order. . . . For countries at the top, this is predictable behavior."[30] Even before reaching the peak of its power, the United States conquered the Philippines on the pretext of bestowing civilization's manifold benefits on a backward people. Economic ambitions have also crouched just behind diplomacy. The Bush-Clinton rhetoric is a pretense in part to justify the American economy as it buys or otherwise acquires additional shares of the world's energy resources, markets, and services.

Still, it does not follow that ideas on world order have simply served to hide or soften the impacts of grasping capital, as asserted by an Amin or Chomsky. The United States is too complex, too contradictory an enterprise to reduce to a simple species of voracious appetite and long reach, all justified by elaborate intellectual cynicism.

However elusive or difficult to pinpoint in the chain of causality, ideas demonstrably matter in U.S. foreign policy. They influence policy makers through such instrumentalities as socialization and training. The broader population is also affected by concepts of liberty and an increasingly confident human rights culture, which in turn exercise some restraint on rulers by democratic means. Citizens and governors are part too of a corporative national body that is permeated by a set of shared notions; these seep back and forth between political elites and the general citizenry. On these points, a few scholars (Gordon Craig, Michael Hunt, Judith Goldstein, Robert Keohane) have made pioneering advances in clearing the thicket of conceptual hazards and narrative pitfalls.[31]

To slight or omit the role of ideas, as in the brief made by pure realism or economic determinism, also misses an important and affirmative aspect of political reality: ideas are intimately connected to U.S. identity and collective conscience, which manifest themselves internationally. The passion of civil rights notably has been felt in foreign affairs—even as solutions to racial conflict have been sought in a domestic context. The 1863 proclamation to rid the United States of slavery helped to foil what might have been substantial Anglo-French efforts on behalf of the Confederacy. The exciting prospect of seeing white overlordship undone in Cuba helped persuade the majority of black Americans to support the 1898 war against Spain. Legal disability previously imposed on black America was lifted, albeit partially and fitfully, by twentieth-century emergencies. The first and second world wars and the Cold War embarrassed U.S. race conscience, prodding it to make practical changes in keeping with the country's creed of equality and freedom. Allied and U.S. morale was in turn strengthened by spirited reiterations of this creed, as in the Fourteen Points, the Atlantic Charter, and Truman Doctrine. The nerve of adversaries was also touched: Germany sued for an armistice in 1918 on the assumption that Wilson's Fourteen Points would form the basis of a nonpunitive peace; anti-Nazi resistance in Germany was buoyed by knowing that an alternative version of life and political organization still lived in the dark age of Hitler; Soviet dissidents knew that they were not ultimately alone, and Kremlin confidence was weakened by U.S. drumming on human rights, begun by Truman. A similar if less dramatic line of influence can be traced in the history of American feminism, running from fulminations against war by Jane Addams and Carrie Chapman Catt to Secretary of State Albright's promise to reinvigorate the human rights agenda in Clinton's second administration.[32] Pesky outsiders to power (Frederick Douglass to Martin Luther King), outlandish idealists (Henry Wallace), irrepressible dissidents (William James to Senator Fulbright), unbudging feminists (not least Eleanor Roosevelt), unblinking prophets (Reinhold Niebuhr), and irritating nonconformists (Randolph S. Bourne to Sidney Hook) have all contributed to U.S. international successes by insisting that a moral fillip be added to the logic and manipulation of power.

Even as attention to the interplay of ideas helps to illuminate the past, such a focus also gives clues to future U.S. behavior. Phrased gloomily, this consideration raises a stark question: Will America in coming decades squander its assets through overextension (à la Steel, Kennedy, Kennan) on behalf of notions that bear tenuous relation to the core value of national security?

American leaders and the public will certainly be eager in coming years to stay on the advantageous side of power, as defined by ordinary security and economic requirements. Such positioning will have little to do with getting on the right side of justice or mercy or compassion for the weak and much to do with anxiety about the consequences of decline.[33] Yet the life of privilege will continue to have its delusional side: power and wealth will always be embarrassed by the spectacle of lording it over others, resulting in the issuance of self-justifying declarations that work as soothing balm on American conscience but that are less availing abroad. Future wars involving the United States will only intensify this search for justification by blithely promising a better future for everyone, in keeping with the history of 1861–1991.

Yet it is unlikely that the claims of better collective conscience will ever be entirely erased or placated. As long as they remain vital in domestic politics—pushing against the limitations of pinched imagination and parochial interests—they will also play a part in the formation and execution of foreign policy. Such claims by their very nature act as a solvent on complacent acceptance of the international status quo or assertion of unbridled power. In the case of future wars, as in the past, untouchable national interest (physical security, economic well-being) and pressure on civil liberties will have to coexist with that unquiet insistence on justice in the public voice. Otherwise popular support will not be reliably forthcoming. Also the conservative virtue, dignified affirmation of self, will become corrupted and give rise to self-righteous chauvinism. The liberal virtue, forbearing tolerance, will likewise fail, producing that counterfeit that cannot affirm a hierarchy of meaningful values. Between these virtues and their corruption lies the difference between U.S. confidence in 1945 and muddle in Vietnam.

The power of American political imagination outside the United States will continue to win respect and occasionally to inspire people—as in 1989, when Chinese students in Tiananmen Square, demonstrating for greater freedom, paraded with a modified version of the Statue of Liberty. Nelson Mandela has praised the Declaration of Independence and the Atlantic Charter as those documents fortified him during the struggle against South African apartheid. His words especially have the same resolute optimism of earlier U.S. experience; they might usefully be recalled by Americans now, bound as they are to try but to fail in transcending themselves: "Men are not capable of doing nothing, of saying nothing, of not reacting to injustice, of not protesting against oppression, of not striving for the good society." Václav Havel of the Czech Republic has also recommended the commitment to responsible freedom contained in the Declaration of Independence. He has reminded Americans that the creation of a new model of coexistence among various cultures, races, and religions is a task for the future. In this case, the U.S. promise of fairness and experiment in self-government still has international relevance. Osama El-Baz, first undersecretary of the Egyptian Foreign ministry, has invoked the moral authority of Abraham Lincoln's Second Inaugural address ("malice toward none and charity for all") as a guide for the proper relations among states, great and poor, in the post–Cold War era. Thus Meriwether Lewis's words—uttered in an altogether different context and when the United States was young and raw—still echo: "As I have always held it a crime to anticipate evils I will believe it a good comfortable road until I am compelled to believe differently."[34]

These testaments can be a source of strength to Americans as they pick their way through Cold War debris and encounter the novel problems of a new era. Necessarily set against past disappointments and betrayals of conscience, collective faith in the future is a sure sign of continuing U.S. vitality.

The other sure sign relates to national enlightenment: the struggle for the emergence from self-incurred immaturity (a narrowly patriotic reading of history) and the cultivation of a detached look at past events. There is no firmer basis on which to meet the twenty-first century's dilemmas of power and conscience.[35]

Notes

Introduction

1. See Kenneth Waltz's durable *Man, the State, and War: A Theoretical Analysis* (New York, 1959) for an explanation of the causes of war. In his account of the Peloponnesian War, Thucydides asserted that people go to war from concerns over honor, fear, and interest. The contemporary historian Donald Kagan largely endorses Thucydides's view. See Kagan's *On the Origins of War and the Preservation of Peace* (New York, 1995), p. 8.
2. Charles Bracelen Flood, *Lee: The Last Years* (Boston, 1981), p. 251.
3. Whether Stalin really made this remark about the Pope and his power is unclear; the story might be apocryphal. See Michael Walzer on Sherman in *Just and Unjust Wars: A Moral Argument with Historical Illustrations* (New York, 1977), pp. 32–33.
4. Judith Goldstein and Robert Keohane, "Ideas and Foreign Policy: An Analytical Framework" in Goldstein and Keohane, eds., *Ideas and Foreign Policy: Beliefs, Institutions, and Political Change* (Ithaca, 1993), p. 30; Francis Fukuyama, "The End of History?," *The National Interest,* reprinted in Foreign Affairs Agenda, *The New Shape of World Politics: Contending Paradigms in International Relations* (New York, 1997), p. 5.
5. The political scientist G. John Ikenberry has made this observation, itself an underlying assumption of my book: "At critical turning points, such as the end of a major war, structures of power and interests matter—just as they always do. But at these turning points, uncertainties about power structures and unhappiness with past or current definitions of interests provide openings for rethinking." See Ikenberry's "Creating Yesterday's New Order: Keynesian 'New Thinking' and the Anglo-American Postwar Settlement" in Goldstein and Keohane, eds., *Ideas and Foreign Policy: Beliefs, Institutions, and Political Change,* p. 59.
6. I enlist Robert Dallek by way of support. In a survey of U.S. diplomacy since 1898, he wrote: "Foreign policy was less a reaction to events abroad than to conditions at home, where economic, political, and social change substantially blotted out overseas affairs and largely made them an irrational extension of internal hopes and fears." See his *The American Style of Foreign Policy: Cultural Politics and Foreign Affairs* (New York, 1983), p. xv.

7. Thomas Schoonover, "Europe, the Spanish-American War and Great Power Activity in the Caribbean and Asia," *SHAFR Newsletter,* September 1997, p. 11.
8. Compare Joseph Nye, *Bound to Lead: The Changing Nature of American Power* (New York, 1990) with Paul Kennedy, *The Rise and Fall of the Great Powers: Economic Change and Military Conflict from 1500 to 2000* (New York, 1987).
9. W. E. B. Du Bois, *Black Reconstruction in America: An Essay Toward a History of the Past Which Black Folk Played in the Attempt to Reconstruct Democracy in America, 1860–1880* (New York, 1935, 1963), p. 714.

Chapter 1

1. Merrill Peterson, ed., *The Portable Thomas Jefferson* (New York, 1986), Jefferson to John Holmes, April 22, 1820, pp. 567–69; Don Fehrenbacker, ed., *Abraham Lincoln: Speeches and Writings, 1832–1858* (New York, 1989), Address to the Young Men's Lyceum of Springfield, Illinois, January 27, 1838, pp. 28–36.
2. B. B. Sideman and Lillian Friedman, eds., *Europe Looks at the Civil War* (New York, 1960), pp. 7, 9, 62, 94–95, 118, 132–33, 141, 173–74, 233, 245, 253, 259.
3. U. S. Grant, *Personal Memoirs* (New York, 1886) Vol. II, pp. 544–45.
4. James McPherson, *Ordeal by Fire: The Civil War and Reconstruction* (New York, 1982), p. 301.
5. Sideman and Friedman, eds., *Europe Looks at the Civil War,* p. 20; Alexandre Tarsaidze, *Czars and Presidents* (New York, 1958), p. 182.
6. Holmes's poem is reproduced in Joseph Loubat, *Gustavus Fox's Mission to Russia in 1866* (New York, 1970), p. 181.
7. David Mayers, *The Ambassadors and America's Soviet Policy* (New York, 1995), pp. 35–43. Useful books on Civil War diplomacy and international relations include the following: D. P. Crook, *The North, the South, and the Powers 1861–1865* (New York, 1974); D. Jordan and E. J. Pratt, *Europe and the American Civil War* (Boston, 1931); Jay Monaghan, *Diplomat in Carpet Slippers: Abraham Lincoln Deals with Foreign Affairs* (Indianapolis, 1945); Frank Lawrence Owsley, *King Cotton Diplomacy* (Chicago, 1959).
8. Lincoln once said of Russia that it made "no pretense of loving liberty . . . [and was a place] where despotism can be taken pure." See Richard Current, ed., *The Political Thought of Abraham Lincoln* (Indianapolis, 1967), p. 83.
9. See Arthur Schlesinger, "War and the Constitution: Abraham Lincoln and Franklin D. Roosevelt" in Gabor S. Boritt, ed., *Lincoln the War President* (New York, 1992), pp. 158–60; Mark Neely, *The Fate of Liberty: Abraham Lincoln and Civil Liberties* (New York, 1991).
10. The law partner of Lincoln characterized his ambition as "an engine that knew no rest." Cited in Richard Neustadt, *Presidential Power and the Modern Presidents* (New York, 1990), p. 205; Frederick Douglass, *Autobiographies,* ed. Henry Louis Gates (New York, 1994), p. 924; David Herbert Donald, *Lincoln* (New York, 1995), pp. 14–15.

11. James McPherson, "When Memorial Day Was No Picnic," *New York Times,* May 26, 1996.

12. The republic of thirty-four states had a population of nearly 31 million people on the eve of the war. This population included substantial numbers of foreign-born immigrants, many of whom were of Irish and German origin. Roughly half a million freed blacks lived in the nation, a small portion of whom lived in the South. A minority of these even had slaves of their own. Eighteen and a half million people lived in the North, more than twice the number of people later embraced by the Confederacy (of whom nearly 40 percent were enslaved). The border states contained three million people, of whom half a million were slaves. Four million blacks were liberated as a result of the Civil War. Estimates on the value of property destroyed by the war range widely from between five and ten billion dollars. See Gabor Boritt, ed., *Lincoln the War President,* pp. 37, 148; Garry Wills, *Lincoln at Gettysburg: The Words that Remade America* (New York, 1992), p. 98; James McPherson, *Abraham Lincoln and the Second American Revolution* (New York, 1990), p. viii; Daniel Boorstin, ed., *An American Primer* (Chicago, 1966), p. 422.

   The statistics on Southern war dead are from McPherson, *Abraham Lincoln and the Second American Revolution,* p. 38, and McPherson, *Ordeal by Fire,* p. 484.

13. In his Second Inaugural address (March 4, 1865), Lincoln said:

   If we shall suppose that American Slavery is one of those offenses which, in the providence of God, must needs come, but which, having continued through His appointed time, He now wills to remove, and that He gives to both North and South, this terrible war, as the woe due to those by whom the offense came, shall we discern therein any departure from those divine attributes which the believers in a Living God always ascribe to Him? Fondly do we hope—fervently do we pray—that this mighty scourge of war may speedily pass away. Yet, if God wills that it continue, until all the wealth piled by the bond-man's two hundred and fifty years of unrequited toil shall be sunk, and until every drop of blood drawn with the lash, shall be paid by another drawn with the sword, as was said three thousand years ago, so still it must be said the judgments of the Lord, are true and righteous altogether.

14. Garry Wills, *Lincoln at Gettysburg,* p. 125; Mark Neely, *The Last Best Hope of Earth: Abraham Lincoln and the Promise of America* (Cambridge, Mass., 1993), pp. 95, 158; Don Fehrenbacher, ed., *Abraham Lincoln: Speeches and Writings, 1859–1865,* Annual Message to Congress, December 1, 1862, p. 415.

15. James, McPherson, "Lincoln and the Strategy of Unconditional Surrender" in Boritt, ed., *Lincoln the War President,* pp. 41–42.

16. Eric Foner, *Reconstruction: America's Unfinished Revolution, 1863–1877* (New York, 1988), p. 74; Donald, *Lincoln,* pp. 560, 583.

17. Lincoln once explained his approach to Reconstruction this way: "The pilots on our Western rivers steer from *point to point* as they call it—setting the

course of the boat no farther than they can see; and that is all I propose to myself in this great problem." Cited in Donald, *Lincoln*, p. 15.

18. Foner, *Reconstruction*, pp. 73–74; William Hesseltine, *Lincoln's Plan of Reconstruction* (Gloucester, Mass., 1963), p. 136.

19. Fehrenbacher, ed., *Lincoln*, Speech on Reconstruction, April 11, 1865, pp. 697–701.

20. Donald, *Lincoln*, pp. 559–60.

21. On completing his inspection tour of the defeated states, the Northern newspaperman Whitelaw Reid observed: "[The Southerners] admit they are whipped, but the honest ones make no pretense of loving the power that whipped them." Cited in Wayne Morgan, ed., *Making Peace with Spain: The Diary of Whitelaw Reid, September-December 1898* (Austin, 1965), p. 6; William Garrett Piston, *Lee's Tarnished Lieutenant: James Longstreet and His Place in Southern History* (Athens, Georgia, 1987), pp. 104–5.

22. Charles Bracelen Flood, *Lee: The Last Years* (Boston, 1981), pp. 120, 221.

23. Piston, *Lee's Tarnished Lieutenant*, p. 106.

24. In addition to Piston's work, see Jeffrey Wert, *General James Longstreet: The Confederacy's Most Controversial Soldier—A Biography* (New York, 1993).

25. Foner, *Reconstruction*, pp. 70–71.

26. LaWanda Cox, *Lincoln and Black Freedom: A Study in Presidential Leadership* (Columbia, South Carolina, 1981), p. 24; C. Vann Woodward, ed., *Mary Chestnut's Civil War* (New Haven, 1981), p. 835; William McFeely, *Frederick Douglass* (New York, 1991), p. 235.

27. Douglass, *Autobiographies*, pp. 798, 811.

28. Philip Foner, *Frederick Douglass: A Biography* (New York, 1969), p. 223; Neely, *The Last Best Hope of Earth*, p. 97.

29. Douglass, *Autobiographies*, pp. 802, 804, 808, 810; Cox, *Lincoln and Black Freedom*, p. 149; McFeely, *Frederick Douglass*, p. 228; Neely, *The Last Best Hope of Earth*, p. 97; Foner, *Frederick Douglass*, p. 233; Albert Castel, *The Presidency of Andrew Johnson* (Lawrence, Kansas, 1979), p. 64.

30. Sideman and Friedman, eds., *Europe Looks at the Civil War*, p. 300.

31. Castel, *The Presidency of Andrew Johnson*, pp. 20, 34.

32. John Hope Franklin, *Reconstruction: After the Civil War* (Chicago, 1961), p. 43.

33. Castel, *The Presidency of Andrew Johnson*, p. 47.

34. Pleasant Stovall, *Robert Toombs: Statesman, Speaker, Soldier, Sage* (New York, 1892), p. 325.

35. Fawn Brodie, *Thaddeus Stevens: Scourge of the South* (New York, 1959), pp. 369–70.

36. Ibid., pp. 26, 53, 56.

37. Ralph Korngold, *Thaddeus Stevens: A Being Darkly Wise and Rudely Great* (New York, 1955), p. viii.

38. Flood, *Lee: The Last Years*, p. 146. For the Fort Pillow episode, see Jack Hurst's account in *Nathan Bedford Forrest: A Biography* (New York, 1993). The details of what occurred are still unknown, as Hurst makes clear. Yet as the officer in charge on the Confederate side, Forrest bore responsibility. In this connection,

it is worth recalling the words of General Douglas MacArthur in 1946, when he confirmed the death sentence on General Tomayuki Yamashita imposed by the United States military commission: "The soldier, be he friend or foe, is charged with the protection of the weak and unarmed. It is the very essence and reason for his being. When he violates this sacred trust, he not only profanes his entire cult but threatens the very fabric of international society. The traditions of fighting men are long and honorable. They are based on the noblest of human traits—sacrifice." Cited in Telford Taylor, *Nuremberg and Vietnam: An American Tragedy* (New York, 1971).

39. Hurst, *Nathan Bedford Forrest*, p. 10.
40. Eric Foner, *Reconstruction,* pp. 558–59.
41. See Jonathan Spence, *God's Chinese Son: The Taiping Heavenly Kingdom of Hong Xiuquan* (New York, 1996), p. 27.
42. W. E. B. Du Bois, *Black Reconstruction in America,* p. 715. Du Bois eventually concluded that meaningful racial justice was impossible in the capitalistic United States. He finally joined the American communist party. He settled in Ghana in 1961 and soon afterward became a citizen of his adopted homeland. He died there in 1963.
43. McPherson, *Ordeal by Fire,* pp. 577–78.
44. Du Bois, *Black Reconstruction,* p. 30. In contrast with Du Bois, Woodrow Wilson wrote in his *A History of the American People* (New York, 1902), Vol. 5, p. 300: "The southern states were [at turn of the century] readjusting their elective suffrage so as to exclude the illiterate Negroes and so in part undo the mischief of Reconstruction."
45. A feminist interpretation of Reconstruction is found in Nina Silber, *The Romance of Reunion: Northerners and the South, 1865–1900* (Chapel Hill, 1994).
46. Jean Edward Smith, *Lucius D. Clay: An American Life* (New York, 1990), pp. 239, 313.
47. John Leekley, ed., *Bruce Catton: Reflections on the Civil War* (New York, 1982), p. 229.

Chapter 2

1. John Crow, *Spain: The Root and the Flower* (Berkeley, 1985), pp. 263, 274; John Offner, *An Unwanted War: The Diplomacy of the United States and Spain over Cuba, 1895–1898* (Chapel Hill, 1992), pp. 137–38, 225–26; Frank Freidel, *The Splendid Little War* (Boston, 1958), p. 43.
2. See Andrew Carnegie, "Wealth," *North American Review* CXLVIII (1889), pp. 653–64; Samuel Eliot Morison, *The Oxford History of the American People* (New York, 1965), pp. 746, 768; Frederick Jackson Turner, "The Significance of the Frontier in American History" *Proceedings of the Forty-first Annual Meeting of the State Historical Society of Wisconsin* (Madison, 1894), pp. 29–112.
3. Robert Dallek, *The American Style of Foreign Policy* (New York, 1983), p. 4; Ernest May, *Imperial Democracy: The Emergence of America as a Great Power* (New York, 1961), p. 268.

4. Akira Iriye, *From Nationalism to Internationalism: U.S. Foreign Policy to 1914* (London, 1977), p. 140; Edward Johnson, *History of Negro Soldiers in the Spanish-American War, and Other Items of Interest* (Raleigh, North Carolina, 1899), p. 17; Woodrow Wilson, *A History of the American People* (New York, 1902), Vol. 5, pp. 273, 275–76, 296.

5. Wayne Andrews, ed., *The Autobiography of Theodore Roosevelt* (New York, 1958), p. 123.

6. Freidel, *The Splendid Little War,* pp. 99, 106; Johnson, *History of Negro Soldiers in the Spanish-American War,* p. 46.

7. Morison, *History of the American People,* p. 802; Theodore Roosevelt, *The Rough Riders* (New York, 1921); Lewis Gould, *The Presidency of Theodore Roosevelt* (Lawrence, Kansas, 1991), p. 7; May, *Imperial Democracy,* p. 219.

8. Gerald Linderman, *The Mirror of War: American Society and the Spanish-American War* (Ann Arbor, 1974), p. 29.

9. Ibid., pp. 25–27.

10. See H. G. Rickover, *How the Battleship* Maine *was Destroyed* (Washington, 1976), for a full evaluation.

11. Johnson, *History of Negro Soldiers in the Spanish-American War,* pp. 10–11.

12. Andrews, ed., *The Autobiography of Theodore Roosevelt,* pp. 118, 141; Richard Hofstadter, *The American Political Tradition* (New York, 1957), pp. 212, 215, 228, 236; Gould, *The Presidency of Theodore Roosevelt,* pp. 6–7; Howard Beale, *Theodore Roosevelt and the Rise of America to World Power* (Baltimore, 1956) pp. 35–38.

13. Richard Challener, *Admirals, Generals, and American Foreign Policy, 1898–1914* (Princeton, 1973), pp. 12–13; Alfred Thayer Mahan, *The Problem of Asia and Its Effect upon International Politics* (Boston, 1900), pp. 142–43, 192–93.

14. The Teller Amendment in 1898 renounced U.S. interest in keeping Cuba. This attitude was revised by the 1901 Platt Amendment, which guaranteed a privileged American position in Cuban affairs. Under pressure from Washington, provisions of Platt were also incorporated into Cuba's 1901 constitution, and confirmed again in a Cuban-U.S. treaty following the withdrawal (1902) of American troops.

    McKinley gave the following reasons for holding the Philippines. These are reproduced in Robert Goldwin and Harry Clor, eds., *Readings in American Foreign Policy* (New York, 1971), p. 107:

    (1) That we could not give them back to Spain—that would be cowardly and dishonorable; (2) that we could not turn them over to France or Germany—our commercial rivals in the Orient—that would be bad business and discreditable; (3) that we could not leave them to themselves—they were unfit for self-government—and they would soon have anarchy and misrule over there worse than Spain's was; and (4) that there was nothing left for us to do but to take them all, and to educate the Filipinos, and uplift and civilize and Christianize them, and by God's grace do the very best we could by them, as our fellow-men for whom Christ also died.

15. The "water cure" was an often fatal torture used to extract information from prisoners. It was administered by forcing gallons of water down the victim's throat; the subsequent swelling made it impossible to breathe normally. A soldier would kick or jump on the victim's stomach to expel the water. See Jim Zwick, ed., Mark Twain's *Weapons of Satire: Anti-Imperialist Writing on the Philippine-American War* (Syracuse, 1992), p. xxiv.

16. Stanley Karnow, *In Our Image: America's Empire in the Philippines* (New York, 1989), p. 140. Roughly 120,000 American troops were assigned to fight in the Philippines. See Walter LaFeber, *The American Age: U.S. Foreign Policy at Home and Abroad* (New York, 1994), Vol. I, p. 215.

17. Akira Iriye, *From Nationalism to Internationalism*, p. 333; May, *Imperial Democracy*, p. 8.

18. Mahan, *The Problem of Asia*, pp. 174–75; William Livezey, *Mahan on Sea Power* (Norman, Oklahoma, 1981), pp. 203–5; Henry Graff, ed., *American Imperialism and the Philippine Insurrection* (Boston, 1969), pp. viii-ix; Thomas Schoonover, "Europe, the Spanish-American War and Great Power Activity in the Caribbean and Asia," *SHAFR Newsletter*, September 1997, p. 12.

19. Iriye, *From Nationalism to Internationalism*, p. 141; Dallek, *The American Style of Foreign Policy*, p. 28.

20. Albert Beveridge, *The Meaning of the Times* (Indianapolis, 1908), p. 57.

21. George Marks, ed., *The Black Press Views American Imperialism, 1898–1900* (New York, 1971), pp. viii, 114, 128, 154; Johnson, *History of Negro Soldiers*, p. 47; Freidel, *The Splendid Little War*, p. 173; Stuart Miller, *Benevolent Assimilation: The American Conquest of the Philippines, 1899–1903* (New Haven, 1982), p. 292, n. 54.

Tributes to the valor of black troops were made by General Nelson Miles, Theodore Roosevelt, and a little- known lieutenant, John J. Pershing.

The following from the *American Baptist* (February 11, 1899) is cited in Marks, *The Black Press*, pp. 114–15:

The annexation of territory as a result of war with Spain is becoming a serious question for discussion and is not confined alone to the right of our government to acquire territory by purchase or conquest. The matter of the treatment of these people who belong to the dark-skinned races is a matter which concerns us. The conduct of men in the future can only be determined by observing their conduct in the past. Experience and not promises weighs more potentially in these matters, and the treatment which the Indians, the Chinese, and the Negroes have received at the hands of white Americans speaks in no uncertain tone—it would be deplorable to have the inhabitants of the Philippine Islands treated as the Indians have been treated or the people of Cuba or Puerto Rico ruled as the Negroes of the South have been ruled . . . This kind of civilization has very little to commend it and it is doubtful whether it ought to be extended to our newly-acquired territory.

22. Sondra Herman, *Eleven Against War* (Stanford, 1969), pp. 33–34.

23. William James, "Moral Equivalent of War" in John Roth, ed., *The Moral Equivalent of War and Other Essays* (New York, 1971), pp. 5, 7; Robert Beisner, *Twelve Against Empire: The Anti-Imperialists, 1898–1900* (New York, 1968), p. 44.

24. Thomas Paterson, ed., "William James on the Suppression of the Philippines, 1899," and "American Anti-Imperialist League Program, 1899," *Major Problems in American Foreign Policy* (Lexington, Mass., 1989), Vol. I, pp. 384–89.

25. Robert Beisner, *Twelve Against Empire,* p. 49.

26. "Mark Twain on American Imperialism," *Atlantic Monthly,* April 1992, pp. 49–65. Funston and a handful of soldiers disguised themselves as prisoners in the escort of Aguinaldo's supposed allies (really Filipino scouts). On delivery to Aguinaldo (March 1901), they overcame his surprised bodyguards and carried him away. Thereafter, Miguel Malvas led the nationalists; he surrendered in April 1902.

27. Zwick, ed., *Mark Twain's Weapons of Satire,* pp. 17, 23, 40, 56, 120, 161, 168–78, 180.

28. Ibid., pp. xxxiv, 27, 40, 42, 56, 64–66, 72, 132; George Hoar, *Autobiography of Seventy Years* (New York, 1903), Vol. II, p. 318.

29. Hoar, *Autobiography,* Vol. II, pp. 304–26.

30. Beisner, *Twelve Against Empire,* p. 162.

31. James Joll, *Europe Since 1870: An International History* (New York, 1973), pp. 80, 94; Wayne Morgan, ed., *Making Peace with Spain: The Diary of Whitelaw Reid, September-December 1898* (Austin, 1965), pp. 11–12.

32. Zwick, *Mark Twain's Weapons of Satire,* p. 4.

33. Lewis Gould, *The Presidency of William McKinley* (Lawrence, Kansas, 1980), pp. 182–83; Stuart Miller, *Benevolent Assimilation: The American Conquest of the Philippines, 1899–1903* (New Haven, 1982), pp. 169–70; Goldwin and Clor, eds., *Readings in American Foreign Policy,* pp. 108–21.

34. Twain was gratified to have the United States on the side of the Cuban rebellion. He told a friend in June 1898: "I have never enjoyed a war—even in written history—as I am enjoying this one . . . It is a worthy thing to fight for one's freedom; it is another sight finer to fight for another man's. And I think this is the first time it has been done." Cited in Zwick, *Mark Twain's Weapons of Satire,* p. xx.

35. Henry Stimson and McGeorge Bundy, *On Active Service in Peace and War* (New York, 1947), pp. 117–52; Robert McNamara with Brian Van De Mark, *In Retrospect: The Tragedy and Lessons of Vietnam* (New York, 1995), p. 171. McNamara has referred to World War I as the chemists' war and to World War II as the physicists' war—in which case Vietnam "might well have to be considered the social scientists' war." See Walter McDougall, "Back to Bedrock: The Eight Traditions of American Statecraft," *Foreign Affairs,* March/April 1997, p. 141.

36. See, for example, Chester Arthur's "The Lessons of Somalia," *Foreign Affairs,* May/June 1995.

37. William Polk has concluded soberly on the damage resulting from twentieth-century interventions by great powers:

However much events and actors [involved in] outside intervention differ from one another, they evince similar patterns: each provoked reactions that usually rendered interventions not only ineffectual but also self-defeating. They caused severe dislocations to societies already split along ethnic, religious, and economic lines and in which institutions of statehood, typically newly established after long periods of foreign domination, were fragile. The results . . . have been decades of violence, sporadic civil war, and impoverishment. And they set in motion tendencies that were certainly unintended and were often costly to those who had made them possible: the spread of the drug trade, international terrorism, and severe social and political disruption as in the Soviet Union (after Afghanistan), America (after Vietnam), and France (after Algeria).

See Polk, *Neighbors and Strangers: The Fundamentals of Foreign Affairs* (Chicago, 1997), p. 272.

38. The historian Ernest May, writing in the era of pre-Vietnam optimism, concluded this about the rise of American power circa 1900: "Some nations achieve greatness; the United States had greatness thrust upon it." See May, *Imperial Democracy*, p. 279.

Chapter 3

1. William Hull, *The Two Hague Conferences and their Contributions to International Law* (Boston, 1908), pp. 464, 496–97, 502–3.
2. Angell was not the first person to conclude that international economic interconnectedness and modern weaponry had made war obsolete. Others before him, who thought along these lines, included: Joseph Priestly, Thomas Paine, John Stuart Mill, Richard Cobden, John Bright. On this point, see Donald Kagan's *On the Origins of War and the Preservation of Peace* (New York, 1995), pp. 1–3. Also see Norman Angell's *The Great Illusion: A Study of the Relation of Military Power in Nations to their Economic and Social Advantage* (London, 1909) and *The Great Illusion 1933* (New York, 1933). Angell's hopeful if naive thesis did not die with him. For a modified version, consult John Mueller's *Retreat from Doomsday: The Obsolescence of Major War* (New York, 1989).
3. Hans Morgenthau recounted in the spirit of lost innocence how as a boy in prewar Germany he happily spent hours playing with lead soldiers. The future theorist of power politics recorded in "Fragment of an Intellectual Autobiography: 1904–1932": "My favorite playthings were toy soldiers in their various historic uniforms, with which I reenacted the historic battles—from Cannae to Waterloo—that we were discussing in school." See Kenneth Thompson and Robert Myers, eds., *Truth and Tragedy: A Tribute to Hans J. Morgenthau* (Washington, D.C., 1977), p. 1.
4. W. B. Yeats, "Nineteen Hundred and Nineteen," *The Collected Poems of W. B. Yeats* (New York, 1970), pp. 204–8.
5. Thomas Kennedy, *Charles A. Beard and American Foreign Policy* (Gainesville, Florida, 1975), p. 29; Allen Davis, *American Heroine: The Life and Legend of*

Jane Addams (New York, 1973), p. 212; H. Wayne Morgan, *Eugene V. Debs: Socialist for President* (Syracuse, 1962), p. 148.

6. Elliot Skinner, *African Americans and U.S. Policy Toward Africa, 1850–1924* (Washington, 1992), pp. 385–86.

7. Carl Resek, ed., *War and the Intellectuals: Essays by Randolph S. Bourne, 1915–1919* (New York, 1964), p. x; Francine Curro Cary, *The Influence of War on Walter Lippmann, 1914–1944* (Madison, Wisconsin, 1967), p. vii; Thomas Knock, *To End All Wars: Woodrow Wilson and the Quest for a New World Order* (New York, 1992), pp. 13, 64.

8. Sondra Herman, *Eleven Against War* (Stanford, 1969), p. 140; Allen Davis, *American Heroine*, pp. 136–38, 214, 240; Knock, *To End All Wars*, pp. 51, 82–83.

9. John Chambers, *The Eagle and the Dove: The American Peace Movement and United States Foreign Policy, 1900–1922* (Syracuse, 1991), p. li; Paolo Coletta, *The Presidency of William Howard Taft* (Lawrence, Kansas, 1973), p. 173; Walter Scholes and Marie Scholes, *The Foreign Policies of the Taft Administration* (Columbia, Missouri, 1970), p. 27.

10. Robert Dallek, *The American Style of Foreign Policy: Cultural and Foreign Affairs* (New York, 1983), p. 84; Richard Hofstadter, *The American Political Tradition* (New York, 1957), pp. 271.

11. Edward House was not a military officer. His title of colonel was honorific.

12. Brian Bond, *War and Society in Europe, 1870–1970* (New York, 1986), p. 114.

13. Richard Challener, *Admirals, Generals, and American Foreign Policy, 1898–1914* (Princeton, 1973), pp. 29, 405; Thomas Schoonover, "Europe, the Spanish-American War and Great Power Activity in the Caribbean and Asia," *SHAFR Newsletter*, p. 17.

14. Knock, *To End All Wars*, pp. 116–17. Foreign Minister Arthur Zimmermann had instructed his ambassador in Mexico to approach his hosts about the following: In the event of German-American fighting, Mexico should declare war on the United States. Mexico's reward would be German support for return of the "lost provinces" of New Mexico, Arizona, and Texas. British intelligence gave a copy of the intercepted telegram to the American ambassador in London, Walter Hines Page. After resolving doubts about its authenticity, Wilson allowed the State Department to make the telegram's contents public.

15. Knock, *To End All Wars*, p. 118; Arthur Link, *Woodrow Wilson: Revolution, War, and Peace* (New York, 1979), p. 85.

16. Rankin, the first woman elected to Congress, also voted against war in December 1941. This Montana pacifist served in Congress in 1917–1919 and 1941–1942. She later organized against the Vietnam War. She led the Rankin Brigade of feminists and pacifists to demonstrate in Washington in 1968.

17. The Fourteen Points provided for the following:

(1) open covenants, openly arrived at; (2) freedom of navigation upon the seas; (3) removal, so far as possible, of all economic barriers; (4) reduction of national armaments; (5) impartial adjustment of colonial claims; (6) evacuation of foreign troops from Russia; (7) restoration of Belgian sover-

eignty; (8) Alsace-Lorraine returned to France, plus the evacuation of German forces from northern France; (9) an adjustment of Italy's frontiers along lines of nationality; (10) autonomous development for the peoples of Austria-Hungary; (11) application of the self-determination principle to the Balkan states; (12) autonomy and safety for the non-Turkish parts of the Ottoman Empire; (13) an independent Poland; (14) an association of nations to guarantee the safety and independence of all states.

18. Marian McKenna, *Borah* (Ann Arbor, 1961), pp. 143, 145.

19. Jane Addams, *Peace and Bread in Time of War* (New York, 1945), p. 71; Davis, *American Heroine,* pp. 245–46; John Chambers, *The Eagle and the Dove,* p. lxi.

20. Knock, *To End All Wars,* pp. 133, 135; Kennedy, *Charles A. Beard,* p. 37.

21. The experience of World War also affected Americans. In 1919, a year after Oswald Spengler published his *Decline of the West,* Senator Henry Cabot Lodge told a friend: "We were all of us in our youth more or less under the spell of the 19th century doctrines that we were in continual evolution, always moving on to something better with perfection as the goal; now it is all over . . . the great war and its legacies, the mental and emotional condition known as pessimism [are] rising up, looking us in the eye and calling upon us to face the hard facts of history and of the world about us." See William Widenor's *Henry Cabot Lodge and the Search for an American Foreign Policy* (Berkeley, 1980), p. 352.

22. Lloyd Gardner, *Safe for Democracy: The Anglo-American Response to Revolution, 1913–1923* (New York, 1987), p. 242.

23. Knock, *To End All Wars,* pp. 112, 138.

24. The Inquiry's primary mission was to compose reports and make recommendations to the administration as it prepared for the Paris peace conference. The Inquiry—organized by Colonel House—consisted of historians, geographers, economists, and other specialists, numbering more than 125. Lippmann became its general secretary. See Lawrence Gelfand's *The Inquiry: American Preparations for Peace, 1917–1919* (New Haven, 1963); Ronald Steel's *Walter Lippmann and the American Century* (Boston, 1980), pp. 134–37; Harold Nicolson's *Peacemaking 1919* (New York, 1965), pp. 8, 223.

25. George Kennan, *Russia and the West Under Lenin and Stalin* (Boston, 1960), pp. 100–2.

26. Wilson made this pronouncement about U.S. diplomats in 1913—a judgment he never revised:

> We find that those who have been occupying the legations and embassies have been habituated to a point of view which is very different, indeed, from the point of view of the present administration. They have had the material interests of individuals in the United Sates very much more in mind than the moral and public considerations which it seems to us ought to control. They have been so bred in a different school that we have found, in several instances, that it was difficult for them to comprehend our point of view and purpose.

> Cited in Arthur Link, *Wilson the Diplomatist: A Look at His Major Foreign Policies* (Baltimore, 1957), pp. 24–25.

27. Nicolson, *Peacemaking*, p. 15. The tension between Wilson and House centered on the latter's greater willingness to make concessions on territory and reparations to the Allies. The decisive point in relations between the two men was reached when House—during Wilson's absence from Paris in February 1919 to visit Washington—defied the president's instructions and accepted French plans to occupy the Rhine's left bank and to separate the League covenant from the preliminary treaty with Germany. Wilson never recovered confidence in House. And House's influence on the president steadily diminished thereafter. See August Heckscher, *Woodrow Wilson* (New York, 1991), pp. 545–47 and Charles Neu's "Edward Mandell House" in Cathal Nolan, ed., *Notable U.S. Ambassadors since 1775* (Westport, Connecticut, 1997), p. 174.

28. Sigmund Freud's "Introduction" in Freud and William Bullitt, *Thomas Woodrow Wilson: A Psychological Study* (Boston, 1966), p. xii.

29. August Heckscher, *Woodrow Wilson*, p. 510.

30. Nicolson, *Peacemaking*, pp. 58, 199–200.

31. The text of Article 10 reads as follows: "The Members of the League undertake to respect and preserve as against external aggression the territorial integrity and existing political independence of all Members of the League. In case of any such aggression or in case of any threat or danger of such aggression the Council shall advise upon the means by which this obligation shall be fulfilled." J. A. S. Grenville, ed., *The Major International Treaties, 1914–1973: A History and Guide with Texts* (London, 1974), p. 60.

32. August Heckscher, *Woodrow Wilson*, p. 521; Samuel Eliot Morison, *The Oxford History of the American People* (New York, 1965), p. 879.

33. Dorothy Jones, *Code of Peace: Ethics and Security in the World of the Warlord States* (Chicago, 1991), pp. 22–23.

34. The decision made by peacemakers in Paris to let Japan retain former German concessions in Shandong sparked off the May Fourth Movement in China. This nationwide protest and reform agenda embraced university students, merchants, and writers against foreign imperialism (especially Japanese). Before concluding that violent revolution was the only cure for China's ills, Mao Zedong had been a disciple of the May Fourth Movement. See John King Fairbank, *China: A New History* (Cambridge, Mass., 1992), pp. 267–69, 276.

35. D. Steven Blum, *Walter Lippmann: Cosmopolitan in the Century of Total War* (Ithaca, 1984), p. 134; Nicolson, *Peacemaking*, p. 35; David Lodge, "The Lives of Graham Greene," *The New York Review of Books*, June 22, 1995, p. 25; David Stevenson, *The First World War and International Politics* (Oxford, 1988), p. 317.

36. Adam Ulam, *Expansion and Coexistence: Soviet Foreign Policy, 1917–73* (New York, 1974), p. 86.

37. Elliott Skinner, *African Americans and U.S. Policy Toward Africa*, pp. 393–95, 398, 404, 408; David Levering Lewis, *W. E. B. Du Bois: Biography of a Race, 1868–1919* (New York, 1993), pp. 561, 564, 569, 578.

38. Herman, *Eleven Against War*, p. 139; Violet Oakley, *Cathedral of Compassion: Dramatic Outline of the Life of Jane Addams, 1860–1935* (Philadelphia, 1935), p. 81; Davis, *American Heroine*, pp. 255, 258–60.

39. Gordon Craig, *Germany, 1866–1945* (New York, 1978), pp. 396–433; Hajo Holborn, *A History of Modern Germany, 1840–1945* (New York, 1969), pp. 533–629.

40. An account of Wilson's medical decline in 1919 is found in Edwin Weinstein, *Woodrow Wilson: A Medical and Psychological Biography* (Princeton, 1981), pp. 333–70.

41. Lodge's fourteen reservations touched on a number of issues, the main ones being who determined whether international obligations were fulfilled; Congress's war-making authority; Congress's attitude toward the League of Nations mandate system; the inviolability of U.S. domestic jurisdiction; the primacy of the Monroe Doctrine; disapproval of the Shandong arrangement; Congress's role in appointing U.S. representatives to the League; Congress's authorization of funds spent by the United States in support of the League; retention by Washington of the right to determine the level of spending on armaments in times of danger.

42. The notion that Lodge's reservations about Versailles and the League sprang primarily from animus against Wilson is challenged by William Widenor in *Henry Cabot Lodge.* Widenor stresses Lodge's pessimistic philosophy of international relations as the important point against Wilson.

43. Knock, *To End All Wars*, p. 124; William Borah, "The Case for Non-Entanglement" in Robert Goldwin and Harry Clor, eds., *Readings in American Foreign Policy* (New York, 1971), pp. 412–22.

44. Marian McKenna, *Borah*, p. 165.

45. Knock, *To End All Wars*, pp. 253–54, 257.

46. Widenor, *Henry Cabot Lodge*, pp. 164, 353.

47. Ernest May, *Lessons of the Past: The Use and Misuse of History in American Foreign Policy* (New York, 1973), p. 10; Dexter Perkins, "Woodrow Wilson's Tour" in Daniel Aaron, ed., *America in Crisis* (New York, 1952), p. 249; Donald Kagan, *On the Origins of War and the Preservation of Peace*, p. 440.

48. Lest I be misunderstood, I am not suggesting that twentieth-century intellectuals engaged in politics always meet a bad end. That would be too foolish. Some intellectuals have been exhilarated by the exercise of power, such as Henry Kissinger. Some have won glory in the context of world events, such as the renowned medievalist Marc Bloch, who fought as a soldier in World War I and died as a member of the Resistance in 1944. His last words before a German firing squad were "Vive la France." See Marc Bloch, *Memoirs of War, 1914–1915*, ed. Carole Fink (New York, 1988), p. 64.

49. Kant wrote in his *Perpetual Peace:* "The possession of power inevitably corrupts the free judgment of reason." See Hans Reiss, ed., *Kant: The Political Writings* (Cambridge, England, 1991), p. 115.

On the dilemmas faced by intellectuals in power, see James Joll's *Three Intellectuals in Politics* (New York, 1960).

50. E. H. Carr characterized Woodrow Wilson as "the most perfect modern example of the intellectual in politics." See Carr's *The Twenty Years' Crisis, 1919–1939* (New York, 1946), p. 14.

51. Dalton Trumbo, *Johnny Got His Gun* (1939; Toronto, 1970), p. 24.

52. One twentieth-century female survivor of persecution is the Burmese Nobel laureate Daw Aung San Suu Kyi. Shortly before the Fourth World Conference on Women was held (September 1995), she declared: "For millennia women have dedicated themselves almost exclusively to the task of nurturing, protecting, and caring for the young and old, striving for the conditions of peace that favor life as a whole. . . . It is time to apply in the arena of the world the wisdom and experience that women have gained." See *New York Times,* September 1, 1995.

    The political scientist J. Anne Tickner has asserted: "A world that is more secure for us all cannot be achieved until the oppressive gender hierarchies that operate to frame the way in which we think about and engage in international politics are dismantled. . . . [A] nongendered perspective could truly offer us a more inclusively human way of thinking about our collective future, a future in which women and men could share equally in the construction of a safer and more just world." See Tickner's *Gender in International Relations: Feminist Perspectives on Achieving Global Security* (New York, 1992), pp. 24–25.

53. It is helpful here to recall Kant's confidence in an organized peace, nowhere more eloquently stated than in his "Idea for a Universal History." He wrote:

> Wars, tense and unremitting military preparations, and the resultant distress which every state must feel within itself, even in the midst of peace—these are the means by which nature drives nations to make initially imperfect attempts, but finally, after many devastations, upheavals and even complete inner exhaustion of their powers, to take the step which reason could have suggested to them without so many sad experiences—that of abandoning a lawless state of savagery and entering a federation of peoples in which every state, even the smallest, could expect to derive its security and rights not from its own power or its own legal judgment, but solely from this great federation, from a united power and the law-governed decisions of a united will.

    Cited in Reiss, ed., *Kant: The Political Writings,* p. 47.

54. Michael Doyle, *Ways of War and Peace: Realism, Liberalism, and Socialism* (New York, 1997), pp. 251–300; Hedley Bull, *The Anarchical Society: A Study of Order in World Politics* (London, 1977), pp. 110, 244, 262.

55. See Bruce Russett, ed., *Grasping the Democratic Peace: Principles for a Post–Cold War World* (Princeton, 1993); Edward Mansfield and Jack Snyder, "Democratization and War," *Foreign Affairs,* May/June 1995; David Hendrickson, "The Recovery of Internationalism: Salvaging Clinton's Foreign Policy," *Foreign Affairs,* September/October 1994.

56. Skinner, *African Americans and U.S. Policy,* p. 389; Lewis, *W. E. B. Du Bois,* pp. 537, 579.

57. Henry Ford authorized his Dearborn newspaper to reprint the *Protocols of the Elders of Zion*. He published his own execrable book, *The International Jew*, in 1920.

58. John Stoessinger, *Crusaders and Pragmatists: Movers of Modern American Foreign Policy* (New York, 1979), pp. 19–20; Richard Hofstadter, *The American Political Tradition*, p. 279.

59. Ronald Schaffer, *America in the Great War: The Rise of the War Welfare State* (New York, 1991), p. 112.

60. Resek, ed., *Randolph S. Bourne*, p. 64.

Chapter 4

1. Willy Brandt, *People and Politics: The Years 1960–1975* (Boston, 1976), p. 457; Terence Prittie, *Willy Brandt: Portrait of a Statesman* (New York, 1974), p. 254; Hermann Otto Bolesch and Hans Dieter Leicht, *Willy Brandt: A Portrait of the German Chancellor* (Tubingen, Germany, 1971), p. 75.

2. Karl Jaspers, *The Question of German Guilt* (New York, 1947), pp. 22, 61, 71–72, 90, 97; Günter Grass, *Two States—One Nation?* (San Diego, 1990), p. 99.

3. Willy Brandt, *In Exile: Essays, Reflections and Letters 1933–1947* (London, 1971), p. 53; Dietrich Bonhoeffer, *Ethics* (New York, 1955), pp. 90, 102;

4. Elie Wiesel, *Night* (New York, 1960), p. 79; Stefan Zweig, *The World of Yesterday* (New York, 1943), p. 9; Gordon Wright, *The Ordeal of Total War, 1939–1945* (New York, 1968), p. 263.

5. Hans Kung declared: "After Auschwitz there can be no more excuses. Christendom cannot avoid a clear admission of its guilt." See his *On Being a Christian* (New York, 1976), pp. 168–70; See Mauriac's preface in Wiesel's *Night*, p. 7; Grass, *Two States—One Nation?*, p. 99.

6. "Internationalism of suffering" is taken from Guy Sajer, who served as an enlisted German soldier on the eastern front. He wrote in his war memoir that "pain is international." See Sajer, *The Forgotten Soldier* (Washington, 1990), p. 465.

7. By "predictable" I do not mean inevitable. There was nothing automatic about victory against Japan or Germany—surely not in 1942—despite Allied advantage in resources and manpower. See Richard Overy, *Why the Allies Won* (New York, 1996). On the intensity of war between Japan and the United States, see John Dower's *War Without Mercy: Race and Power in the Pacific War* (New York, 1986).

8. D. Clayton James, "American and Japanese Strategies in the Pacific War" in Peter Paret, ed., *Makers of Modern Strategy from Machiavelli to the Nuclear Age* (Princeton, 1986), p. 720; Winston Churchill, *Triumph and Tragedy* (Boston, 1953), p. 545; Gandhi, "The Atom Bomb, America and Japan" in John Vasquez, ed., *Classics of International Relations* (Englewood Cliffs, New Jersey, 1990), p. 50.

9. Michael Walzer, *Just and Unjust Wars: A Moral Argument with Historical Illustrations* (New York, 1977), pp. xvi, 332; Studs Terkel, *The Good War: An Oral*

History of World War Two (New York, 1984), p. vi; Robert Schulzinger, *American Diplomacy in the Twentieth Century* (New York, 1990), p. 191.

10. Rochelle Chadakoff, ed., *Eleanor Roosevelt's My Day* (New York, 1989), p. 389. President Roosevelt died on April 12, 1945—before the scheduled date of his speech. It was released to the newspapers before his funeral on April 14.

11. David Fromkin represents critical-minded historians in his endorsement of FDR, who in 1940 "made up his mind to throw isolationism overboard . . . to set about saving the world." See Fromkin, *In the Time of the Americans: The Generation that Changed America's Role in the World* (New York, 1995), p. 551. See David Long and Peter Colin, *Thinkers of the Twenty Years' Crisis: Inter-War Idealism Reassessed* (New York, 1995), for an evaluation of interwar internationalist thought. Much of it has been disparaged by self-styled realists, beginning with E. H. Carr in his *The Twenty Years' Crisis, 1919–1939* (New York, 1946).

12. Jacqueline Van Voris, *Carrie Chapman Catt: A Public Life* (New York, 1987), pp. 187, 197–98, 206–7; Robert Booth Fowler, *Carrie Catt: Feminist Politician* (Boston, 1986), pp. 35–36.

13. Harold Josephson, *James T. Shotwell and the Rise of Internationalism in America* (Rutherford, New Jersey, 1975), pp. 175, 177, 234–36.

14. Robert Dallek, *Franklin D. Roosevelt and American Foreign Policy, 1932–1945* (New York, 1979), pp. 176–77; James Shotwell, *Autobiography* (Indianapolis, 1961), pp. 296–97.

15. See Robert Conquest, *The Harvest of Sorrow: Soviet Collectivization and the Terror-Famine* (New York, 1986); David Mayers, *The Ambassadors and America's Soviet Policy* (New York, 1995), chapter 4.

16. Igor Lukes, *Czechoslovakia between Stalin and Hitler: The Diplomacy of Edvard Benes in the 1930s* (New York, 1996), pp. 174–79, 225–29.

17. For a review of the Soviet side of responsibility for the Molotov-Ribbentrop pact, see Geoffrey Roberts's *The Unholy Alliance: Stalin's Pact with Hitler* (Bloomington, 1989).

18. Dallek, *Franklin Roosevelt and American Foreign Policy*, pp. 85, 285.

19. Thomas Paterson, ed., *Major Problems in American Foreign Policy: Since 1914* (Lexington, Mass., 1989), p. 167.

20. Schulzinger, *American Diplomacy in the Twentieth Century*, p. 132; Charles Beard, "Giddy Minds and Foreign Quarrels" in Robert Goldwin and Harry Clor, eds., *Readings in American Foreign Policy* (New York, 1971), p. 133.

21. Harry Ashmore, *Unseasonable Truths: The Life of Robert Maynard Hutchins* (Boston, 1989), p. 216.

22. Chadakoff, ed., *Eleanor Roosevelt's My Day*, pp. 130, 159–60; Richard Fox, *Reinhold Niebuhr: A Biography* (New York, 1985), p. 194; Voris, *Catt*, pp. 174, 215.

23. See Charles Beard's *President Roosevelt and the Coming of the War, 1941: A Study in Appearances and Realities* (New Haven, 1948); Arnold Offner, "Misperception and Reality: Roosevelt, Hitler, and the Search for a New Order in Europe," *Diplomatic History*, Fall 1991, p. 613; Dallek, *Franklin Roosevelt and American Foreign Policy*, p. 129; Ashmore, *Unseasonable Truths,* p. 211.

24. Fox, *Reinhold Niebuhr*, p. 199; Reinhold Niebuhr, *Christianity and Power Politics* (New York, 1940), p. 47.

25. Whether imaginative diplomacy in 1941 could have averted a Japanese-American war remains an open question. There were diplomats on both sides who worked hard for such an end, notably Ambassador Joseph Grew posted in Tokyo and Ambassador Kichisaburo Nomura assigned to Washington. The latter, however, was not deeply influential with such avowed expansionists as Foreign Minister Yosuke Matsuoka. As for the Americans, they would have preferred continued negotiations and peace in the Pacific, allowing the United States to concentrate maximum power against Germany. See Waldo Heinrichs's two books: *Threshold of War: Franklin D. Roosevelt and American Entry into World War II* (New York, 1988) and *American Ambassador: Joseph C. Grew and the Development of the United States Diplomatic Tradition* (New York, 1966). Also see Arthur Waldron, ed., *How the Peace Was Lost* (Stanford, 1992).

26. Mark Mazower, "Hitler's New Order, 1939–45," *Diplomacy and Statecraft*, March 1996, pp. 30–31, 34, 36, 38.

27. Peter Duus, "Imperialism Without Colonies: The Vision of a Greater East Asia Co-Prosperity Sphere," *Diplomacy and Statecraft*, March 1996, pp. 62–65, 70.

28. An account in English of Japanese misdeeds in China is Iris Chang's *The Rape of Nanking: The Forgotten Holocaust of World War II* (New York, 1997). Torture or outright executions accounted for the deaths of 300,000 civilians and surrendered Chinese soldiers in Nanjing during late 1937 through early 1938.

29. Nicholas Cull, "Selling Peace: The Origins, Promotion and Fate of the Anglo-American New Order During the Second World War," *Diplomacy and Statecraft*, March, 1996, p. 3.

30. Not all scholarship agrees with my characterization of British aims and policy. John Charmley, for example, is critical of Churchill and charges him with abject accommodation to FDR's wishes. This misconceived policy smoothed the way, argues Charmley, for America's superpower status and Britain's decline. See Charmley, *Churchill's Grand Alliance: The Anglo-American Special Relationship, 1940–1957* (New York, 1995). On the Soviet Union's ideological goals, see Geoffrey Swain, "Stalin's Wartime Vision of the Postwar World," *Diplomacy and Statecraft*, March 1996, pp. 73–74, 94; Vladimir Pechatnov, "The Big Three After World War II: New Documents on Soviet Thinking about Post War Relations with the United States and Great Britain," Cold War International History Project, *Working Paper No. 13*, Woodrow Wilson Center, (Washington, July 1995), p. 2.

31. The Atlantic Charter's reference to freedom from fear and want came from FDR's speech to Congress, January 6, 1941; the other two freedoms were freedom of worship and speech.

32. Ernest May, *Lessons of the Past: The Use and Misuse of History in American Foreign Policy* (New York, 1973), p. 12; Lloyd Gardner, *Architects of Illusion: Men and Ideas in American Foreign Policy, 1941–1949* (Chicago, 1970), p. 52; Michael Sherry, *In the Shadow of War: The United States Since the 1930s* (New Haven, 1995), p. 72; Dallek, *Franklin Roosevelt and American Foreign Policy*, p.

439; Gerhard Weinberg, *A World at Arms: A Global History of World War II* (Cambridge, England, 1994), p. 829; Warren Kimball, *The Juggler: Franklin Roosevelt as Wartime Statesman* (Princeton, 1991), pp. 85, 103.

33. On the world federalists see: Grenville Clark and Louis Sohn, *Introduction to World Peace through World Law* (Cambridge, Mass., 1973); Jon Yoder, "The United World Federalists: Liberals for Law and Order" in Charles Chatfield, ed., *Peace Movements in America* (New York, 1973); Charles DeBenedetti, *The Peace Reform in American History* (Bloomington, 1980), pp. 149–51.

34. Dallek, *Franklin Roosevelt and American Foreign Policy,* p. 421; Sumner Welles, *The World of the Four Freedoms* (New York, 1943), p. 102; John Morton Blum, ed., *The Price of Vision: The Diary of Henry A. Wallace, 1942–1946* (Boston, 1973), pp. 25–26, 31, 36; Henry Wallace, *The Century of the Common Man* (New York, 1943), pp. 36, 40; Henry Wallace, *Democracy Reborn* (New York, 1944), pp. 74–75; Edward Schapsmeier and Frederick Schapsmeier, *Prophet In Politics: Henry A. Wallace and the War Years, 1940–1945* (Ames, Iowa, 1970), pp. 26, 35–36, 75, 88–89. For a full treatment of Wallace's career, see Graham White and John Maze, *Henry A. Wallace: His Search for a New World Order* (Chapel Hill, 1995).

35. Chester Bowles, *Promises to Keep: My Years in Public Life, 1941–1969* (New York, 1971), p. 156; Chadakoff, ed., *Eleanor Roosevelt's My Day,* pp. 137, 348–49; Fowler, *Carrie Catt,* p. 34; Josephson, *James T. Shotwell,* p. 241.

36. Wendell Willkie, *One World* (New York, 1943), p. 206.

37. Herbert Agar et al., *The City of Man: A Declaration on World Democracy* (New York, 1941), p. 47; Ronald Steel, *Walter Lippmann and the American Century* (Boston, 1980), p. 404; Fox, *Reinhold Niebuhr,* pp. 202, 213, 219, 223; Reinhold Niebuhr, *The Children of Light and the Children of Darkness* (New York, 1945), pp. 160–61, 178, 181, 185.

38. Edward Schapsmeier and Frederick Schapsmeier, *Prophet in Politics,* p. 55; Steel, *Walter Lippmann,* pp. 405–7, 409–10.

39. David Mayers, *George Kennan and the Dilemmas of U.S. Foreign Policy* (New York, 1988), p. 96; Patterson, *Mr. Republican,* pp. 290–91; Steel, *Walter Lippmann,* pp. 404, 410.

40. Nearly 40 percent of Americans polled in 1945 felt that their country would become involved in another world war in fewer than twenty-five years. See Dallek, *Franklin Roosevelt and American Foreign Policy,* p. 522.

41. Melvyn Leffler, *A Preponderance of Power: National Security, the Truman Administration, and the Cold War* (Stanford, 1992), p. 2; Sherry, *In the Shadows of War,* pp. 48, 89–92, 109; Frances Perkins, *The Roosevelt I Knew* (New York, 1946), pp. 368–69; Dallek, *Franklin Roosevelt and American Foreign Policy,* pp. 220, 373, 443–44; Forrest Pogue, *George C. Marshall: Statesman, 1945–1959* (New York, 1987), p. 6.

42. Japanese Canadians were also badly dealt with by their government. They numbered 23,000. They mostly lived along the coast of British Columbia; they were forcibly moved inland. See K. Adachi, *The Enemy That Never Was: A History of the Japanese Canadians* (Toronto, 1976).

The worst treatment of suspect minorities during World War II occurred in the Soviet Union. Approximately 3.5 million people from many nationalities were deported to the east. Fatalities were high. One-quarter of the people deported may have died en route. Crimean Tartars, Volga Germans, Chechens, Turks, Greeks, and Bulgarians were among the displaced. See Norman Davies and Martin McCauley, "Deportations" in I. C. B. Dear and M. R. D. Foot, eds., *The Oxford Companion to World War II* (Oxford, 1995), pp. 295–96.

43. Patterson, *Mr. Republican,* p. 216; Steel, *Walter Lippmann,* p. 395; Chadakoff, ed., *Eleanor Roosevelt's My Day,* p. 172; Blum, ed., *The Price of Vision,* p. 32; Edward Schapsmeier and Frederick Schapsmeier, *Prophet in Politics,* p. 52; Sherry, *In the Shadows of War,* p. 67, 98; Dallek, *Franklin Roosevelt and American Foreign Policy,* pp. 227, 289–90; Bruce Porter, *War and the Rise of the State: The Military Foundations of Modern Politics* (New York, 1994), pp. 284–85.

44. Chadakoff, ed., *Eleanor Roosevelt's My Day,* pp. 292–93.

45. Neil Wynn, *The Afro-American and the Second World War* (New York, 1993), pp. 30, 33, 36, 134; Porter, *War and the Rise of State,* p. 285; Henry Stimson and McGeorge Bundy, *On Active Service in Peace and War* (New York, 1947), pp. 461–64; Walter White, *A Man Called White: The Autobiography of Walter White* (New York, 1948), pp. 242–52, 293.

46. Adam Clayton Powell, Jr., *Adam by Adam: The Autobiography* (New York, 1971), p. 71.

47. White, *A Man Called White,* p. 187; Charles Hamilton, *Adam Clayton Powell, Jr.: The Political Biography of an American Dilemma* (New York, 1991), pp. 118, 120, 134; Powell, *Adam by Adam,* p. 81.

48. Chadakoff, ed., *Eleanor Roosevelt's My Day,* p. 299; Joseph Lash, *Eleanor and Franklin: The Story of Their Relationship, Based on Eleanor Roosevelt's Private Papers* (New York, 1971), p. 684; Welles, *The World of the Four Freedoms,* p. 75; Willkie, *One World,* pp. 188, 190–92, 195; Blum, *The Diary of Henry A. Wallace,* p. 21; Wallace, *Democracy Reborn,* p. 260.

49. Gunnar Myrdal, *An American Dilemma: The Negro Problem and Modern Democracy* (New York, 1944), p. 997; Wynn, *The Afro-American and the Second World War,* pp. 68, 131–33, 141; Sherry, *In the Shadow of War,* pp. 94, 102, 108; Weinberg, *A World at Arms,* p. 495; Porter, *War and the Rise of the State,* p. 285; Powell, *Adam by Adam,* p. 79; White, *A Man Called White,* pp. 260–61.

50. See Winston Churchill's magisterial—if not wholly reliable as history—*The Grand Alliance* (Boston, 1950); George Kennan, *American Diplomacy, 1900–1950* (Chicago, 1951), pp. 85–86; Churchill spoke of "the natural contrariness" of allies. See Dallek, *Franklin D. Roosevelt and American Foreign Policy,* p. 393; W. Averell Harriman and Elie Abel, *Special Envoy to Churchill and Stalin, 1941–1946* (New York, 1975), pp. 264–69; Maurice Matloff's "Allied Strategy in Europe, 1939–1945" in Paret, ed., *Makers of Modern Strategy,* p. 689; Leffler, *A Preponderance of Power,* p. 2. For a comprehensive treatment of Anglo-U.S. wartime relations, consult Warren Kimball, ed., *Churchill and Roosevelt: The Complete Correspondence* 3 vols. (Princeton, 1984), and Warren

Kimball, *Forged in War: Roosevelt, Churchill, and the Second World War* (New York, 1997).

51. John Stoessinger, *Crusaders and Pragmatists: Movers of Modern American Foreign Policy* (New York, 1979), p. 43.

52. David Holloway, *Stalin and the Bomb: The Soviet Union and Atomic Energy, 1953–1956* (New Haven, 1994), pp. 105–8, 222–23.

53. C. L. Sulzberger, *A Long Row of Candles: Memoirs and Diaries, 1934–1954* (Toronto, 1969), p. 307.

54. Bernard Brodie, *War and Politics* (New York, 1973), p. 49; Michael Schaller, *The American Occupation of Japan: The Origins of the Cold War in Asia* (New York, 1985), p. 4. Morgenthau expected that "when the majority of the German people are small farmers, they will be a bit less susceptible to the lure of militarism." See his *Germany Is Our Problem* (New York, 1945), p. 146.

55. Patterson, *Mr. Republican,* p. 50; John F. Kennedy, *Profiles in Courage* (New York, 1956), pp. 190–92; Ashmore, *Unseasonable Truths,* pp. 250–51.

56. A thoughtful American view on Nuremberg is found in Telford Taylor's *The Anatomy of the Nuremberg Trials* (New York, 1992).

57. See "First Hague Trial For Bosnia Crimes Opens On Tuesday," *New York Times,* May 6, 1996.

58. By this same reasoning, Daniel Jonah Goldhagen's indictment of the German nation in the murder of Jews is too sweeping. Goldhagen does not seriously acknowledge gradations of responsibility or shadings of traditional German attitude toward Jewry, ranging from acceptance to mild distaste to exterminating Nazi fervor. See his fascinating but ultimately unconvincing *Hitler's Willing Executioners: Ordinary Germans and the Holocaust* (New York, 1996).

59. Mayers, *George Kennan and the Dilemmas of U.S. Foreign Policy,* p. 84; Grass, *Two States—One Nation?,* p. 96; Jaspers, *The Question of German Guilt,* pp. 59–60; Brandt, *In Exile,* p. 130.

   The International Military Tribunal for the Far East met in Tokyo in May 1946-November 1948. It was considerably less satisfactory than Nuremberg from the standpoint of setting legal precedent. See C. Hosoya, N. Ando, Y. Onuma, and R. H. Minear, eds., *The Tokyo War Crimes Trial: An International Symposium* (New York, 1986).

60. Grass, *Two States—One Nation?,* p. 96.

61. Arnold Offner, "Roosevelt, Hitler, and the Search for a New Order in Europe," *Diplomatic History,* Fall 1991, pp. 615–16; Fox, *Reinhold Niebuhr,* pp. 200–1; Chadakoff, ed., *Eleanor Roosevelt's My Day,* p. 344; Voris, *Carrie Chapman Catt,* p. 214; David Wyman, *The Abandonment of the Jews: America and the Holocaust, 1941–1945* (New York, 1985), pp. xiv-xv. Also see Fred Israel, ed., *The War Diary of Breckinridge Long: Selections from the Years 1939–1944* (Lincoln, Nebraska, 1966), pp. 128, 216–17, 225–26.

62. Standard fare for English literature classes in American high schools are Anne Frank's *Diary* and John Hersey's *Hiroshima.*

63. Elie Wiesel told Reagan shortly before his Bitburg visit with Chancellor Helmut Kohl: "That place, Mr. President, is not your place. Your place is with the

victims of the SS." See George Shultz, *Turmoil and Triumph: My Years as Secretary of State* (New York, 1993), p. 551. Also see "Plans for Market at Auschwitz Dropped," *New York Times,* March 26, 1996 and "French Far-Right Leader Convicted of Slighting Holocaust," *New York Times,* December 27, 1997. The right-wing leader referred to in the above *New York Times* article is Jean-Marie Le Pen, who was quoted: "If you take a book of 2,000 pages on [WW II], the concentration camps fill two pages and the gas chambers take up 10 to 12 lines. That's what you call a detail."

64. Even a small sample of scholarship on the use of the atomic bombs in August 1945 shows interpretive diversity. See, for example, Gar Alperovitz, *Atomic Diplomacy: Hiroshima and Potsdam* (New York, 1985); Bernard Brodie, *War and Politics (New York,* 1973); Herbert Feis, *The Atomic Bomb and the End of World War II* (Princeton, 1966); Gregg Herken, *The Winning Weapon: The Atomic Bomb in the Cold War, 1945–1950* (New York, 1980); Martin Sherwin, *A World Destroyed: The Atomic Bomb and the Grand Alliance* (New York, 1975); Barton Bernstein, "The Atomic Bombings Reconsidered," *Foreign Affairs,* January/February 1995; J. Samuel Walker, "The Decision to Use the Bomb," *Diplomatic History,* Winter 1990. J. Samuel Walker has produced an exceptionally balanced account in his *Prompt and Utter Destruction: Truman and the Use of Atomic Bombs Against Japan* (Chapel Hill, 1997).

65. Pogue, *George Marshall,* p. 22; Alonzo Hamby, *Man of the People: A Life of Harry S. Truman* (New York, 1995), pp. 331–37.

66. Bernstein, "The Atomic Bombings Reconsidered," p. 136.

67. Pogue, *George Marshall,* p. 17; Sherry, *In the Shadows of* War, pp. 114–15; Terkel, *The Good War,* p. 560; Arthur Schlesinger, Jr., "History as Therapy: A Dangerous Idea," *New York Times,* May 3, 1996.

68. G. John Ikenberry, "Creating Yesterday's New World Order: Keynesian 'New Thinking' and the Anglo-American Postwar Settlement" in Judith Goldstein and Robert Keohane, eds., *Ideas and Foreign Policy: Beliefs, Institutions, and Political Change* (Ithaca, 1993), pp. 57–58. Vojtech Mastny contrasts the West's "overwhelming material superiority" with the Soviet Union's less substantial assets at the end of World War II. See Mastny's *The Cold War and Soviet Insecurity: The Stalin Years* (New York, 1996), p. 29.

69. See Porter, *War and the Rise of the State,* pp. 279–83.

70. Seyom Brown, *International Relations in a Changing World: Toward a Theory of the World Polity* (Boulder, Colorado, 1992), p. 78.

71. Weinberg, *A World at Arms,* p. 894; Sherry, *In the Shadow of War,* pp. 114–15; Ashmore, *Unseasonable Truths,* pp. 249–50; Manfred Jonas, *Isolationism in America, 1935–1941* (Ithaca, 1966), p. 267.

72. Cited in Chadakoff, ed., *Eleanor Roosevelt's My Day,* p. 248.

73. Reinhold Niebuhr, *Christian Realism and Political Problems* (New York, 1953), p. 15; Niebuhr, *The Children of Light and the Children of Darkness,* pp. 163, 173, 189. Machiavelli wrote centuries ago "that we never try to escape one difficulty without running into another." *The Prince* (New York, 1964), p. 191, edited and translated by Mark Musa.

74. Heda Margolius Kovaly, Czech Jew and survivor of Auschwitz, wrote this about the war's ending and prospects: "The war ended the way a passage through a tunnel ends. From far away you could see the light ahead, a gleam that kept growing, and its brilliance seemed ever more dazzling to you huddled there in the dark the longer it took to reach it. But when at last the train burst out into the glorious sunshine, all you saw was a wasteland full of weeds and stones, and a heap of garbage." Kovaly, *Under a Cruel Star: A Life in Prague 1941–1968* (New York, 1989), p. 39.

Chapter 5

1. Richard Haass of the Brookings Institution has argued along such lines: "The Cold War was a relatively structured era of international relations dominated by two great powers and disciplined by nuclear weapons. Rules of the road developed governing competition that reduced the chance the two superpowers would find themselves in direct confrontation involving military forces of any sort. Most other states had their freedom of action circumscribed by their respective superpower patron." See Haass, *The Reluctant Sheriff: The United States After the Cold War* (New York, 1997), p. 1.

2. See Mearsheimer's "Back to the Future: Instability in Europe After the Cold War" in *International Security* (Summer 1990), reprinted in Foreign Affairs Agenda, *The New Shape of World Politics* (New York, 1997), p. 152. Mearsheimer wrote: "The West has an interest in maintaining peace in Europe. It therefore has an interest in maintaining the Cold War order, and hence has an interest in the continuation of the Cold War confrontation; developments that threaten to end it are dangerous. The Cold War antagonism could be continued at lower levels of East-West tension, but a complete end to the Cold War would create more problems than it would solve."

3. See John Lewis Gaddis, *The Long Peace: Inquiries into the History of the Cold War* (New York, 1987), pp. 215–45. George Bush declared in his 1992 State of the Union address that the United States won the Cold War through tenacity and God's grace (cited in *New York Times,* January 29, 1992). Henry Kissinger has also spoken glowingly of "America's victory in the Cold War," per his "The Foreign Service of the United States" April 15, 1996, attached to Press Notice of the American Academy of Diplomacy, April 22, 1996. Mikhail Gorbachev endorsed Richard Ned Lebow and Janice Gross Stein, *We All Lost the Cold War* (Princeton, 1994) with this comment: "It is a dangerous conclusion that the West won the Cold War. The argument that one side won the Cold War is mistaken. We all lost the Cold War, particularly the USA and USSR. We all won by ending it. That is the scientific conclusion." Anatoly Dobrynin, former Soviet ambassador to the United States, also claims that the Cold War produced neither victors nor vanquished. See his *In Confidence: Moscow's Ambassador to America's Six Cold War Presidents, 1962–1986* (New York, 1995), p. 639.

4. Korean and Vietnam war casualties are from Robert Famighetti, ed., *The World Almanac and Book of Facts 1996* (Mahwa, New Jersey, 1995); the 11 trillion dollars is from Greg Treverton cited in Michael Doyle, *Ways of War and Peace: Realism, Liberalism, and Socialism* (New York, 1997), p. 458.

5. Karl Jaspers, *The Future of Mankind* (Chicago, 1958), p. ix; William Faulkner, "Speech on Acceptance of the Nobel Prize," in Daniel Boorstin, ed., *An American Primer* (Chicago, 1966), p. 899; Reinhold Niebuhr, *The Irony of American History* (New York, 1952), p. 2; John Lewis Gaddis, "Morality and the American Experience in the Cold War" in Cathal Nolan ed., *Ethics and Statecraft: The Moral Dimension of International Affairs* (Westport, Connecticut, 1995), p. 174.

6. Soviet conduct in eastern Germany during the occupation years was severe. See Norman Naimark, *The Russians in Germany: A History of the Soviet Zone of Occupation, 1945–1949* (Cambridge, Mass., 1995).

7. It is worth recalling the observation by Britain's Lord Ismay: NATO was created to keep the Soviets out, the Germans down, and the Americans in Europe.

8. That the quality of Sino-Soviet-North Korean relations was more ambiguous than most people in the West appreciated in 1950 is shown in such post–Cold War scholarship as S. Goncharov, J. Lewis, and X. Litai, *Uncertain Partners: Stalin, Mao, and the Korean War* (Stanford, 1993).

9. The extent of Cuban danger in 1962 is nowhere better documented than in the book edited by Ernest May and Philip Zelikow, *The Kennedy Tapes: Inside the White House During the Cuban Missile Crisis* (Cambridge, Mass., 1997).

10. See John Lewis Gaddis, *We Now Know: Rethinking Cold War History* (Oxford, 1997); Anders Stephanson, "The United States" in David Reynolds, ed., *The Origins of the Cold War in Europe: International Perspectives* (New Haven, 1994); Michael Hogan, ed., *America in the World: The Historiography of American Foreign Relations Since 1941* (Cambridge, England, 1996); Melvyn Leffler, "Inside Enemy Archives: The Cold War Reopened," *Foreign Affairs,* July/August 1996; Vladislav Zubok and Constantine Pleshakov, *Inside the Kremlin's Cold War: From Stalin to Khrushchev* (Cambridge, Mass., 1996); "Symposium: Soviet Archives: Recent Revelations and Cold War Historiography," *Diplomatic History,* Spring 1997. The *Bulletin* of the Cold War International History Project published by the Woodrow Wilson Center for Scholars is an indispensable resource for new Cold War scholarship.

11. Thomas Paterson, ed., *Major Problems in American Foreign Policy,* Volume II: *Since 1914,* (Lexington, Mass., 1989), p. 298.

12. James Patterson, *Mr. Republican: A Biography of Robert A. Taft* (Boston, 1972), pp. 369–72; Ronald Steel, *Walter Lippmann and the American Century* (Boston, 1980), pp. 438–39, 578; David Mayers, *George Kennan and the Dilemmas of U.S. Foreign Policy* (New York, 1988), pp. 136–37.

13. Charles Bohlen, *The Transformation of American Foreign Policy* (New York, 1969), p. 55; Forrest Pogue, *George C. Marshall: Statesman* (New York, 1987), p. 167.

14. George Marshall, "The Marshall Plan," in Boorstin, ed., *An American Primer,* pp. 886–87.
15. George Kennan "X," "The Sources of Soviet Conduct," *Foreign Affairs,* July 1947, p. 582.
16. Michael Hunt, *Crises in U.S. Foreign Policy: An International History Reader* (New Haven, 1996), p. 163; Melvyn Leffler, *A Preponderance of Power: National Security, the Truman Administration, and the Cold War* (Stanford, 1992), p. 495.
17. See David Mayers's *Cracking the Monolith: U.S. Policy Against the Sino-Soviet Alliance, 1949–1955 (Baton Rouge, 1986)* and especially Thomas Christensen's excellent *Useful Adversaries: Grand Strategy, Domestic Mobilization, and Sino-American Conflict, 1947–1958* (Princeton, 1996).
18. Graham White and John Maze, *Henry A. Wallace: His Search for a New World Order* (Chapel Hill, 1995), pp. 233, 239, 257.
19. Ibid., pp. 219–22, 228, 246, 253, 262–64, 269; John Morton Blum, *The Price of Vision: The Diary of Henry A. Wallace, 1942–1946* (Boston, 1973), pp. 661–68; Edward Schapsmeier and Frederick Schapsmeier, *Prophet in Politics: Henry A. Wallace and the War Years, 1940–1945* (Ames, Iowa, 1970), pp. 189–91, 193; Richard Fox, *Reinhold Niebuhr: A Biography* (New York, 1985), 236.
20. Reinhold Niebuhr, *The Irony of American History,* pp. 146–47, 170; White and Maze, *Henry A. Wallace,* pp. 245–46, 250, 253, 255, 278–79; Frederick Schapsmeier and Edward Schapsmeier, *Prophet in Politics,* p. 195.
21. Charles Hamilton, *Adam Clayton Powell, Jr: The Political Biography of an American Dilemma* (New York, 1991), p. 190; Paul Robeson, *Here I Stand* (Boston, 1958), pp. 82–83; Dorothy Butler Gilliam, *Paul Robeson: All-American* (Washington, 1976), pp. 124, 137, 141, 158, 160; Martin B. Duberman, *Paul Robeson* (New York, 1988), pp. 342, 354, 358, 394, 406.
22. Stephen Ambrose, *Eisenhower: The President* (New York, 1984), p. 94.
23. Eisenhower and Wallace had some admiration for each other. See White and Maze, *Henry A. Wallace,* pp. 300–1.
24. *Foreign Relations of the United States, 1952–1954* (Washington, 1988), Vol. viii, pp. 1147–55.
25. Public Papers of the Presidents of the United States. *Dwight D. Eisenhower, 1960–1961* (Washington, 1961), pp. 1035–40.
26. Nat Hentoff, ed., *The Essays of A. J. Muste* (Indianapolis, 1967), p. 14.
27. Ibid., p. 392; Jo Ann Ooiman Robinson, *Abraham Went Out: A Biography of A. J. Muste* (Philadelphia, 1981), p. 185.
28. Sidney Hook, "A Foreign Policy For Survival," *The New Leader,* April 7, 1958, pp. 10–11.
29. See Bertrand Russell, "World Communism and Nuclear War," *The New Leader,* May 26, 1958; Sidney Hook, "A Free Man's Choice," *The New Leader,* May 26, 1958; Bertrand Russell, "Freedom to Survive," *The New Leader,* July 7–14, 1958; Sidney Hook, "Bertrand Russell Retreats," *The New Leader,* July 7–14, 1958; David Mayers, *George Kennan and the Dilemmas of U.S. Foreign Policy,* pp. 310–11.

30. Sidney Hook, comments in *Partisan Review,* Winter 1962, pp. 24–25.

31. Hook, "A Foreign Policy For Survival," pp. 9–10, 12.

32. Sidney Hook, *Out of Step: An Unquiet Life in the Twentieth Century* (New York, 1987), pp. 583–85; Norman Podhoretz, *Why We Were In Vietnam* (New York, 1982), p. 173.

33. Robert Dallek, *Lone Star Rising: Lyndon Johnson and His Times, 1908–1960* (New York, 1991), p. 4; Hunt, *Crises in U.S. Foreign Policy,* p. 312; Thomas Paterson, *Major Problems in American Foreign Policy: Since 1914,* p. 568.

34. Lyndon Baines Johnson, *The Vantage Point: Perspectives of the Presidency, 1963–1969* (New York, 1971), p. 136; Bruce Schulman, *Lyndon B. Johnson and American Liberalism: A Brief Biography with Documents* (Boston, 1995), p. 101.

35. Public Papers of the Presidents of the United States. *Lyndon B. Johnson, 1965* (Washington, 1966), p. 398.

36. George Herring, *America's Longest War: The United States and Vietnam, 1950–1975* (New York, 1986), p. 256; Henry Kissinger, *Years of Upheaval* (Boston, 1982), p. 372.

37. Larry Berman, *Planning a Tragedy: The Americanization of the War in Vietnam* (New York, 1982), pp. 79–129; George Ball, *The Past Has Another Pattern* (New York, 1982), pp. 366, 384–85, 400–2.

38. Greg Russell, *Hans J. Morgenthau and the Ethics of American Statecraft* (Baton Rouge, 1990), pp. 119, 200, 204–5; Hans Morgenthau, *Truth and Power: Essays of a Decade, 1960–1970* (New York, 1970), pp. 197, 398, 400, 407; Michael Hunt, *Crises in U.S. Foreign Policy,* 335–36; Richard Fox, *Reinhold Niebuhr: A Biography* (New York, 1985), pp. 283–90; David Mayers, *George Kennan and the Dilemmas of U.S. Foreign Policy,* pp. 282–87; Steel, *Walter Lippmann and the American Century,* pp. 487, 490, 541, 566, 571, 575, 577, 580, 586; Tom Engelhardt, *The End of Victory Culture: Cold War America and the Disillusioning of a Generation* (New York, 1995), p. 274.

39. See McNamara's reflections on the Vietnam War, *In Retrospect: The Tragedy and Lessons of Vietnam* (New York, 1995).

40. Mary McCarthy, *The Seventeenth Degree* (New York, 1974), p. 7; Abraham Feinberg, *Hanoi Diary* (Don Mills, Ontario, 1968), p. 66; Hannah Arendt, *Crises of the Republic,* (New York, 1972), p. 27.

41. Schulman, *Lyndon B. Johnson and American Liberalism,* p. 209; Robert Mullen, *Blacks and Vietnam* (Lanham, Maryland, 1981), pp. 63, 66; David Garrow, *Bearing the Cross: Martin Luther King, Jr., and the Southern Christian Leadership Conference* (New York, 1986), pp. 539, 546, 549, 555, 561, 572.

42. J. William Fulbright, *The Arrogance of Power* (New York, 1966), pp. 22, 134, 219; Robert Goldwin and Harry Clor, eds., *Readings in American Foreign Policy* (New York, 1971), p. 697.

43. Amalrik wrote that the Soviet leadership was incapable of implementing necessary reforms. Therefore, the country was bound for failure—sparked, perhaps, by a protracted war against China. See Amalrik's *Will the Soviet Union Survive Until 1984?* (New York, 1970).

44. Dobrynin, *In Confidence: Moscow's Ambassador to America's Six Cold War Presidents*, p. 193.

45. Raymond Garthoff, *Détente and Confrontation: American-Soviet Relations from Nixon to Reagan* (Washington, 1985), pp. 290–94; Robert Pranger, ed., *Détente and Defense: A Reader* (Washington, 1976), pp. 114–16.

46. Aleksandr Solzhenitsyn, *Détente: Prospects for Democracy and Dictatorship* (New Brunswick, New Jersey, 1980), p. 78; Strobe Talbott, *The Master of the Game: Paul Nitze and the Nuclear Peace* (New York, 1988), pp. 146–47.

47. Dobrynin, *In Confidence: Moscow's Ambassador to America's Six Cold War Presidents*, p. 513.

48. George Kennan, *The Nuclear Delusion: Soviet-American Relations in the Atomic Age* (New York, 1983), pp. 235–36; Helen Caldicott, *A Desperate Passion: An Autobiography* (New York, 1996), pp. 249–50, 354; Also see Robert Scheer, *With Enough Shovels: Reagan, Bush and Nuclear War* (New York, 1983) and Helen Caldicott, *Missile Envy: The Arms Race and Nuclear War* (New York, 1984).

49. Robin Marantz Henig, *The People's Health: A Memoir of Public Health and Its Evolution at Harvard* (Washington, 1997), pp. 114–18.

50. Author's conversation with Helmut Sonnenfeldt at Boston University on April 19, 1995.

51. See Kennan to State Department, February 22, 1946, *Foreign Relations of the United States: 1946* (Washington, 1969), Vol. VI, p. 709, and the last two paragraphs of Kennan's "The Sources of Soviet Conduct" in *Foreign Affairs,* July 1947.

52. Dean Acheson, *Present at the Creation: My Years in the State Department* (New York, 1969), p. 375. "The task of a public officer seeking to explain and gain support for a major policy is not that of the writer of a doctoral thesis. Qualification must give way to simplicity of statement, nicety and nuance to bluntness, almost brutality, in carrying home a point. If we made our points clearer than truth, we did not differ from most other educators and could hardly do otherwise."

53. Jeff Broadwater, "Ralph J. Bunche" in Cathal Nolan, ed., *Notable U.S. Ambassadors Since 1776* (Westport, Connecticut, 1997), p. 44; George Kennan, *At a Century's Ending: Reflections 1982–1995* (New York, 1996), p. 77.

54. Seyom Brown, *International Relations in a Changing Global System: Toward a Theory of the World Polity* (Boulder, Colorado, 1992), p. 78; Michael Walzer, *Just and Unjust Wars: A Moral Argument with Historical Illustrations* (New York, 1977) p. 281.

55. Bernard-Henri Levy, *Barbarism with a Human Face* (New York, 1979), p. ix.

56. Michael Sherry, *In the Shadow of War: The United States Since the 1930s* (New Haven, 1995), p. 146.

57. See Gregg Herken's study of U.S. foreign policy during the period of U.S. atomic monopoly, *The Winning Weapon: The Atomic Bomb in the Cold War, 1945–1950* (New York, 1982).

Chapter 6

1. Ronald Steel wrote: "During the Cold War we [Americans] had a vocation; now we have none . . . The world we knew has collapsed around us." See his *Temptations of a Superpower* (Cambridge, Mass., 1995), p. 1. Walter Mc-Dougall observed: "Americans today seem at a loss." See his "Back to Bedrock: The Eight Traditions of American Statecraft," *Foreign Affairs*, March/April 1997, p. 142. C. William Maynes said that the United States without the Soviet Union had lost the sextant needed to steer its foreign policy—cited in Richard Haass, *The Reluctant Sheriff: The United States After the Cold War* (New York, 1997), p. 3.

2. Francis Fukuyama wrote in his teaser, "The End of History?," *National Interest*, Summer 1989:

   The end of history will be a very sad time. The struggle for recognition, the willingness to risk one's life for a purely abstract goal, the world-wide ideological struggle that called forth daring, courage, imagination, and idealism, will be replaced by economic calculation, the endless solving of technical problems, environmental concerns, and the satisfaction of sophisticated consumer demands. In the post-historical period there will be neither art nor philosophy, just the perpetual caretaking of the museum of human history. I can feel in myself, and see in others around me, a powerful nostalgia for the time when history existed. Such nostalgia, in fact, will continue to fuel competition and conflict even in the post-historical world for some time to come. Even though I recognize its inevitability, I have the most ambivalent feelings for the civilization that has been created in Europe since 1945, with its north Atlantic and Asian offshoots. Perhaps this very prospect of centuries of boredom at the end of history will serve to get history started once again.

   Reprinted in Foreign Affairs Agenda, *The New Shape of World Politics* (New York, 1997), p. 25. The managing editor of *Foreign Affairs*, Fareed Zakaria, has also hinted at disappointment with rampaging blandness when he wrote in *The New Shape of World Politics*, p. vii: "[The post–Cold War world] may not have the drama and life-threatening urgency of a nuclear arms race. . . ."

   Samuel Huntington's apt retort to Fukuyama was: "So long as human beings exist, there is no exit from the traumas of history." See Huntington, "No Exit: The Errors of Endism," originally published in *The National Interest* (Fall 1989), reprinted in *The New Shape of World Politics*, p. 38.

3. See John Gerard Ruggie, *Winning the Peace: America and World Order in the New Era* (New York, 1996), pp. 77, 104; Joseph Nye, *Bound to Lead: The Changing Nature of American Power* (New York, 1990), p. 232; Noam Chomsky, *World Orders Old and New* (New York, 1994), p. 3; "Searching for an Enemy and Finding China," *New York Times*, April 6, 1997.

4. Congressmen Lee Hamilton voiced this commonly held idea as the Cold War passed into history: "We've got to begin to lay an intellectual base for U.S. involvement in the world, a rationale that people understand and support and

around which you can build a consensus, as was done with containment." Richard Melanson, "'This Will Not Be Another Vietnam': George Bush and the Persian Gulf War," *Occasional Paper #9,* Thomas Watson, Jr., Institute for International Studies, Brown University, 1991, p. 26.

5. The United States remains the chief barrier against mishap in the post–Cold War era, Joseph Nye wrote in 1990: "If the most powerful country fails to lead, the consequences for the rest of the world may be disastrous." The country has to muster a will commensurate with its resources:

> The critical question is whether [the United States] will have the political leadership and strategic vision to convert [its economic-technological-military] resources into real influence in a transitional period of world politics. The implications for stability in the nuclear era are immense. A strategy for managing the transition to complex interdependence over the next decades will require the United States to invest its resources in the maintenance of the geopolitical balance, in an open attitude to the rest of the world, in the development of new international institutions, and in major reforms to restore the domestic sources of U.S. strength. The twin dangers that Americans face are complacency about the domestic agenda and an unwillingness to invest in order to maintain confidence in their capacity for international leadership. Neither is warranted. The United States remains the largest and richest power with the greatest capacity to shape the future.

> See Nye, *Bound to Lead,* pp. x, 260–61. Also see Haass for a similar argument made in 1997, *The Reluctant Sheriff,* p. 6.

6. Richard Melanson, *American Foreign Policy Since the Vietnam War: The Search for Consensus from Nixon to Clinton* (Armonk, New York, 1996), p. 222; Samir Amin, *Empire of Chaos* (New York, 1992), p. 16; Michael Sherry, *In the Shadow of War: The United States Since the 1930s* (New Haven, 1995), p. 432; Steel, *Temptations of a Superpower,* pp. 55, 126; Ruggie, *Winning The Peace,* p. 162.

7. Casualty figures in the Gulf War are reliable on the U.S./coalition side. Authoritative figures for Iraqi losses are unavailable in the public domain as of this writing. See Harry Summers, *Persian Gulf War Almanac* (New York, 1995), p. 90; *International Military and Defense Encyclopedia* (Washington, 1993), p. 1115; Ritchie Ovendale, *The Middle East Since 1914* (London, 1992), p. 135. Also see Sherry's *In the Shadow of War,* pp. 465, 471, 474, 477.

8. Tom Engelhardt, *The End of Victory Culture: Cold War America and the Disillusioning of a Generation* (New York, 1995), p. 299.

9. Lawrence Freedman, "Order and Disorder in the New World," and Strobe Talbott, "Post-Victory Blues," *Foreign Affairs,* America and the World 1991/92, pp. 21–22, 58; Richard Melanson, *American Foreign Policy Since the Vietnam War,* pp. 219–21, 225, 232–34; Steel, *Temptations of a Superpower,* p. 83.

10. Sherry, *In the Shadow of War,* p. 474.

11. See, for example, Warren Christopher's outline for foreign policy goals, *New York Times,* January 21, 1995, and Clinton's speech, "America Must Continue

to Bear the Responsibilities of World Leadership," *Washington Post,* October 6, 1995. Also consult Lawrence Eagleburger and Robert Barry, "Dollars and Sense Diplomacy," *Foreign Affairs,* July/August 1996. Finally, see the text of Clinton's Second Inaugural address, *New York Times,* January 21, 1997 and Madeleine Albright's "Blueprint for a Bipartisan Foreign Policy," *New York Times,* January 26, 1997.

By late 1997 the United States owed $1.5 billion to the United Nations. Yet according to the Pew Research Center, popular attitude toward the UN was shifting in a favorable direction—a majority of people polled held the organization in favorable regard. See "Idealism, Past and Present," *New York Times,* January 4, 1998.

12. "On Global Stage, Clinton's Pragmatic Turn," *New York Times,* July 29, 1996; William Pfaff, "The Future of the United States As a Great Power," *Fifteenth Morgenthau Memorial Lecture on Ethics and Foreign Policy* (New York, Carnegie Council on Ethics and International Affairs, 1996) p. 6; Strobe Talbott, "Democracy and the National Interest," *Foreign Affairs,* November/December 1996, p. 49.

13. The administration's case for constructive engagement has not stressed only the projected benefits of improved Sino-U.S. economic involvement. During Jiang Zemin's White House visit (October 1997) the Chinese president and Clinton agreed to cooperate on nearly a dozen issues. These ranged from easing the crisis in North Korea to fighting air pollution in China (*Boston Globe,* October 30, 1997, p. A28). My thanks here to Sheng-ping Hu, Boston University doctoral candidate, for drawing my attention to these agreements in his seminar paper (December 1997) on Sino-U.S. relations and game theory.

Clinton's retreat from a firm human rights policy and reticence about Chinese misdeeds in Tibet were reflected in what Stephen Graubard (editor of *Daedalus,* journal of the American Academy of Arts and Sciences) said and did not say at the time of Jiang's visit. Graubard's only complaint was that leading American scholars of China were not invited to a White House fete for Jiang. See "Guess Who Wasn't Invited to Dinner?," *New York Times,* November 1, 1997.

14. James Chace, "Safe and Sound," *New York Times,* January 2, 1997; Ruggie, *Winning the Peace,* p. 2. See also David Ricci, *The Tragedy of Political Science: Politics, Scholarship, and Democracy* (New Haven, 1984), p. 72.

15. Melanson, *American Foreign Policy Since the Vietnam War,* p. 276.

16. Henry Kissinger, *Diplomacy* (New York, 1994), p. 806.

17. Ibid., p. 813; Gordon Craig, "Looking for Order," *New York Review of Books,* May 12, 1994, p. 14.

18. George Kennan, "The Failure in Our Success," *New York Times,* March 14, 1994; George Kennan, "On American Principles," *Foreign Affairs,* March/April 1995, pp. 118, 124–25; David Mayers, *George Kennan and the Dilemmas of U.S. Foreign Policy* (New York, 1988), p. 279.

19. Ronald Steel, "The Domestic Core of Foreign Policy," *Atlantic Monthly,* June 1995, pp. 85–86; Steel, *Temptations of a Superpower,* pp. 121, 123, 125–26, 131, 139; William Hyland, "The Case For Pragmatism," *Foreign Affairs,*

America and the World 1991/92, pp. 41, 52; James Schlesinger, "Quest for a Post–Cold War Foreign Policy," *Foreign Affairs*, America and the World 1992/93, p. 20.

20. Samuel Huntington, *The Clash of Civilizations and the Remaking of World Order* (New York, 1996), p. 66: "It is sheer hubris to think that because Soviet communism has collapsed, the West has won the world for all time and that Muslims, Chinese, Indians, and others are going to rush to embrace Western liberalism as the only alternative." Also see Huntington, "The West Unique, Not Universal," *Foreign Affairs*, November/December 1996, p. 40.

21. Paul Kennedy, *The Rise and Fall of the Great Powers: Economic Change and Military Conflict from 1500 to 2000* (New York, 1987), pp. 514–15; Matthew Connelly and Paul Kennedy, "Must It Be The Rest Against the West?," *Atlantic Monthly*, December 1994, pp. 76, 79, 82, 84.

22. Lawrence Freedman, "Order and Disorder in the New World," *Foreign Affairs*, America and the World 1991/92, p. 36; "French-American Ties Mostly Untied for Now," *New York Times*, November 10, 1996.

23. Andrei Kozyrev, "Don't Threaten US," *New York Times*, March 18, 1994; Gennadi Zyuganov, "Junior Partner? No Way," *New York Times*, February 1, 1996; "Russia Is True to West, in Its Fashion," *New York Times*, May 1, 1997; Alexi Arbatov, "As NATO Grows, Start 2 Shudders," *New York Times*, August 26, 1997.

24. Richard Solomon, former assistant secretary of state for East Asian and Pacific affairs, has placed the number of dead from the famine as between 30 and 40 million (from his remarks on "Is the Press Demonizing China?" at the School of Advanced International Studies, Johns Hopkins University, May 20, 1997). Writer Jung Chang accepts a death toll of 30 million people. See her *Wild Swans: Three Daughters of China* (New York, 1991), p. 234. Historian Jonathan Spence, writing in 1990, estimated at least 20 million fatalities: "Half of those dying in China [in 1963] were under ten years old. The Great Leap Forward, launched in the name of strengthening the nation by summoning all the people's energies, had turned back on itself and ended by devouring its young." See Spence, *The Search for Modern China* (New York, 1990), p. 583.

   Chinese casualty figures from World War II are nowhere reliably reported. The estimate of 35 million dead is from "China Makes a Vow on '37 Invasion," *International Herald Tribune*, July 8, 1997. Also see "demography of the war" in I. C. B. Dear and M. R. D. Foot, eds., *Oxford Companion to World War II* (New York, 1995), p. 290.

25. "China Turns the Tables, Faulting U.S. on Rights," *New York Times*, March 5, 1997.

26. Samir Amin, *Empire of Chaos* (New York, 1992), pp. 16, 18, 30, 81.

27. Chomsky, *World Orders Old and New*, pp. 6, 9, 19, 25, 82, 178–79, 185, 188, 271–72; Muammer El-Qadhafi, "A Revolutionary Perspective on the New World Order" in Keith Lepor, ed., *After the Cold War: Essays on the Emerging World Order* (Austin, 1997), p. 237. In Qadhafi's words:

The concept of the 'New World Order' . . . is nothing more than another attempt at hiding the bitter truth of the way the world is being ruled these days—a world still languishing in the chains of the inherited world order, shackled by its old values, its barren ideas, and poor solutions. Maybe the only difference between the old and the new orders is that the old order has lost its balance and no longer has any resistance against desires, lusts, and evils.

28. "U.S. Won't Offer Trade Testimony on Cuba Embargo," *New York Times*, February 21, 1997.

29. From Alexis de Tocqueville's *Democracy in America* in Robert Goldwin and Harry Clor, eds., *Readings in American Foreign Policy* (New York, 1971), p. 6.

30. Kenneth Waltz, *Theory of International Politics* (Reading, Mass., 1979), p. 200; Ruggie, *Winning the Peace*, p. 23.

31. The historian Gordon Craig has noted: "To establish the relationship between ideas and foreign policy is always a difficult task, and it is no accident that it has attracted so few historians." See Craig sympathetically cited in Michael Hunt, *Ideology and U.S. Foreign Policy* (New Haven, 1987), p. xi. Political scientists Judith Goldstein and Robert Keohane have also maintained that ideas, as well as interests, have weight in explaining foreign policy, however murky the connections or difficult to disentangle. See Goldstein and Keohane, eds., *Ideas and Foreign Policy: Beliefs, Institutions, and Political Change* (Ithaca, 1993), pp. 4, 29. Goldstein and Keohane write on p. 3 of their book: "Our argument is that ideas influence policy when the principled or causal beliefs they embody provide road maps that increase actors' clarity about goals or ends-means relationships, when they affect outcomes of strategic situations in which there is no unique equilibrium, and when they become embedded in political institutions."

32. See Rhodri Jeffreys-Jones's *Changing Differences: Women and the Shaping of American Foreign Policy, 1917–1994* (New Brunswick, New Jersey, 1995) for a variation on the theme that women and peace are closely associated.

33. One historian who writes on U.S. power has given this premature notice of national demise: "The United States was preeminent for only a moment of history, one powerful state among nations and empires over time, holding land, propagating population, making science, producing wealth, raising armies, waging war, espousing beliefs and faith." See Donald White, *The American Century: The Rise and Decline of the United States as a World Power* (New Haven, 1996), pp. 437–38; also see pp. 426, 430.

34. Jonathan Spence, *The Search for Modern China*, p. 742; Nelson Mandela, *Long Walk to Freedom* (Boston, 1995), pp. 95–96, 174, 331; Address of the President of the Czech Republic, His Excellency Vaclav Havel, on the Occasion of the Liberty Medal Ceremony, Philadelphia, July 4, 1994; Osama El-Baz "The Third World and the Post–Cold War Order" in Lepor, ed., *After the Cold War*, p. 204; Stephen Ambrose, *Undaunted Courage: Meriwether Lewis, Thomas Jefferson, and the Opening of the American West* (New York, 1996), p. 227.

35. I have lifted from and forced into my own purposes Kant's essay, "An Answer to the Question: 'What Is Enlightenment?'" His famous short answer to the question is: "*Enlightenment is man's emergence from his self-incurred immaturity. Immaturity* is the inability to use one's own understanding without the guidance of another. This immaturity is *self-incurred* if its cause is not lack of understanding, but lack of resolution and courage to use it without the guidance of another. The motto of enlightenment is therefore: *Sapere aude!* Have courage to use your own understanding!" See Hans Reiss, ed., *Kant: Political Writings* (Cambridge, England, 1994), p. 54.

Bibliography

Aaron, Daniel, ed. *America in Crisis: Fourteen Crucial Episodes in American History* (New York, 1952).

Addams, Jane. *Newer Ideals of Peace* (New York, 1915).

———. *Peace and Bread in Time of War* (New York, 1945).

Agar, Herbert, et al. *The City of Man: A Declaration on World Democracy* (New York, 1941).

Alperovitz, Gar. *Atomic Diplomacy: Hiroshima and Potsdam* (New York, 1985).

Amalrik, Andrei. *Will the Soviet Union Survive Until 1984?* (New York, 1970).

Ambrose, Stephen. *Eisenhower: The President* (New York, 1984).

———. *Undaunted Courage: Meriwether Lewis, Thomas Jefferson, and the Opening of the American West* (New York, 1996).

Ambrosius, Lloyd. *Wilsonian Statecraft: Theory and Practice of Liberal Internationalism During World War I* (Wilmington, Del., 1991).

Amin, Samir. *Empire of Chaos* (New York, 1992).

Andrews, Wayne, ed. *The Autobiography of Theodore Roosevelt* (New York, 1958).

Angell, Norman. *The Great Illusion 1933* (New York, 1933).

———. *The Great Illusion: A Study of the Relations of Military Power in Nations to their Economic and Social Advantage* (London, 1911).

Arendt, Hannah. *Crises of the Republic* (New York, 1972).

Ashmore, Harry. *Unseasonable Truths: The Life of Robert Maynard Hutchins* (Boston, 1989).

Ball, George. *The Past Has Another Pattern* (New York, 1982).

Barry, Kathleen. *Susan B. Anthony: A Biography of a Singular Feminist* (New York, 1988).

Beale, Howard. *Theodore Roosevelt and the Rise of America to World Power* (Baltimore, 1956).

Beard, Charles. *President Roosevelt and the Coming of the War, 1941: A Study in Appearances and Realities* (New Haven, 1948).

Beisner, Robert. *Twelve Against Empire: The Anti-Imperialists, 1898–1900* (New York, 1968).

Berman, Larry. *Planning a Tragedy: The Americanization of the War in Vietnam* (New York, 1982).

Bernstein, Barton. "The Atomic Bombings Reconsidered." *Foreign Affairs,* January/February 1995.

Beschloss, Michael, and Strobe Talbott. *At the Highest Levels: The Inside Story of the End of the Cold War* (Boston, 1993).

Beveridge, Albert. *The Meaning of the Times* (Indianapolis, 1908).

Bloch, Marc. *Memoirs of War, 1914–1915.* Trans. Carole Fink (Cambridge, England, 1988).

Blum, D. Steven. *Walter Lippmann: Cosmopolitanism in the Century of Total War* (Ithaca, 1984).

Blum, John Morton, ed. *The Price of Vision: The Diary of Henry A. Wallace, 1942–1946* (Boston, 1973).

Boegelsack, Brigitte, ed. *Paul Robeson: For His 80th Birthday* (Berlin, 1978).

Bohlen, Charles. *The Transformation of American Foreign Policy* (New York, 1969).

Bond, Brian. *War and Society in Europe, 1870–1970* (New York, 1986).

Bonhoeffer, Dietrich. *Ethics* (New York, 1955).

Boritt, Gabor, ed. *Lincoln, the War President* (New York, 1992).

Bowen, David Warren. *Andrew Johnson and the Negro* (Knoxville, Tenn., 1989).

Bradsher, Henry. *Afghanistan and the Soviet Union* (Durham, North Carolina, 1985).

Brands, H. W. *TR: The Last Romantic* (New York, 1997).

Brandt, Willy. *In Exile: Essays, Reflections and Letters, 1937–1947* (London, 1971).

———. *People and Politics: The Years 1960–1975* (Boston, 1978).

Brodie, Fawn. *Thaddeus Stevens: Scourge of the South* (New York, 1959).

Brown, Seyom. *International Relations in a Changing Global System: Towards a Theory of the World Polity* (Boulder, Colorado, 1992).

Bull, Hedley. *The Anarchical Society: A Study of Order in World Politics* (London, 1977).

Cahill, Kevin, ed. *Preventive Diplomacy: Stopping Wars Before They Start* (New York, 1997).

Caldicott, Helen. *A Desperate Passion: An Autobiography* (New York, 1996).

———. *Missile Envy: The Arms Race and Nuclear War* (New York, 1984).

Carnegie, Andrew. "Wealth." *North American Review* CXLVIII (1889).

Carr, Edward Hallett. *The Twenty Years' Crisis, 1919–1939* (New York, 1946).

Cary, Francine Curro. *The Influence of War on Walter Lippmann, 1914–1944* (Madison, Wisconsin, 1967).

Castel, Albert. *The Presidency of Andrew Johnson* (Lawrence, Kansas, 1979).

Chadakoff, Rochelle, ed. *Eleanor's Roosevelt's My Day* (New York, 1989).

Challener, Richard. *Admirals, Generals, and American Foreign Policy, 1898–1914* (Princeton, 1973).

Chambers, John Whiteclay. *The Eagle and the Dove: The American Peace Movement and United States Foreign Policy, 1900–1922* (Syracuse, 1991).

Chang, Iris. *The Rape of Nanking: The Forgotten Holocaust of World War II* (New York, 1997).

Chang, Jung. *Wild Swans: Three Daughters of China* (New York, 1991).

Charmley, John. *Churchill's Grand Alliance: The Anglo-American Special Relationship, 1940–1957* (New York, 1995).

Chatfield, Charles, ed. *Peace Movements in America* (New York, 1973).

Chomsky, Noam. *World Orders Old and New* (New York, 1994).

Christensen, Thomas. *Useful Adversaries: Grand Strategy, Domestic Mobilization, and Sino-American Conflict, 1947–1958* (Princeton, 1996).

Clark, Grenville, and Louis Sohn. *Introduction to World Peace through World Law* (Cambridge, Mass., 1973).

Clifford, Clark, with Richard Holbrooke. *Counsel to the President: A Memoir* (New York, 1991).

Cold War International History Project, *Bulletin* (Washington series).

Coletta, Paolo E. *The Presidency of William Howard Taft* (Lawrence, Kansas, 1973).

Connelly, Matthew, and Paul Kennedy. "Must It Be the Rest Against The West?" *Atlantic Monthly*, December 1994.

Cooper, John Milton. *The Warrior and the Priest: Woodrow Wilson and Theodore Roosevelt* (Cambridge, Mass., 1983).

Cox, LaWanda. *Lincoln and Black Freedom: A Study in Presidential Leadership* (Columbia, South Carolina, 1981).

Craig, Gordon, and Felix Gilbert, eds. *The Diplomats, 1919–1939* (Princeton, 1953).

Craig, Gordon, and Francis Lowenheim, eds. *The Diplomats, 1939–1979* (Princeton, 1994).

Craig, Gordon. "Looking for Order." *The New York Review of Books*, May 12, 1994.

Crocker, Chester. "The Lessons of Somalia." *Foreign Affairs*, May/June 1995.

Crook, D. P. *The North, the South, and the Powers, 1861–1865* (New York, 1974).

Crow, John. *Spain: The Root and the Flower: An Interpretation of Spain and the Spanish People* (Berkeley, 1985).

Cull, Nicholas. "Selling Peace: The Origins, Promotion and Fate of the Anglo-American New Order During the Second World War." *Diplomacy and Statecraft*, March 1996.

Current, Richard, ed. *The Political Thought of Abraham Lincoln* (Indianapolis, 1967).

———. *Those Terrible Carpetbaggers* (New York, 1988).

Dallek, Robert. *Franklin D. Roosevelt and American Foreign Policy, 1932–1945* (New York, 1979).

———. *Lone Star Rising: Lyndon Johnson and His Times, 1908–1960* (New York, 1991).

———. *The American Style of Foreign Policy: Cultural Politics and Foreign Affairs* (New York, 1983).

Davis, Allen. *American Heroine: The Life and Legend of Jane Addams* (New York, 1973).

DeBenedetti, Charles. *An American Ordeal: The Antiwar Movement of the Vietnam Era* (Syracuse, 1990).

———. *Origins of the Modern American Peace Movement, 1915–1929* (Milkwood, New York, 1978).

———. *The Peace Reform in American History* (Bloomington, 1980).

Divine, Robert, ed. *The Johnson Years: LBJ at Home and Abroad* (Lawrence, Kansas, 1994).

————. *The Johnson Years: Vietnam, the Environment, and Science* (Lawrence, Kansas, 1987).

Dobrynin, Anatoly. *In Confidence: Moscow's Ambassador to America's Six Cold War Presidents, 1962–1986* (New York, 1995).

Dobson, John. *Reticent Expansion: The Foreign Policy of William McKinley* (Pittsburgh, 1988).

Donald, David Herbert. *Charles Sumner and the Rights of Man* (New York, 1970).

————. *Lincoln* (New York, 1995).

Douglass, Frederick. *Autobiographies* Ed. Henry Louis Gates, Jr. (New York, 1994).

Dower, John. *War Without Mercy: Race and Power in the Pacific War* (New York, 1986).

Doyle, Michael. *Ways of War and Peace: Realism, Liberalism, and Socialism* (New York, 1997).

Drew, Elizabeth. *On the Edge: The Clinton Presidency* (New York, 1994).

Du Bois, W. E. B. *Black Reconstruction in America: An Essay Toward a History of the Past Which Black Folk Played in the Attempt to Reconstruct Democracy in America, 1860–1880* (New York, 1935, 1963).

Duberman, Martin. *Paul Robeson* (New York, 1988).

Duus, Peter. "Imperialism Without Colonies: The Vision of a Greater East Asia Co-Prosperity Sphere." *Diplomacy and Statecraft,* March 1996.

Eagleburger, Lawrence, and Robert Barry. "Dollars and Sense Diplomacy." *Foreign Affairs,* July/August 1996.

Engelhardt, Tom. *The End of Victory Culture: Cold War America and the Disillusioning of a Generation* (New York, 1995).

Fairbank, John King. *China: A New History* (Cambridge, Mass., 1992).

Fehrenbacher, Don, ed. *Abraham Lincoln: Speeches and Writings, 1832–1858* (New York, 1989).

————. *Abraham Lincoln: Speeches and Writings, 1859–1865* (New York, 1989).

Feinberg, Abraham. *Hanoi Diary* (Don Mills, Ontario, 1968).

Feis, Herbert. *The Atomic Bomb and the End of World War II* (Princeton, 1966).

Ferrell, Robert, ed. *The Eisenhower Diaries* (New York, 1981).

Flood, Charles Bracelen. *Lee: The Last Years* (Boston, 1981).

Foner, Eric. *Reconstruction: America's Unfinished Revolution, 1863–1877* (New York, 1988).

Foner, Philip. *Frederick Douglass* (New York, 1969).

Foreign Affairs Agenda. *The New Shape of World Politics: Contending Paradigms in International Relations* (New York, 1997).

Fowler, Robert. *Carrie Catt: Feminist Politician* (Boston, 1986).

Fox, Richard. *Reinhold Niebuhr: A Biography* (New York, 1985).

Franklin, John Hope. *Reconstruction: After the Civil War* (Chicago, 1961).

Freedman, Lawrence. "Order and Disorder in the New World." *Foreign Affairs,* 1991/92.

Freidel, Frank. *The Splendid Little War* (Boston, 1958).

Freud, Sigmund, and William C. Bullitt. *Thomas Woodrow Wilson: A Psychological Study* (Boston, 1966).

Fromkin, David. *In the Time of the Americans: The Generation that Changed America's Role in the World* (New York, 1995).

Fukuyama, Francis. "The End of History?" *National Interest,* Summer 1989.

Fulbright, J. William. *The Arrogance of Power* (New York, 1966).

Fussell, Paul. *The Great War and Modern Memory* (London, 1975).

Gaddis, John Lewis, et al. "The Soviet Side of the Cold War: A Symposium." *Diplomatic History,* Fall 1991.

Gaddis, John Lewis. *The Long Peace: Inquiries into the History of the Cold War* (New York, 1987).

———. *The United States and the End of the Cold War* (New York, 1992).

———. *We Now Know: Rethinking Cold War History* (Oxford, 1997).

Gardner, Lloyd. *Architects of Illusion: Men and Ideas in American Foreign Policy 1941–1949* (Chicago, 1970).

———. *Safe for Democracy: The Anglo-American Response to Revolution, 1913–1923* (New York, 1987).

Garrow, David. *Bearing the Cross: Martin Luther King, Jr., and the Southern Christian Leadership Conference* (New York, 1986).

Garthoff, Raymond. *Détente and Confrontation: American-Soviet Relations From Nixon to Reagan* (Washington, 1985).

Gelfand, Lawrence. *The Inquiry: American Preparations for Peace, 1917–1919* (New Haven, 1963).

Gilliam, Dorothy Butler. *Paul Robeson: All-American* (Washington, 1976).

Goldhagen, Daniel Jonah. *Hitler's Willing Executioners: Ordinary Germans and the Holocaust* (New York, 1996).

Goldstein, Judith, and Robert Keohane, eds. *Ideas and Foreign Policy: Beliefs, Institutions, and Political Change* (Ithaca, 1993).

Goncharov, S., J. Lewis, and X. Litai. *Uncertain Partners: Stalin, Mao, and the Korean War* (Stanford, 1993).

Gould, Lewis. *The Presidency of Theodore Roosevelt* (Lawrence, Kansas, 1991).

———. *The Presidency of William McKinley* (Lawrence, Kansas, 1980).

Graff, Henry, ed. *American Imperialism and the Philippine Insurrection* (Boston, 1969).

Grant, U. S. *Personal Memoirs.* Vol. II (New York, 1886).

Grass, Günter. *Two States—One Nation?* (San Diego, 1990).

Haass, Richard. *The Reluctant Sheriff: The United States After the Cold War* (New York, 1997).

Hamby, Alonzo. *Man of the People: A Life of Harry S. Truman* (New York, 1995).

Hamilton, Charles. *Adam Clayton Powell: The Political Biography of an American Dilemma* (New York, 1991).

Harriman, W. Averell and Elie Abel. *Special Envoy to Churchill and Stalin, 1941–1946* (New York, 1975).

Havel, Václav. "The Responsibility of Intellectuals." *The New York Review of Books,* June 22, 1995.

Heckscher, August. *Woodrow Wilson* (New York, 1991).

Heinrichs, Waldo. *American Ambassador: Joseph Grew and the Development of the United States Diplomatic Tradition* (New York, 1966).

————. *Threshold of War: Franklin D. Roosevelt and American Entry into World War II* (New York, 1988).

Hendrickson, David. "The Recovery of Internationalism: Salvaging Clinton's Foreign Policy." *Foreign Affairs,* September/October 1994.

Henig, Robin Marantz. *The People's Health: A Memoir of Public Health and Its Evolution at Harvard* (Washington, 1997).

Hentoff, Nat, ed. *The Essays of A. J. Muste* (Indianapolis, 1967).

Herken, Gregg. *The Winning Weapon: The Atomic Bomb in the Cold War, 1945–1950* (New York, 1982).

Herman, Sondra. *Eleven Against War: Studies in American Internationalist Thought, 1898–1921* (Stanford, 1969).

Herring, George. *America's Longest War: The United States and Vietnam, 1950–1975* (New York, 1986).

Hesseltine, William. *Lincoln's Plan of Reconstruction* (Gloucester, Mass., 1963).

Hixson, Walter. *George F. Kennan: Cold War Iconoclast* (New York, 1989).

Hoar, George. *Autobiography of Seventy Years.* Vol. 2 (New York, 1903).

Hobson, John. *Imperialism: A Study* (Ann Arbor, 1902, 1965).

Hofstadter, Richard. *The American Political Tradition* (New York, 1957).

Hogan, Michael, ed. *America in the World: The Historiography of American Foreign Relations Since 1941* (Cambridge, England, 1996).

Holloway, David. *Stalin and the Bomb: The Soviet Union and Atomic Energy, 1939–1956* (New Haven, 1994).

Hook, Sidney. "A Free Man's Choice." *The New Leader,* May 26, 1958.

————. "A Foreign Policy for Survival." *The New Leader,* April, 7, 1958.

————. "Bertrand Russell Retreats." *The New Leader,* July 7–14, 1958.

————. Comments, *Partisan Review,* Winter 1962.

————. *Convictions* (Buffalo, New York, 1990).

————. *Out of Step: An Unquiet Life in the Twentieth Century* (New York, 1987).

Hosoya, C., N. Ando, Y. Onuma, and R. H. Minear, eds. *The Tokyo War Crimes Trial: An International Symposium* (New York, 1986).

Hull, William. *The Two Hague Conferences and their Contributions to International Law* (Boston, 1908).

Hunt, Michael. *Crises in U.S. Foreign Policy: An International History Reader* (New Haven, 1996).

————. *Ideology and U.S. Foreign Policy* (New Haven, 1987).

Huntington, Samuel. "If Not Civilizations, What?" *Foreign Affairs,* November/December 1993.

————. *The Clash of Civilizations and the Remaking of World Order* (New York, 1996).

————. "The West: Unique, Not Universal." *Foreign Affairs,* November/December 1996.

Hurst, Jack. *Nathan Bedford Forrest: A Biography* (New York, 1993).

Hutton, Graham. *The War as a Factor in Human Progress* (Chicago, 1942).

Hyland, William. "The Case for Pragmatism." *Foreign Affairs,* 1991/92.

Ikenberry, G. John. "The Myth of Post–Cold War Chaos." *Foreign Affairs,* May/June 1996.

Iriye, Akira. *From Nationalism to Internationalism: U.S. Foreign Policy to 1914* (London, 1977).

Israel, Fred, ed. *The War Diary of Breckinridge Long: Selections from the Years 1939–1944* (Lincoln, Nebraska, 1966).

James, William. *The Moral Equivalent of War and Other Essays.* Ed. John Roth (New York, 1971).

Jaspers, Karl. *The Future of Mankind* (Chicago, 1958).

———. *The Question of German Guilt* (New York, 1947).

Jeffreys-Jones, Rhodri. *Changing Differences: Women and the Shaping of American Foreign Policy, 1917–1994* (New Brunswick, New Jersey, 1995).

Johnson, Edward. *History of Negro Soldiers in the Spanish-American War, and Other Items of Interest* (Raleigh, North Carolina, 1899).

Johnson, Lyndon Baines. *The Vantage Point: Perspectives of the Presidency, 1963–1969* (New York, 1971).

Joll, James. *Europe Since 1870: An International History* (New York, 1973).

———. *The Origins of the First World War* (London, 1992).

———. *Three Intellectuals in Politics* (New York, 1960).

Jonas, Manfred. *Isolationism in America 1935–1941* (Ithaca, 1966).

Jones, Dorothy V. *Code of Peace: Ethics and Security in the World of Warlord States* (Chicago, 1991).

Jordan, D., and E. J. Pratt. *Europe and the American Civil War* (Boston, 1931).

Josephson, Harold. *James T. Shotwell and the Rise of Internationalism in America* (London, 1975).

Kagan, Donald. *On the Origins of War and the Preservation of Peace* (New York, 1995).

Kapstein, Ethan. "Workers and the World Economy." *Foreign Affairs,* May/June 1996.

Karnow, Stanley. *In Our Image: America's Empire in the Philippines* (New York, 1989).

———. *Vietnam: A History* (New York, 1983).

Kearns, Doris. *Lyndon Johnson and the American Dream* (New York, 1976).

Kennan, George "X." "The Sources of Soviet Conduct" *Foreign Affairs,* July 1947.

———. *American Diplomacy 1900–1950* (Chicago, 1951).

———. *At a Century's Endings: Reflections, 1982–1995* (New York, 1996).

———. "On American Principles." *Foreign Affairs,* March/April 1995.

———. *Russia and the West Under Lenin and Stalin* (Boston, 1960).

———. *The Cloud of Danger: Current Realities of American Foreign Policy* (Boston, 1977).

———. *The Nuclear Delusion: Soviet-American Relations in the Atomic Age* (New York, 1983).

Kennedy, John. *Profiles in Courage* (New York, 1955).

Kennedy, Paul. *The Rise and Fall of the Great Powers: Economic Change and Military Conflict from 1500 to 2000* (New York, 1987).

Kennedy, Thomas. *Charles A. Beard and American Foreign Policy* (Gainesville, Florida, 1975).

Kimball, Warren, ed. *Churchill and Roosevelt: The Complete Correspondence.* 3 vols. (Princeton, 1984).

————. *Forged in War: Roosevelt, Churchill, and the Second World War* (New York, 1997).

————. *The Juggler: Franklin Roosevelt as Wartime Statesman* (Princeton, 1991).

Kindsvatter, Peter. "Exploring the 'New' Cold War History and Missed Opportunities for Conflict Resolution." *SHAFR Newsletter,* December 1996.

Kissinger, Henry. *Diplomacy* (New York, 1994).

————. "Foreign Service of the United States," April 15, 1996, attached to Press Notice of the American Academy of Diplomacy newsletter, April 22, 1996.

————. "Reflections on Containment." *Foreign Affairs,* May/June 1994.

————. *White House Years* (Boston, 1979).

————. *Years of Upheaval* (Boston, 1982).

Knock, Thomas. *To End All Wars: Woodrow Wilson and the Quest for a New World Order* (New York, 1992).

Kolko, Gabriel. *The Politics of War: Allied Diplomacy and the World Crisis of 1943–945* (London, 1969).

Korngold, Ralph. *Thaddeus Stevens: A Being Darkly Wise and Rudely Great* (New York, 1955).

Kovaly, Heda Margolius. *Under a Cruel Star: A Life in Prague, 1941–1968* (New York, 1989).

Kung, Hans. *On Being a Christian* (New York, 1976).

Kurtz, Paul. *Sidney Hook: Philosopher of Democracy and Humanism* (Buffalo, New York, 1983).

Kurtz, Paul, ed. *Sidney Hook and the Contemporary World: Essays on the Pragmatic Intelligence* (New York, 1968).

LaFeber, Walter. *The New Empire: An Interpretation of American Expansion, 1860–1898* (Ithaca, 1963).

Lash, Joseph. *Eleanor and Franklin: The Story of Their Relationship, Based on Eleanor Roosevelt's Private Papers* (New York, 1971).

Lebow, Richard Ned, and Janice Gross Stein. *We All Lost the Cold War* (Princeton, 1994).

Leekley, John, ed. *Bruce Catton: Reflections on the Civil War* (New York, 1982).

Leffler, Melvyn. *A Preponderance of Power: National Security, the Truman Administration, and the Cold War* (Stanford, 1992).

————. "Inside Enemy Archives: The Cold War Reopened." *Foreign Affairs,* July/August 1996.

Lepor, Keith, ed. *After the Cold War: Essays on the Emerging World Order* (Austin, 1997).

Levin, N. Gordon. *Woodrow Wilson and World Politics: America's Response to War and Revolution* (London, 1968).

Lewis, David Levering. *W. E. B. Du Bois: A Biography of a Race, 1868–1919* (New York, 1993).

Linderman, Gerald. *The Mirror of War: American Society and the Spanish-American War* (Ann Arbor, 1974).

Link, Arthur. *Wilson the Diplomatist: A Look at His Major Foreign Policies* (Baltimore, 1957).

————. *Woodrow Wilson: Revolution, War, and Peace* (New York, 1979).

Link, Arthur, ed. *The Papers of Woodrow Wilson* (Princeton, 1965-series).

Livezey, William. *Mahan On Sea Power* (Norman, Oklahoma, 1981).

Lodge, David. "The Lives of Graham Greene." *The New York Review of Books,* June 22, 1995.

Long, David, and Peter Wilson. *Thinkers of the Twenty Years' Crisis: Inter-War Idealism Reassessed* (Oxford, 1995).

Lukes, Igor. *Czechoslovakia between Stalin and Hitler: The Diplomacy of Edvard Benes in the 1930s* (New York, 1996).

Mahan, Alfred Thayer. *The Problem of Asia and Its Effect upon International Policies* (Boston, 1900).

Mandela, Nelson. *Long Walk to Freedom* (Boston, 1995).

Mansfield, Edward, and Jack Snyder. "Democratization and War." *Foreign Affairs,* May/June 1995.

Marchand, C. Roland. *The American Peace Movement and Social Reform, 1898–1918* (Princeton, 1972).

Marks, George, ed. *The Black Press Views American Imperialism, 1898–1900* (New York, 1971).

Mastny, Vojtech. *Russia's Road to the Cold War* (New York, 1979).

————. *The Cold War and Soviet Insecurity: The Stalin Years* (New York, 1996).

Matlock, Jack. *Autopsy of an Empire: The American Ambassador's Account of the Collapse of the Soviet Union* (New York, 1995).

May, Ernest. *Imperial Democracy: The Emergence of America as a Great Power* (New York, 1961).

————. *Lessons of the Past: The Use and Misuse of History in American Foreign Policy* (London, 1973).

May, Ernest, ed. *American Cold War Strategy: Interpreting NSC 68* (New York, 1993).

May, Ernest, and Philip Zelikow, eds. *The Kennedy Tapes: Inside the White House During the Cuban Missile Crisis* (Cambridge, Mass., 1997).

Mayer, Arno. *Political Origins of the New Diplomacy, 1917–1918* (New Haven, 1959).

————. *Politics and Diplomacy of the Peacemaking: Containment and Counterrevolution at Versailles, 1918–1919* (New York, 1967).

Mayers, David. *Cracking the Monolith: U.S. Policy Against the Sino-Soviet Alliance, 1949–1955* (Baton Rouge, 1986).

————. *George Kennan and the Dilemmas of U.S. Foreign Policy* (New York, 1988).

————. *The Ambassadors and America's Soviet Policy* (New York, 1995).

Mazower, Mark. "Hitler's New Order, 1939–45." *Diplomacy and Statecraft,* March 1996.

McCarthy, Mary. *The Seventeenth Degree* (New York, 1974).

McDougall, Walter. "Back to Bedrock: The Eight Traditions of American Statecraft." *Foreign Affairs,* March/April 1997.

McFeely, William. *Frederick Douglass* (New York, 1991).

————. *Grant: A Biography* (New York, 1981).

McKenna, Marian. *Borah* (Ann Arbor, 1961).

McKitrick, Eric. *Andrew Johnson and Reconstruction* (Chicago, 1960).

McNamara, Robert, with Brian VanDeMark. *In Retrospect: The Tragedy and Lessons of Vietnam* (New York, 1995).

McNeill, William. "Decline of the West?" *The New York Review of Books,* January 9, 1997.

McPherson, James. *Abraham Lincoln and the Second American Revolution* (New York, 1990).

———. *Ordeal By Fire: The Civil War and Reconstruction* (New York, 1982).

Melanson, Richard, and David Mayers, eds. *Reevaluating Eisenhower: American Foreign Policy in the 1950s* (Urbana, Illinois,1987).

Melanson, Richard. *American Foreign Policy Since the Vietnam War: The Search for Consensus from Nixon to Clinton* (Armonk, New York, 1996).

———. "'This Will Not Be Another Vietnam': George Bush and the Persian Gulf War." *Occasional Paper #9,* Thomas J. Watson, Jr. Institute for International Studies, Brown University, 1991.

Miller, Richard, ed. *American Imperialism in 1898: The Quest for National Fulfillment* (New York, 1970).

Miller, Stuart Creighton. *Benevolent Assimilation: The American Conquest of the Philippines, 1899–1903* (New Haven, 1982).

Miscamble, Wilson. *George F. Kennan and the Making of American Foreign Policy, 1945–1950* (Princeton, 1992).

Monaghan, Jay. *Diplomat in Carpet Slippers: Abraham Lincoln Deals with Foreign Affairs* (Indianapolis, 1945).

Morgan, H. Wayne. *Eugene V. Debs: Socialist for President* (Syracuse, 1962).

Morgan, Wayne, ed. *Making Peace with Spain: The Diary of Whitelaw Reid, September-December 1898* (Austin, 1965).

Morgenthau, Hans. *Politics in the Twentieth Century* (Chicago, 1971).

———. *Truth and Power: Essays of a Decade, 1960–1970* (New York, 1970).

Morgenthau, Henry. *Germany Is Our Problem* (New York, 1945).

Mueller, John. *Retreat from Doomsday: The Obsolescence of Major War* (New York, 1989).

Mullen, Robert. *Blacks and Vietnam* (Lanham, Maryland, 1981).

Myrdal, Gunnar. *An American Dilemma: The Negro Problem and Modern Democracy* (New York, 1944).

Naimark, Norman. *The Russians in Germany: A History of the Soviet Zone of Occupation, 1945–1949* (Cambridge, Mass., 1995).

Nardin, Terry, and David Mapel, eds. *Traditions of International Ethics* (Cambridge, England, 1992).

Neal, Fred Warner, ed. *Détente or Debacle: Common Sense in U.S.-Soviet Relations* (New York, 1979).

Neely, Mark. *The Fate of Liberty: Abraham Lincoln and Civil Liberties* (New York, 1991).

———. *The Last Best Hope of Earth: Abraham Lincoln and the Promise of America* (Cambridge, Mass., 1993).

Nicolson, Harold. *Peacemaking 1919* (New York, 1965).

Niebuhr, Reinhold. *Christian Realism and Political Problems* (New York, 1953).
————. *Christianity and Power Politics* (New York, 1940).
————. *The Children of Light and the Children of Darkness: A Vindication of Democracy and a Critique of Its Traditional Defense* (New York, 1945).
————. *The Irony of American History* (New York, 1952).
Nitze, Paul. *Tension Between Opposites: Reflections on the Practice and Theory of Politics* (New York, 1993).
Nixon, Richard M. *RN: The Memoirs of Richard Nixon* (New York, 1978).
Nolan, Cathal, ed. *Ethics and Statecraft: The Moral Dimension of International Affairs* (Westport, Connecticut, 1995).
————. *Notable U.S. Ambassadors since 1775* (Westport, Connecticut, 1997).
Nye, Joseph. *Bound to Lead: The Changing Nature of American Power* (New York, 1990).
Nye, Joseph, et al. *Global Cooperation After the Cold War: A Reassessment of Trilateralism* (New York, 1991).
Oakley, Violet. *Cathedral of Compassion: Dramatic Outline of the Life of Jane Addams, 1860–1935* (Philadelphia, 1955).
Offner, Arnold. *American Appeasement: United States Foreign Policy and Germany, 1933–1938* (Cambridge, Mass., 1969).
————. "Roosevelt, Hitler, and the Search for a New World Order." *Diplomatic History,* Fall 1991.
Offner, John. *An Unwanted War: The Diplomacy of the United States and Spain Over Cuba, 1895–1898* (Chapel Hill, 1992).
Overy, Richard. *Why the Allies Won* (New York, 1996).
Owsley, Frank Lawrence. *King Cotton Diplomacy* (Chicago, 1959).
Patterson, James. *Mr. Republican: A Biography of Robert A. Taft* (Boston, 1972).
Pechatnov, Vladimir. "The Big Three After World War II: New Documents on Soviet Thinking about Post War Relations with the United States and Great Britain." *Working Paper No. 13,* Cold War International History Project, Woodrow Wilson Center (Washington, July 1995).
Perkins, Frances, *The Roosevelt I Knew* (New York, 1946).
Perlmutter, Amos. *Making the World Safe for Democracy: A Century of Wilsonianism and Its Totalitarian Challengers* (Chapel Hill, 1997).
Peterson, Merrill, ed. *The Portable Thomas Jefferson* (New York, 1986).
Pfaff, William. "The Future of the United States as a Great Power." *Fifteenth Morgenthau Memorial Lecture on Ethics and Foreign Policy* (New York, 1996).
Piston, William Garrett. *Lee's Tarnished Lieutenant: James Longstreet and His Place in Southern History* (Athens, Georgia, 1987).
Plummer, Brenda Gayle. *Rising Wind: Black Americans and U.S. Foreign Affairs, 1935–1960* (Chapel Hill, 1996).
Podhoretz, Norman. *Why We Were In Vietnam* (New York, 1982).
Pogue, Forrest. *George C. Marshall: Statesman 1945–1959* (New York, 1987).
Polk, William. *Neighbors and Strangers: The Fundamentals of Foreign Affairs* (Chicago, 1997).
Porter, Bruce. *War and the Rise of the State: The Military Foundations of Modern Politics* (New York, 1994).

Powell, Adam Clayton, Jr. *Adam by Adam* (New York, 1971).

Pranger, Robert, ed. *Détente and Defense: A Reader* (Washington, 1976).

Prittie, Terrence. *Willy Brandt: Portrait of a Statesman* (New York, 1974).

Public Papers of the Presidents of the United States. *Dwight D. Eisenhower, 1960–1961* (Washington, 1961).

Public Papers of the Presidents of the United States. *Lyndon B. Johnson, 1965* (Washington, 1966).

Resek, Carl, ed. *War and the Intellectuals: Essays by Randolph S. Bourne, 1915–1919* (New York, 1964).

Reynolds, David, ed. *The Origins of the Cold War in Europe: International Perspectives* (New Haven, 1994).

Rickover, H. G. *How the Battleship Maine Was Destroyed* (Washington, 1976).

Robeson, Paul. *Here I Stand* (Boston, 1971).

Robinson, Jo Ann Ooiman. *Abraham Went Out: A Biography of A. J. Muste* (Philadelphia, 1981).

Roosevelt, Theodore. *The Rough Riders* (New York, 1921).

Ruggie, John Gerard. *Winning the Peace: America and World Order in the New Era* (New York, 1996).

Russell, Bertrand. "Freedom to Survive." *The New Leader,* July 7–4, 1958.

———. "World Communism and Nuclear War." *The New Leader,* May 26, 1958.

Russell, Greg. *Hans J. Morgenthau and the Ethics of American Statecraft* (Baton Rouge, 1990).

Russett, Bruce, ed. *Grasping the Democratic Peace: Principles for a Post–Cold War World* (Princeton, 1993).

Sajer, Guy. *The Forgotten Soldier* (Washington, 1990).

Salvatore, Nick. *Eugene V. Debs: Citizen and Socialist* (Urbana, 1982).

Schaffer, Ronald. *America in the Great War: The Rise of the War Welfare State* (New York, 1991).

Schaller, Michael. *The American Occupation of Japan: The Origins of the Cold War in Asia* (New York, 1985).

Schapsmeier, Edward, and Frederick Schapsmeier. *Prophet in Politics: Henry A. Wallace and the War Years, 1940–1945* (Ames, Iowa, 1970).

Scheer, Robert. *With Enough Shovels: Reagan, Bush and Nuclear War* (New York, 1983).

Schlesinger, James. "Quest for a Post–Cold War Foreign Policy." *Foreign Affairs,* 1993.

Scholes, Walter, and Marie Scholes. *The Foreign Policies of the Taft Administration* (Columbia, Missouri, 1970).

Schoonover, Thomas. "Europe, the Spanish-American War and Great Power Activity in the Caribbean and Asia." *SHAFR Newsletter,* September 1997.

Schulman, Bruce. *Lyndon B. Johnson and American Liberalism: A Brief Biography with Documents* (Boston, 1995).

Schulzinger, Robert. *Henry Kissinger: Doctor of Diplomacy* (New York, 1989).

Sherry, Michael. *In the Shadow of War: The United States Since the 1930s* (New Haven, 1995).

Sherwin, Martin. *A World Destroyed: The Atomic Bomb and the Grand Alliance* (New York, 1975).

Sherwood, Robert. *Roosevelt and Hopkins: An Intimate History* (New York, 1948).

Shotwell, James. *Autobiography* (Indianapolis, 1961).

Shultz, George. *Turmoil and Triumph: My Years as Secretary of State* (New York, 1993).

Sideman, B. B., and L. Friedman, eds. *Europe Looks at the Civil War* (New York, 1960).

Silber, Nina. *The Romance of Reunion: Northerners and the South, 1865–1900* (Chapel Hill, 1994).

Skinner, Elliott. *African Americans and U.S. Policy Toward Africa, 1850–1924* (Washington, D.C., 1992).

Smith, Jean Edward. *Lucius D. Clay: An American Life* (New York, 1990).

Smith, Michael Joseph. *Realist Thought from Weber to Kissinger* (Baton Rouge, 1986).

Smith, Page. *Democracy on Trial: The Japanese American Evacuation and Relocation in World War II* (New York, 1995).

———. *Trial By Fire: A People's History of the Civil War* (New York, 1982).

Solzhenitsyn, Aleksandr. *Détente: Prospects for Democracy and Dictatorship* (New Brunswick, New Jersey, 1980).

Spence, Jonathan. *God's Chinese Son: The Taiping Heavenly Kingdom of Hong Xiuquan* (New York, 1996).

———. *The Search for Modern China* (New York, 1990).

State Department. *Foreign Relations of the United States* (Washington, series).

Steel, Ronald. "America Remains No. 1." *The New York Times Magazine,* September 29, 1996.

———. *Temptations of a Superpower* (Cambridge, Mass., 1995).

———. "The Domestic Core of Foreign Policy." *Atlantic Monthly,* June 1995.

———. *Walter Lippmann and the American Century* (Boston, 1980).

Stephanson, Anders. *Kennan and the Art of Foreign Policy* (Cambridge, Mass., 1989).

Stevenson, David. *The First World War and International Politics* (Oxford, 1988).

Stimson, Henry, and McGeorge Bundy. *On Active Service in Peace and War* (New York, 1948).

Stoessinger, John. *Crusaders and Pragmatists: Movers of Modern American Foreign Policy* (New York, 1979).

Stovall, Pleasant. *Robert Toombs: Statesman, Speaker, Soldier, Sage* (New York, 1892).

Sulzberger, C. L. *A Long Row of Candles: Memoirs and Diaries, 1934–1954* (Toronto, 1969).

Swain, Geoffrey. "Stalin's Wartime Vision of the Postwar World." *Diplomacy and Statecraft,* March 1996.

"Symposium: Soviet Archives: Recent Revelations and Cold War Historiography." *Diplomatic History,* Spring 1997.

Talbott, Strobe. "Democracy and the National Interest." *Foreign Affairs,* November/December 1996.

———. "Post-Victory Blues" *Foreign Affairs,* 1991/92.

———. *The Master of the Game: Paul Nitze and the Nuclear Peace* (New York, 1988).

Tarsaidze, Alexandre. *Czars and Presidents* (New York, 1958).

Taubman, William. *Stalin's American Policy: From Entente to Détente to Cold War* (New York, 1982).

Taylor, Telford. *Nuremberg and Vietnam: An American Tragedy* (New York, 1971).

———. *The Anatomy of the Nuremberg Trials* (New York, 1992).

Terkel, Studs. *The Good War* (New York, 1984).

Thompson, Kenneth, and Robert Myers, eds. *Truth and Tragedy: A Tribute to Hans J. Morgenthau* (Washington, D.C., 1977).

Tickner, J. Anne. *Gender in International Relations: Feminist Perspectives on Achieving Global Security* (New York, 1992).

Trefousse, Hans. *Andrew Johnson: A Biography* (New York, 1989).

Trumbo, Dalton. *Johnny Got His Gun* (1939; Toronto, 1970).

Tucker, Robert W., and David Hendrickson. *The Imperial Temptation: The New World Order and America's Purpose* (New York, 1992).

Turner, Frederick Jackson. "The Significance of the Frontier in American History." *Proceedings of the Forty-first Annual Meeting of the State Historical Society of Wisconsin* (Madison, 1894).

Twain, Mark. "On American Imperialism" (previously unpublished) *Atlantic Monthly,* April 1992.

Ulam, Adam. *Dangerous Relations: The Soviet Union in World Politics, 1970–1982* (New York, 1983).

———. *Expansion and Coexistence: Soviet Foreign Policy, 1917–1973* (New York, 1974).

Van Voris, Jacqueline. *Carrie Chapman Catt: A Public Life* (New York, 1987).

Waldron, Arthur, ed. *How the Peace Was Lost* (Stanford, 1992).

Walker, J. Samuel. *Prompt and Utter Destruction: Truman and the Use of the Atomic Bombs Against Japan* (Chapel Hill, 1997).

———. "The Decision to Use the Bomb." *Diplomatic History,* Winter 1990.

Wallace, Henry. *Democracy Reborn.* Ed. Russell Lord (New York, 1944).

———. *The Century of the Common Man* (New York, 1943).

Waltz, Kenneth. *Man, the State, and War: A Theoretical Analysis* (New York, 1959).

———. *Theory of International Politics* (Reading, Mass., 1979).

Walworth, Arthur. *Woodrow Wilson.* Vol. II: *World Prophet* (New York, 1958).

Walzer, Michael. *Just and Unjust Wars: A Moral Argument with Historical Illustrations* (New York, 1977).

Weinberg, Gerhard. *A World at Arms: A Global History of World War II* (Cambridge, England, 1994).

Weinstein, Edwin. *Woodrow Wilson: A Medical and Psychological Biography* (Princeton, 1981).

Welch, Richard. *George Frisbie Hoar and the Half-Breed Republicans* (Cambridge, Mass., 1971).

Welles, Sumner. *The World of the Four Freedoms* (New York, 1943).

Wert, Jeffrey. *General James Longstreet: The Confederacy's Most Controversial Soldier— A Biography* (New York, 1993).

White, Donald. *The American Century: The Rise and Decline of the United States as a World Power* (New Haven, 1996).

White, Graham, and John Maze. *Henry A. Wallace: His Search for a New World Order* (Chapel Hill, 1995).

White, Walter. *A Man Called White* (New York, 1948).

Widenor, William. *Henry Cabot Lodge and the Search for an American Foreign Policy* (Berkeley, 1980).

Wiesel, Elie. *Night* (New York, 1960).

Willkie, Wendell. *One World* (New York, 1943).

Wills, Garry. *Lincoln at Gettysburg: The Words that Remade America* (New York, 1992).

Wilson, Woodrow. *A History of the American People* Vol. 5 (New York, 1902).

Woodward, C. Vann, ed. *Mary Chestnut's Civil War* (New Haven, 1981).

Wyman, David. *The Abandonment of the Jews: America and the Holocaust, 1941–1945* (New York, 1984).

Wynn, Neil. *The Afro-American and the Second World War* (New York, 1993).

Young, Marilyn Blatt, ed. *American Expansion: The Critical Issues* (Boston, 1973).

Zubok, Vladislav, and Constantine Pleshakov. *Inside the Kremlin's Cold War: From Stalin to Khrushchev* (Cambridge, Mass., 1996).

Zweig, Stefan. *The World of Yesterday: An Autobiography* (New York, 1943).

Zwick, Jim, ed. *Mark Twain's Weapons of Satire: Anti-Imperialist Writings on the Philippine-American War* (Syracuse, 1992).

Index